DISCOVERING **MISSIONS**

BY CHARLES R. GAILEY / HOWARD CULBERTSON

BEACON HILL PRESS
OF KANSAS CITY

ISBN 978-0-8341-2257-4

Printed in the United States of America

Cover Design: Brandon H. Hill
Interior Design: Sharon Page

Library of Congress Cataloging-in-Publication Data

Gailey, Charles R., 1937-
Discovering missions / Charles R. Gailey and Howard Culbertson.
p. cm.
Includes bibliographical references.
ISBN-13: 978-0-8341-2257-4 (pbk.)
ISBN-10: 0-8341-2257-X (pbk.)
1. Missions. I. Culbertson, Howard, 1946- II. Title.

BV2061.3.G35 2007
266—dc22

2007019830

10 9 8 7 6 5 4 3

CONTENTS

PREFACE

This is an exciting time to study global mission. It was not supposed to be this way because half a century ago respected church leaders were talking about the demise of mission. A few even proposed a moratorium on mission. With the passing of time, however, the number of missionaries and the finances spent on missionary work have increased to higher levels than ever. A new appreciation of missionaries and the world Christian movement has developed, typified by Harvard University historian William Hutchison's *Errand to the World.* Not long ago, *TIME* magazine featured "The New Missionary" as a cover story. In 2002, Philip Jenkins, a history professor at Penn State University, wrote *The Next Christendom: The Coming of Global Christianity,* which chronicled the stunning growth of the Christian faith in the non-Western world. A lead story in *Newsweek* recounted "how the explosion of Christianity in developing nations is transforming the world's largest religion."[1] The view that global mission outreach would become a relic has itself become a relic.

Mission is a topic that concerns the whole church. A primary audience of this volume is students at the university and seminary level. For easy use in semester-long classes, the book has 14 chapters. However, it has also been written with pastors and laypeople in mind. We have tried to help readers with sidebars and boxed quotes to amplify the subject matter and to give contrasting views. Questions are given at the end of each chapter to provoke further discussion and analysis. The glossary at the end of the book defines those words that are in bold type the first time they appear in the text.

We are grateful to all who helped with the preparation of this book. The project would have stalled out had it not been for the persistent nudging, encouragement, and help of Bonnie Perry, director of Beacon Hill Press of Kansas City, and Alex Varughese, managing editor of the Centennial Initiative.

Missionaries Amy Crofford, Barbara Culbertson, and John Seaman read two successive drafts of the entire manuscript, each time offering real-life examples for illustrations and suggesting clarifications in wording. Helping track down and verify numerous details were librarians, archivists, and researchers Joseph Achipa, Stacy Barber, Debra Bradshaw, Stan Ingersol, Dale Jones, and Vernell Posey. Sarah Bean, Elaine Cunningham, Roger Hahn, and Pam Rider helped with editing the manuscript. Missionaries who critiqued most or all of the full manuscript include Doris Gailey, Steve Heap, Tim Mercer, Terry Read, Scot Riggins, Craig and Anita Sheppard, and Brian and Julie Woolery.

We are also grateful to Donnamie Ali, Hal Cauthron, Franklin Cook, David Cooper, Greg Crofford, Tim Crutcher, John Hall, Marty Hoskins, Brint Montgomery, Dan Psaute, Jirair Tashjian, David Wesley, and John and Sandy Cunningham for their valuable comments and help on specific chapters. A word of thanks goes to a missionary who gave valuable input but must remain anonymous because he ministers in a **creative access** country.

Thanks to Missions Advanced Research and Communications Center (MARC), Global Mapping International, InterDev, and Patrick Johnstone of WEC International for permission to use their graphics.

Charles Gailey
Howard Culbertson

1
MISSION
AN INTRODUCTION

Objectives

Your study of this chapter should help you to:

- Define mission
- Get an overview of key components of missiology
- Reflect on the nuances of *mission* and *missions*
- Explore definitions of the term *missionary*
- Acquire a feel for foundational concepts in missiology
- Conceptualize the changing global context

Key Words to Understand

missionary
missiology
mission
missiologist
Missio Dei
closure
missionary call
globalization
glocalization
paradigm shifts

Fiction writers and movie producers have not often been kind when portraying Christian missionaries. Most missionary characters they dream up are bigoted, arrogant, and anthropologically challenged. Many of those fictional missionaries have been self-serving with very base motivations. For instance, one of W. Somerset Maugham's more famous short stories was "Rain." At the center of that story was a **missionary** who disintegrated morally while trying to convert a Pacific island prostitute.

James Michener's 1959 *Hawaii* weaves a tale that includes not-so-angelic 18th-century missionaries messing up the lives of charmingly simple islanders. Forty years later, a novel called *The Poisonwood Bible* was a Pulitzer prize runner-up and an Oprah Book Club selection. For that book author Barbara Kingsolver conceived a less-than-ideal missionary family living in the Congo. Nathan Price, the husband and father, is physically and emotionally abusive to his family. The strident and intransigent Rev. Price poorly represents the Lord he purports to serve.

Peter Matthiessen's 1965 book *At Play in the Fields of the Lord* is another example of a work that is very unflattering to missionaries. Matthiessen's missionary characters were destructive to themselves as well as to the Amazonian tribe they went to evangelize. A similarly negative picture of missionaries was painted in 1966 by the movie *Seven Women.* That film plays on the conflicting inner desires of some American female missionaries in China. The stereotypes spawned by such fictional missionary figures have opened up Christian missionaries to withering criticism and even caused missiologist J. Herbert Kane to ask, "What happened to the halo?" as a chapter title of his *Winds of Change in the Christian Mission.*

Fortunately, there is another side to this issue. Three films—*Inn of the Sixth Happiness, The Mission,* and *End of the Spear*[1]—based on true missions stories have been positive. Way on the opposite end of the spectrum from most fiction writers are those people for whom real-life missionaries are saintly folk living close to heaven. Such people who put missionaries up on pedestals find inspiration in missionary hero books such as *The Missionary Hero of Kuruman,* a biography of **Robert Moffat** and *The Missionary Hero of the New Hebrides,* the life story of John G. Paton. Such biographies have used glowing superlatives to describe those who have borne the label *missionary.* The Roman Catholics have gone even further than Protestants in their adulation of missionaries. Having conferred official sainthood on several missionaries, Roman Catholics have everyone referring to *Saint* Paul, *Saint* Boniface, *Saint* Anskar, *Saint* Francis Xavier, and *Saint* Isaac Jogues. Even Patrick, missionary to Ireland, was sainted by the Roman Catholics although his branch of Celtic Christianity was not under the authority of the Bishop of Rome.

The Study of Mission

How should believers respond to the caricatures—good and bad—of Christian missionaries and the fruits of their work? Between the extremes of withering criticism and uncritical adulation, where does the truth lie?

Missiology

One way to sift through both the muck and the fluff about missionaries is to use discernment grounded in good **missiology.** Though the word *missiology* is not in the average English speaker's vocabulary, many will know that the suffix *-ology* means "language about" or "the study of." Indeed, missiology is the study of, or conscious reflection upon, the practice of Christian **mission.** The first part of *missiology* comes from the Latin word *mission,* which means "sending out" or "assigned task" (thus, *mission*). *Missio* is a participle of the verb *mittere,* the Latin equivalent of *apostello,* a Greek verb meaning "to send" from which *apostle* comes. Based on this etymology, missiology can be said to be the study of sending. Because that definition may not communicate much to anyone other than a **missiologist,** it may help to think of missiology as "mission-ology."

I Wasn't God's First Choice

I wasn't God's first choice for what I've done for China. There was somebody else. I don't know who it was—God's first choice. It must have been a man—a wonderful man. A well-educated man. I don't know what happened. Perhaps he died. Perhaps he wasn't willing . . . and God looked down . . . and saw Gladys Aylward.[2]

—Gladys Aylward

Missiology looks at more than missionary biographies. While **expatriate** missionaries are important players in world evangelization, they are only temporary agents seeking to accomplish some specific things. At the heart of missiology is reflection on the outreach, growth, and development of the Christian Church as it is planted and bears fruit in new cultural contexts. As a field of study, missiology draws on several other academic disciplines. As one might guess, missiology uses material from theology, biblical studies, and church history. It also gleans insights from communications theory, **cultural anthropology,** geography, linguistics, psychology, and sociology. These diverse threads of missiology's fabric are reflected in missions courses taught at colleges and universities around the world:

- Christian Theology and Religions in African Contexts
- Communicating Christ in Animistic Contexts

- Cross-cultural Adjustment
- Cross-cultural Communication of the Gospel
- Cultural Anthropology
- Ethnomusicology in Christian Missions
- Folk Islam
- Intercultural Communication
- Linguistics
- Religions of the World

Like other academic disciplines, missiology has its own specialized vocabulary. Examples of missiology's words and phrases include **4-14 window, 10/40 Window, contextualization, dynamic equivalence, excluded middle, homogenous unit, inclusivism, indigenous church, modality**, people movements, reamateurization, **sodality, Theological Education by Extension,** and **unreached people groups.**

"Doing" Mission

The Church did not coin the word *missiology* because it finally recognized that it had a missionary task or even because it wanted to start doing serious reflection on the missions enterprise. Just as Christian missionary work did not begin with **William Carey** (who is often called the father of the modern missionary movement), so missiology did not begin when Ludwig J. Van Rijckevorsel first used the word in 1915.[3]

> All good missiology should be able to be translated into action. If there is no action, you're missing something.[4]
>
> —Johannes Verkuyl, professor of missiology
> Free University of Amsterdam

In the 5th century, Patrick was doing missiology in Ireland when he used local metaphors, such as the shamrock for illustrating the Trinity. Ulfilas, "apostle to the Goths," made a missiological decision not to translate the books of Samuel and Kings when he decided their material would not be helpful in his ministry among combative and warlike peoples. Ramon Llull[5] reflected on missiological principles in the 13th century as he wrote books and pamphlets to prepare missionaries for Muslim North Africa. Not long before that, Francis of Assisi decided he would approach Egypt's Muslim leaders by searching for common ground rather than simply regarding Islam as enemy territory. In the late 16th century, Matteo Ricci was struggling with whether Chinese veneration of ancestors transgressed Christian principles. As Jesuit Francis Xavier evangelized in Asia, he sought to reduce Christianity to its core essentials, that is, what a person of any culture had to know and to do to be a Christian. These missionaries were all doing mission and reflecting on it long before missiology became the subject of university and seminary courses.

Missions or Mission?

Anyone looking at recent missiological literature would conclude that *mission* is an important word. Seventy-five years ago the more dominant word would have been *missions.* The change from *missions* to *mission* began in the 1960s, although the roots of the shift go back to 1934 when German missiologist Karl Kartenstein started referring to ***Missio Dei.*** This Latin phrase, which means "mission of God," became a major theme for the 1952 World Missionary Conference in Willingen, Germany, and has since become a common way to describe global mission work. Its use, which some say originated with Augustine's frequent use of *missio,* caused many to begin using *mission* almost exclusively.

Mission and *Mission Board*

Missionaries sometimes use the word *mission* as a shortened form of *the mission board,* a sending agency supervising and facilitating the work of missionaries and national churches. Even though saying "the mission" was common in Haiti when Paul Orjala was a missionary there, he opposed its usage because he felt it fostered feelings of **dependency.**[6]

For many people, *mission* and *missions* mean almost the same thing and are often used interchangeably. Each of those two words, however, has some unique nuances. Those advocating for the use of *mission* felt that *missions* emphasized too much the human side while the singular word *mission* would be a needed reminder that missionary work is trying to accomplish God's mission. Some thought that *missions* overemphasized a **Western** perspective of world evangelism and that its focus on the expatriate individuals doing mission resulted in a weakened **ecclesiology,** the theological understanding of the Church that John Howard Yoder, missionary to Nigeria, saw as inseparable from missiology.[7] A pragmatic and linguistically sound way of approaching the use of the two words is to see *mission* as the comprehensive label for the Church's response to God's calling while *missions* are the particular ways and organizational structures through which the Church's global outreach is carried out.[8]

Even the change from *missions* to *mission* has not been enough for everyone. In attempts to shed negative baggage that *missions, missionary,* and even *mission* might carry, some academicians downplay the usage of all three words. Many schools put *intercultural studies* on diplomas instead of *missions* or *missiology.* The neutral-sounding *intercultural studies* was chosen because it would be vague and seemingly innocuous in places where Christianity is suspect and restricted.

> Do we claim to believe in God? He's a missionary God. You tell me you're committed to Christ. He's a missionary Christ. Are you filled with the Holy Spirit? He's a missionary Spirit. Do you belong to the church? It's a missionary society. And do you hope to go to heaven when you die? It's a heaven into which the fruits of world mission have been and will be gathered.[9]
>
> —John R. Stott

Whose Mission Is It?

The sending and purposeful going that is mission did not begin in 1907 when Harmon Schmelzenbach sailed for Africa with financial backing and prayer support of students and faculty at Peniel College. Christian mission did not begin in 1793 when William Carey went to India. Mission did not even begin with the apostle Paul.

Though it is common to think Christian missionary outreach began in obedience to the **Great Commission,** mission did not originate with Jesus' words, "Therefore go" (Matthew 28:19). To be sure, Christ's Great Commission is a powerful call to the Church to win and disciple those of all people groups. That was not where mission began, however. Rather than originating in the final chapter of Matthew, mission is rooted in the words of Genesis 1. That should not be surprising. Scholars call Genesis the seedbed from which the rest of Scripture sprouts. If that be so, then Genesis should be where the missionary enterprise germinates and indeed it is. The declaration that God is Creator of all is the seed for proclaiming God's wish to be worshiped by all human beings. Mission does not start with human beings getting burdened about spreading the Good News, as laudable as that is. Mission starts with God, and thus believers should joyfully echo missionary Paul Orjala's book title: *God's Mission Is My Mission.* Since mission begins with the declaration that God is Creator, it can be said that Christians are not evangelizing the world because of what the Bible says; they are evangelizing the world because of who God is.

> The church exists by mission as a fire exists by burning.[10]
>
> —Emil Brunner

To continue with the seedbed metaphor, mission is more than a few plants—even robust ones—scattered among other good things in Scripture. Mission is the soil of Scripture in which everything else is rooted. The inescapable conclusion is that if Christians are going to call themselves "people of the Book," they must be gripped by that Book's passion for global mission.

Is Mission Everything the Church Does?

The importance that Scripture gives to mission must influence how Christians think about the church. Missionary outreach is not simply one more good thing that churches can do. Because mission is so integral to what it means for the Church to be the Church, those who do not fervently espouse global mission are failing to embrace a core essential of the faith. Brooke Brown, mission volunteer in Slovenia, emphasized how indispensable involvement in global mission is for all believers when she said, "People think you have to be called to missions. You're already called from the moment you become a Christian."[11]

Getting believers of the 20th and 21st centuries to see how foundational mission is to the nature and purpose of the Church has been a rocky road. In some cases, people have used *mission* or *missions* to label anything and everything even remotely related to outreach. Sadly, such a broadening of meaning may have been facilitated by moving to using *mission* instead of *missions.* A negative consequence of the broadening of meaning beyond cross-cultural outreach efforts is that putting everything under the same umbrella tempts Christians and churches to forget their global responsibilities. It is human nature to get most excited about things and people that are close by. One consequence is that without a specific focus on faraway places and people groups, those faraway places and least-evangelized groups get less and less attention. At some point, even for those who acknowledge the sinful predicament of all human beings, it becomes easy to say "that is not my problem" about unreached peoples.

One danger with calling everything *mission* (and putting the label *missionary* on every Christian) is that, as Stephen Neill has said, "When everything is mission, nothing is mission."[12] Neill's point was that when *mission* gets broadened beyond its original usage, pleas to get involved in mission to unreached peoples can be ignored or shrugged off as someone else's responsibility.

Too often the idea of outreach itself has been broadened even further to include every single thing that churches do. Charles Van Engen, former missionary to Mexico, said that such broadening is precisely what happened in mainline denominations during the last half of the 20th century. Van Engen noted that when churches began defining mission in all-inclusive ways, it brought "church and mission so close as to nearly eclipse each other." Van Engen further commented, "The intention of the players in this drama was laudable. But . . . we face some disastrous consequences of their perspectives."[13]

On the local church level, one disastrous consequence of saying "everything we do is mission" is that congregations have raised money to replace carpet as a mission or local evangelism expense. Indeed, if everything is mission, then buying toilet bowl cleaner can be called a mission expense. Sadly, as Van Engen has noted, there seems to be a cause-and-effect link between (1) the declaration that everything the church does is mission and (2) a loss of passion for global missionary outreach. "In such a situation," Van Engen concluded, "both church and mission can get lost."[14] The dimming and even loss of global mission vision and passion can result, as it has, in more money being spent each year in America on chewing gum than is given to world evangelism.[15]

Kingdom of God and Closure

Pastor John Piper has reminded the Church that the world mission enterprise is not an end in itself; mission is a means to an end. That end is the worship of God by all peoples.[16] Because mission is the means and not the end, missiologists have used the word **closure** when talking about fulfilling the Great Commission of Matthew 28:19-20. Closure looks to establishing communities of Christian faith within every culture. Closure looks for where the gospel is not being preached and asks how proclamation and discipling can begin there. However, with more than 1 billion people never having heard about Jesus of Nazareth, closure could seem way out of reach. Nevertheless, convinced that Matthew 24:14 is a declaration that the Great Commission will be fulfilled, many missionaries today echo the words of Howie Shute, missionary in Africa: "We didn't come to work at the Great Commission. We're here to finish it."[17]

To truly understand the Church's global mission, one must conceive of it in a kingdom of God paradigm. Doing mission with a kingdom of God paradigm invites God's people to play a significant role in history. In a Kingdom way of looking at things, mission is not just about saving individual souls from hell, as important as that is. Mission is about proclaiming a **holistic** gospel of the kingdom of God in the tradition of Jesus (Mark 1:15) and Paul (Acts 28:31), both of whom preached healing that was spiritual, physical, emotional, and even political. Using kingdom of God terms to talk about world mission puts a focus on the righteousness, justice, and peace that God wants for all the peoples of earth. Thinking in kingdom of God terms provides a framework for integrating evangelism and societal transformation. It reminds believers that the Lordship of Jesus has societal as well as personal implications. Thinking in kingdom of God terms will enable people to grasp the missionary implications of a key phrase of the Lord's Prayer: "Your kingdom come, your will be done" (Matthew 6:10).

Who Is a Missionary?

> I believe that in each generation God has "called" enough men and women to evangelize all the yet unreached peoples of the earth . . . everywhere I go, I constantly meet with men and women who say to me, "When I was young, I wanted to be a missionary, but I got married instead" or "My parents dissuaded me" or some such thing. No, it is not God who does not call. It is persons who will not respond![18] —Isobel Kuhn, missionary to the Lisu of Thailand and China

While awe-inspiring wonders of nature often evoke feelings of worship, God uses something more personal than natural revelation when He seeks to call humanity into fellowship with himself. As Dean Nelson wrote in a tribute to missiologist Paul Orjala, "When God wants to send a message, He wraps it up in a person and sends that person."[19] God's willingness to entrust the Good News to human messengers is why within a short period after Jesus' resurrection, the Holy Spirit prompted the Church to send evangelists across geographic and cultural boundaries. Over the years, people thus sent out have been called missionaries. People bearing this missionary title have had two clear identifying marks: First, they have been specifically selected or chosen, and second, they have taken the gospel to other cultural groups. Former missionary to the Muslim world Ray Tallman tied these two thoughts together when he defined a missionary as: "A ministering agent sent by God and His church to communicate the gospel message across any and all cultural boundaries for the purpose of leading people to Christ and establishing them into viable fellowships that are also capable of reproducing themselves."[20]

While Paul Little and others have called for every believer to be seen as a missionary,[21] Tallman's definition keeps it narrowed to people with a distinct vocation and who are sent by the Church to take the gospel to other cultural groups. Not everyone is a missionary in this way any more than every believer is a pastor in the way *pastor* is used in Ephesians 4:11. While all believers are to be witnesses and while they may utilize missiological insights in their ministries, not all are missionaries if the message is correctly understood from Ephesians 4 that believers have different callings and gifts.

Mission is also not about auto-sending, that is, people deciding on their own to go. *Mittere* and *apostello* both imply that there is someone doing the "sending." Indeed, that is what happens. Missionaries are sent by a mission board as well as by the Holy Spirit and by the Church. Acts 14:1-4 gives an example of that happening when it says the church in Antioch laid hands on Paul and Barnabas and sent them to the cities of what is now Turkey.

The *Evangelical Dictionary of World Missions* defines *missionary* in a way that fits the experience of Paul and Barnabas and echoes what Tallman wrote. That dictionary says that a missionary is one who is called of God and sent by the Church "to serve God in a **culture,** a geographic location, and very likely, in a language different from the missionary's own."[22] This does not mean that the only way to be a missionary is to go halfway around the world. In its most biblical expression, a "mission field" is simply where the "sent ones" go. The cultural and ethnic diversity that exists within many nations means that a **missionary call** may be the sending of someone to another culture or language group within that person's home country. India, Nigeria, and Papua New Guinea are typical of countries that are complex mosaics of cultural and ethnic groupings. India, for example, is made up of about 4,600 distinct people groups speaking more than 400 different languages. Though not a very large nation, Papua New Guinea is one of the world's most culturally complex ones with more than 1,000 people groups speaking 816 different languages.

Sometimes those who cross national boundaries to minister to immigrants from their native countries are said to be doing missionary work. They are not. By definition, missionaries are outsiders among those with whom they work. Thus, a Haitian going to Paris to pastor a congregation of Haitian immigrants would not be doing missionary work. Likewise, a Mexican going to the U.S. to pastor Mexican immigrants would not be considered a missionary. In a biblically rooted ecclesiology, pastors or elders plant or shepherd individual congregations within their own cultural group while missionaries or apostles are those who develop church planting and discipleship movements in other cultures.

On occasion people have speculated that youth pastors should be considered missionaries because they work with the youth culture. While there are special gifts and graces needed for youth ministry and some new words or ways of saying things need to be learned, cultural anthropologists would say that youth ministers are working with a subgroup of a larger culture, not a totally different culture. Thus, youth ministers do not really fit within the definition of *missionary.*

To try to delineate the cultural and language barriers and distances that call for people with particular missionary gifts using missionary thinking and strategies, missiologists came up with an E-Scale (for Evangelism Scale). In this E-Scale, E0 is the evangelism aimed at spiritually dead churchgoers. Traditional spiritual renewal events in local churches are one way that E0 evangelism is done. E1 evangelism is what believers are doing when they reach out within the culture or cultures of the people of their own congregation. E1 evangelism is aimed at people not currently involved in a church but who are of the same general language and cultural group as the congregation doing the evangelism. E1 evangelism is not cross-cultural missionary evangelism because the only boundaries the gospel encounters are the theological ones separating Christians from non-Christians. In Acts 1:8, Jerusalem and Judea are symbols of E1 evangelism.

E2 evangelism happens when some cultural boundaries are crossed, as would have been the case between Jews and Samaritans. Thus, the Acts 1:8 symbol of E2 evangelism is Samaria. In E2 evangelism, the language is often the same, but evangelism has a missionary tint because of the cultural differences involved. Evangelism that crosses the greatest cultural distances is called E3 evangelism. In E3 evangelism, a language barrier almost always has to be crossed. This ends-of-the-earth missionary evangelism is considerably more complex than E0, E1, or even E2 evangelism.

Globalization: The New Context of Mission

(see plate 1.1)

Things are different now from 1871 when journalist Henry Stanley ventured into the heart of Africa looking for David Livingstone. The 21st-century Church exists in a world where **globalization** has produced never-before-seen interconnectedness. In his book *The World Is Flat: A Brief History of the Twenty-First Century,* Thomas Friedman described the monumental convergence of technological changes that has produced an unprecedented economic and cultural intertwining of individuals and societies. Globalization and its effects on societies of the world is discussed and debated by business executives, politicians, and even terrorists. It is something that will also affect Christian mission.

Today's context of economic and cultural togetherness has resulted from several things:

1. Instantaneous Global Communication

Not long ago, international mail correspondence took weeks or even months. It used to be very costly to get complex documents, photos, and video to faraway destinations in two days or less. Now, that material can arrive electronically in seconds. In milliseconds, cell phone technology links up any two users anywhere on the globe. E-mail and instant messages zip to and from computers around the world. There are positives and negatives to this. Whizzing along optic fiber cables are messages from those preaching the gospel and from those promoting violent guerilla warfare. Global connectivity means that a blog written in frustration by someone in the small Oklahoma town of Hartshorne can be read immediately in the little Tuscan village of Montevettolini, Italy. Consequently, mission organizations as well as businesses have had to become sensitized to global audiences in regard to what they put into print and on Web sites.

2. Movements of People and Goods (see plate 1.2)

Freer access across what used to be tightly controlled national boundaries has made some areas of the globe seem what business strategist Kenichi Ohmae calls "the borderless world."[23] People are aware of and have access to greater amounts of information, goods, services, and images than ever before. Such access has been fostered by things like the European Union and the North American Free Trade Agreement. The resulting borderless world is both a dream and a nightmare with freedom of movement often applying to people as well as commercial products. Each day, hundreds of thousands of people cross national boundaries on footbridges and in airplanes, ferries, buses, and private vehicles. Many of those travelers are on one-way trips to start a new life in another country. Among other things, such emigration influences evangelism and church planting patterns. Thus, the fastest-growing churches in some places are made up of immigrants. Some of the most vibrant evangelical congregations in Paris, for example, are filled with African and Caribbean immigrants rather than with native Parisians.

3. The Revolution in Technology

"Innovate or disappear" is a key dictum of today's commercial world. A few years ago mechanical systems morphed into electronic ones that are now being ever more miniaturized. There was a time when a single computer filled an entire room. Today, the average automobile uses 50 microprocessors, each with more computing power than the room-sized computers of 50 years ago. Friedman says recent technological advances have "flattened" the world, allowing, for instance, the Grameen Bank (whose founder won the 2006 Nobel Peace Prize) to furnish solar-powered cell phones and computers to rural poor in Bangladesh who are doing computer programming for major global corporations. Globalization thus means that competition for jobs is moving from being local to being global.

4. Interdependence of the Nations of the World

Up until the 16th century very few people ever traveled more than 10 miles from their home. As a result, societies were very localized. Today, societies thousands of miles from each other are interlocked in communication, commerce, and even popular culture. Sociologist and economist Saskia Sassen said that today's world has become "a worldwide grid of strategic places . . . constituting a new economic geography of centrality, one that cuts across national boundaries and across the old North-South divide."[24] This has given rise to the phrase *global village* and sparked fears that unique cultural features will be obliterated by uniformity and homogenization. Others such as anthropologist Brian Howell combine the words *local* and *global* into **glocalization,** noting that rather than tossing everything into a blender, globalization has actually promoted "the development of difference, but within a mutually intelligible system."[25] No one knows how such flattening will ultimately affect efforts in the **indigenization** of the church. However, the thought that glocalization is promoting differences may allay the fears of some that a McChurch world is coming, in which churches will look and feel much the same anywhere on the globe.

Result: Paradigm Shifts

The enormous changes wrought by globalization are happening at a time when the face of Christianity is undergoing dramatic changes. For his book *The Next Christendom,* Philip Jenkins looked at dizzying demographic changes in Christianity and concluded that the world is seeing the arrival of a true "global Christianity."[26]

Both Sassen and Jenkins describe **paradigm shifts** that future generations may regard as hinge points in world history. Such paradigm changes could significantly alter the contexts in which the gospel will be proclaimed. The thought of that can be unsettling, but David Bosch, a South African who ministered among the Xhosa in Transkei, sounded hopeful when he spoke to this issue in *Transforming Mission:*

> The events we have been experiencing at least since World War II and the consequent crisis in Christian mission are not to be understood as merely incidental and reversible. Rather, what has unfolded is the result of a fundamental paradigm shift, not only in mission or theology, but in the experience and thinking of the whole world. In earlier ages the church has responded imaginatively to paradigm changes: we are challenged to do the same for our time and context.[27]

Through the centuries, when confronted with new contexts, the Church's missionary outreach has been agile enough to adapt and even increase its level of effectiveness. May it be so again. As it moves forward, the Church will need to be sure of its foundations. It will need to use its resources wisely, and it will, as much as ever, need to be empowered and directed by the Holy Spirit.

Questions for Reflection

1. How is *mission* defined by this book?
2. Does every Christian need to consider whether he or she has a missionary call?
3. Some people consider *mission* to be a reference to God's mission and *missions* to refer to human activity. Is this distinction helpful? Why or why not?

4. In what way is missionary work different from the work of a pastor or of an evangelist?
5. Who is the author of mission? What is God's relationship to humans and how does mission fit into that relationship?
6. What are the overall positives and negatives of globalization and glocalization?
7. How might globalization and glocalization negatively or positively affect Christian mission?

2
THE HEART OF GOD
THE BIBLICAL AND THEOLOGICAL BASIS OF MISSION

Objectives

Your study of this chapter should help you to:

- Recognize that global mission finds its meaning in the very nature and character of God
- Grasp how significant Abraham is to the theology of mission
- Articulate the evidence showing that mission was on God's mind throughout Old Testament times
- See the missionary DNA of the New Testament
- Reflect on the need for each believer to respond to mission as a central theme of Scripture

Key Words to Understand

Great Commission
Abrahamic covenant
Sinai covenant
gôyim
nations
apostle
Paul of Tarsus

A few hundred years ago, scholars divided the Old and New Testament writings into 1,189 chapters and about 32,000 verses. If asked to come up with Bible verses that speak about global mission, the average Christian would list about half a dozen. Though that short list would likely include powerful statements like the Great Commission, 6 verses out of 32,000 are not very many. Looking at that ratio, many believers conclude that world evangelization is barely mentioned in Scripture and thus think it to be something optional for Christians. In the eyes of many Christians, while involvement in world evangelism may be a good thing, it is not necessary for a believer to be a believer or even for the Church to be the Church.

They are wrong in that conclusion. There are far more than a half dozen Bible verses about global mission. Sacred Scripture is full of references to God's desire that all nations would know and worship Him. Again and again the Bible speaks of the ends of the earth hearing of God's glory and of His wish that all peoples be reconciled to Him. Indeed, the middle chapter of the Protestant canon, Psalm 117, begins with the words: "Praise the LORD, all you nations; extol him, all you peoples."

Of course, understanding what the Bible has to say about global mission involves more than listing all the verses that relate to it. The Bible is such a thoroughly missionary book that Ralph Winter, director of the U.S. Center for World Mission, has said: "The Bible is not the basis of missions; missions is the basis of the Bible."[1]

Blessing All Peoples

Abraham: *"All peoples on earth* will be blessed through you" (Genesis 12:3; cf. 18:18; 22:18).

David: "Declare his glory *among the nations"* (1 Chronicles 16:24; cf. Psalm 96:3).

"That your ways may be known on earth, your salvation *among all nations"* (Psalm 67:2).

Solomon: Temple dedication prayer: "That *all the peoples* of the earth may know that the LORD is God and that there is no other" (1 Kings 8:60).

Isaiah: "I will also make you a *light for the Gentiles,* that you may bring my salvation to *the ends of the earth"* (Isaiah 49:6, NIV; cf. chapters 9 and 42).

A strong case for world evangelism can be made from God's interaction with four key Old Testament characters: Abraham, David, Solomon, and Isaiah. God's covenant with Abraham was about global mission. Many of the lyrics in David's Hebrew hymnal (the Book of Psalms) point to God's heart for the nations. The Temple built by Solomon was to be a worship center for all peoples and not just for those born as Hebrews. Isaiah, perhaps Israel's greatest prophet, declares that God's people were to "bring my salvation to the ends of the earth" (Isaiah 49:6, NIV). The sidebar "Blessing All Peoples" gives the key missions passages that involve those four figures.

Old Testament

The reason Winter, former missionary to Guatemala, says that "missions is the basis of the Bible" is that God has revealed himself in Scripture to be desirous of a holy, loving relationship with all people. Both Hebrew and Christian Scriptures tell of a God who initiated, and continues to initiate, communication with people. After earth's first inhabitants sinned (Genesis 3:14-15), Yahweh launched a campaign to salvage His lost creation. That salvage campaign is a major focal point of the Bible. *The Living Bible*'s paraphrase of 2 Chronicles 20:17 refers to God's "incredible rescue operation" (TLB). The ultimate success of the rescue operation that is global mission was glimpsed by John who said in Revelation 7:9 that he saw "a great multitude that no one could count, from every nation, tribe, people and language, standing before the throne and in front of the Lamb."

The Mission Implications of Genesis 1—11

While much of the Old Testament focuses on the Israelites, it begins by describing God's relationship to all of humanity. In Genesis 1—11 the Creator involves himself with all peoples. Thus, before Yahweh became identified as the God of Israel, He had revealed himself as the God of all humankind. The way in which the Hebrew word *'adam* is used shows that the Old Testament is about the whole human race and not just about Israel. *'Adam,* which appears more than 20 times in Genesis 1—5, can mean humanity as a whole as well as the very first human being. More than two-thirds of the times *'adam* is used in Genesis, it appears with the definite article as *ha-'adam.* When that is done, the word does mean all of humanity or humankind instead of a particular person.[2]

This dual use of *'adam* reflects the collective worldview prevalent among the cultures of Old Testament times. That collective worldview means that the first readers of Genesis would have seen all human beings as bound together in a corporate unity. This corporate outlook, which has significant implications for Christian mission, is reinforced by the genealogies of Genesis 5 and 10, which point to the solidarity of all human families before and after the Flood. The first readers of Genesis would have understood its early part to be about

God's desire for a relationship not just with a man and a woman named Adam and Eve and other people specifically mentioned but with every member of the human race. The loving relationship that 21st-century believers say they have with God should be a powerful motivation for them to do global mission so that His desire for a relationship with all peoples can become a reality.

The Promise to Abraham

Genesis 1—11 closes with the dispersal or scattering of the human race at the end of the Tower of Babel story. From that point on, the narrative focuses on one of Noah's sons (Shem) and his descendants and then even more narrowly on Abraham and Sarah and their descendants. This narrowing of focus is not an abrupt turn toward exclusivism. By zeroing in on Abraham and Sarah's family, God moved to turn His desire for a relationship with all peoples into a reality.

It is fairly common knowledge that Abraham's family was the one into which the Messiah was to be born. What is less often noted is that Abraham's family was charged with perpetuating the vision of God's desire to bless all families of the earth. When God says in Genesis 12:1-3 that He is choosing Abraham and his family, He makes clear the relevance of this choice to the whole human race. In verse 1, Yahweh tells Abraham to go from his homeland to a place he will be shown. That encounter was about more than Abraham moving from point A to point B. Because God's command included words of promise, the Yahweh/Abraham encounter was a covenant-making moment that is repeatedly mentioned in both Testaments.

God's Claim on the Whole World

God's election of Abraham and Israel concerns the whole world. He deals so intensely with Israel precisely because He is maintaining His personal claim on the whole world. To speak to this world in the fullness of time, He needed a people.[3]

—Johannes Verkuyl

In verse 2, God promises to make Abraham into a great nation. God tells Abraham that he will be blessed and that his name will become great. The final promise of the **Abrahamic covenant** is that through Abraham all peoples on earth will be blessed. This promise in verse 3 is the climax of the covenant, not its afterthought. In this "all peoples on earth will be blessed through you" promise, Israel was clearly being asked to play a key role in God's world mission **strategy** where doing mission fulfills the Genesis 12 covenant. That is why many missiologists say that Jesus' Great Commission becomes most significant when it is seen as a reiteration of the human responsibilities of the Abrahamic covenant. Don Richardson, the author of *Peace Child* and *Eternity in Their Hearts,* has put the Abrahamic covenant in accounting terms: The top line of divine blessings means that the recipients have a bottom line of responsibilities.[4]

Changing Abram's name to Abraham in Genesis 17 further emphasized that the blessings promised in Genesis 12 would reach out to future generations in ever-widening circles. When God told Abraham that he would have a new name, "father of many nations" (17:4, 5), God also told him that he was being offered "an everlasting covenant between me and you and your descendants" (v. 7). The Genesis narrative keeps emphasizing that the promised blessing of all peoples was not limited to Abraham's time. To Abraham's son Isaac God proclaimed: "Through your offspring all nations on earth will be blessed" (26:4). When God renewed the Abrahamic covenant with Isaac's son, Jacob, He added the phrase about "offspring" that He had earlier said to Isaac: "All peoples on earth will be blessed through you and your offspring" (28:14). Abraham and Sarah and their descendants, spiritual as well as biological, were thus blessed in order to be a blessing.

The Sinai Vision of Mission

Following their escape from Egypt, Abraham's descendants encountered Yahweh at Sinai. In that desert setting, God renewed His call to Israel for a covenant relationship: "Now if you obey me fully and keep my covenant, then out of all nations you will be my treasured possession" (Exodus 19:5*ab*). The phrase "treasured possession" has caused some to conclude that Yahweh wanted to relate to Israel in ways that excluded other peoples. Such people fail to see that "treasured possession" was not all that God said about Israel in the **Sinai covenant.** After saying "treasured possession," God went on to say, "Although the whole earth is mine, you will be for me a kingdom of priests and a holy nation" (vv. 5*c*-6).

Centuries later, as Peter wrote to Christian believers, he quoted Exodus 19 and then explained to his readers that the reason God chose a people was so "that you may declare the praises of him who called you out of darkness into his wonderful light" (1 Peter 2:9). Thus, for Israel to be asked at Sinai to serve as a kingdom of priests (or "priestly kingdom" [Exodus 19:6] as the *New Revised Standard Version* puts it) meant that God wanted this people to be an active bearer of His grace to the world.

Just before the people of Israel arrived at Sinai, they camped at Elim, an oasis with "twelve springs" of water "and seventy palm trees" (Exodus 15:27). Jewish scholars have noted that the number of springs equaled the number of Israelite tribes,[5] though it is usually said that the palm trees were for the elders. Elim had the same number of trees as the number of Noah's descendants listed in Genesis 10. Calling Genesis 10 the table of nations, Jewish tradition has treated these 70 people as the forebears of 70 nations from which all human beings descended. The Jewish Midrash also says that the earth's people were divided into 70 language groups. Thus, the image of Elim's 70 palm trees being watered by 12 springs creates a fascinating backdrop for the Sinai covenant and its priestly kingdom concept. At the Israelites' previous encampment, the water was bitter; at Elim where 12 springs watered 70 palm trees, the water was sweet.

The Prophets' Vision of Israel's Mission

The Bible tells how Israel consistently failed in being both the holy people and the priestly kingdom called for in the Sinai covenant. Because Israel's prophets talked repeatedly about global mission, it cannot be said that the Israelites did not know the desires of God's heart that were clearly announced by passages such as Psalm 113:3: "From the rising of the sun to the place where it sets, the name of the LORD is to be praised." Though some take the phrase about the rising and setting of the sun to mean "from sunup to sundown," the reference is geographical and means from as far eastward as one can imagine to as far westward as can be imagined.

Nothing Left But the Covers

If you take missions out of the Bible, there is little left but the covers.[6] —Nina Gunter, former director of Nazarene Missions International

Furthermore, the Old Testament prophets' use of two Hebrew words, ***gôyim*** and *'am,* makes plain God's wish that His people participate in global mission. *Gôyim,* a word meaning groups of people with distinct political, ethnic, or territorial identities, is rendered in English as *nations* or *peoples* (see Isaiah 11:10; 12:4; 66:19; Jeremiah 16:19; Ezekiel 36:22-24; Daniel 7:13-14; Micah 1:2; 4:2; Zephaniah 2:11; Haggai 2:7; Zechariah 2:11; 9:10; and Malachi 1:11). Those who think the Old Testament focuses exclusively on Israel need to know that *gôyim* ("peoples") appears about 500 times in the Hebrew Bible. It often is used together with and in contrast to *'am,* a word that means people in the sense of them having descended from the same ancestor. Thus, *gôyim* most frequently means non-Israelite peoples while *'am* is more often the label for Israel.

The latter part of Isaiah shows Israelite reflection on God's desire for a relationship with neighboring Gentile peoples. Isaiah 42:1-4 speaks of a Servant of Yahweh who will have a global mission. It begins with the words, "Here is my servant, whom I uphold, my chosen one in whom I delight; I will put my Spirit on him, and he will bring justice to the nations *[gôyim]"* (v. 1). The passage then concludes by observing, "In his teaching the islands will put their hope" (v. 4). It may have startled some Jews to hear one of their prophets declare that "islands," which can also be rendered as "coastlands," were going to hear the message of Yahweh's servant. The Hebrews were not much of a seafaring people. To be sure, they fished in a body of water that they called a "sea" even though it—the Sea of Galilee—is a great deal smaller than many of the world's lakes. On the other hand, the Jews rarely ventured out on the real sea to their west, the Mediterranean. Yet, this passage in Isaiah pointed to a Hebrew messianic figure who would become known and welcomed by the Gentile world far beyond the shores of the Jewish homeland.

Isaiah 55:4-5 also develops this vision of God's desire for mission to the nations. Speaking on behalf of God, the prophet refers to an unidentified ruler: "See, I have made him a witness to the peoples, a ruler and commander of the peoples" (v. 4). The Hebrew word translated as "peoples" in this verse is neither *gôyim* nor *'am.* It is *le'ōm,* a word that encompasses the other two Hebrew words, thus implying that God would have a future Witness whose work would be with both Jewish and Gentile peoples.[7]

Verse 5 continues, "Surely you will summon nations you know not, and nations that do not know you will come running to you, because of the LORD your God, the Holy One of Israel, for he has endowed you with splendor." Since the author has returned to using *gôyim,* it is clear that this special Servant was going to invite the world's nations and people groups to enter into a glorious relationship with Yahweh, Creator of all.

Calling God "the Holy One of Israel" may also be one more way for the prophet to point to Israel's calling to be a "holy nation" that would model for all peoples what an adoring relationship with the Holy One should look like. Isaiah 55:6-7 contains a gospel message for all the peoples of the earth: "Seek the LORD while he may be found; call on him while he is near. Let the wicked forsake their ways and the unrighteous their thoughts. Let them turn to the LORD, and he will have mercy on them, and to our God, for he will freely pardon." The responsibility of God's people to proclaim to the whole world Yahweh's coming work of restoration also appears in 60:1-3. There, the result of God's work among His people is said to result in additional nations and people groups coming to the light. Isaiah concludes his book with a vision of God's final work of gathering peoples and nations from all the world:

> And I, because of what they have planned and done, am about to come and gather the people of all nations and languages, and they will come and see my glory. I will set a sign among them, and I will send some of those who survive to the nations—to Tarshish, to the Libyans and Lydians (famous as archers), to Tubal and Greece, and to the distant islands that have not heard of my fame or seen my glory. They will proclaim my glory among the nations. And they will bring all your people, from all the nations, to my holy mountain in Jerusalem as an offering to the LORD *(66:18-20).*

The *gôyim,* which here appears to mean language groups, will be gathered by God who will reveal His glory to them. In an affirmation of the "blessed to be a blessing" principle, some from these gathered nations will then be commissioned to proclaim God's glory to other nations, gathering even more into the family of God.

World missions was on God's mind from the beginning.[8]

—Dave Davidson

About a century after Isaiah, God's call came to Jeremiah, "Before I formed you in the womb I knew you, before you were born I set you apart; I appointed you as a prophet to the nations" (Jeremiah 1:5). It is noteworthy that God says He is appointing Jeremiah as a prophet to the *gôyim* rather than just to Israel. At that point in time, God's people were being menaced by the Babylonians. However, when God spoke to Jeremiah it was not about Israel's survival; it was to point Jeremiah toward a mission among the nations of the world. Furthermore, the wording indicates that commissioning Jeremiah to the nations was not a fleeting afterthought.

Unlike Paul or even Jonah, Jeremiah did not make any missionary journeys. Perhaps one might argue that Jeremiah was supposed to prophesy *about* Gentile nations like Egypt, Assyria, and Babylon and the way those nations would impact the southern kingdom of Judah. That interpretation, however, is hard to reconcile with the wording of Jeremiah 1:10: "See, today I appoint you over nations and kingdoms to uproot and tear down, to destroy and overthrow, to build and to plant." Words like *build* and *plant* would seem to include more than simply pronouncing divine judgment on various people groups. Would this building include announcing to the nations God's desire for a relationship? How all that played out in Jeremiah's lifetime is hard to see, although Jeremiah 43 and 44 do tell of Jeremiah being taken into Egypt where he declared the word of God to the Egyptians as well as to the Judean refugees living there. Of course, the inclusion of Jeremiah and Lamentations in the biblical canon has meant that long after his death, Jeremiah's ministry has indeed had wide global influence.

An Obstinate Missionary

God sent a Hebrew prophet to Nineveh, the capital of the violent and brutal Assyrian empire, to call that city to repentance. By sending Jonah to Nineveh, God confirms His desire for a relationship with all peoples, including Israel's enemies.

Jonah's reluctance to go to Nineveh mirrored Israel's reluctance to be used by God to draw the Gentiles to himself. Jonah eventually went to Nineveh and preached his message. At that point, instead of rejoicing at the Ninevites' marvelous turning to God, Jonah complained because destruction was not raining down on Nineveh. God responded by chastising Jonah for not sharing His compassionate heart.

Sadly, this brief story epitomizes what has often happened to mission theology and practice:

1. God's will and heart are clearly committed to mission to all peoples through a priestly ministry by His people.
2. His people resist engaging in the mission to which they have been called in the Abrahamic covenant.

In "Coming Around," Thomas Carlisle expresses that thought in a more poetic way:

> And Jonah stalked
> to his shaded seat and waited for God
> to come around
> to his way of thinking.
>
> And God is still waiting for a host of Jonahs
> in their comfortable houses
> to come around
> to his way of loving.[9]

Jonah is an example of a point of view often prevalent among God's people (see sidebar "An Obstinate Missionary"). Most likely Jonah did not want to preach in Nineveh because it was not a Jewish city and he did not want God to deal graciously with non-Jews. Outraged at that prejudicial attitude, God asks a haunting question that is left unanswered: "Should I not have concern for the great city Nineveh?" (Jonah 4:11). It is clear that God cared for the people of Nineveh even if Jonah did not. Behind Jonah's story is the idea that permeates the entire Bible—that Yahweh is a missionary God who desires that His people share His missionary heart.

The New Testament

Ultimately, God sent one "greater than Jonah" and "greater than Solomon" (Matthew 12:41-42). When Matthew introduced this greater one as "the son of David, the son of Abraham" (1:1), he was connecting Jesus with the Abrahamic covenant. It should not, therefore, be surprising that this promised Messiah started and ended His earthly ministry with words about all peoples. At the onset of Jesus' ministry came the marvelous words of John 3:16: "God so loved the world." Then, with Jesus' time on earth drawing to a close, He pointed out a connection between the world mission enterprise of His followers and the consummation of all things: "This gospel of the kingdom will be preached in the whole world as a testimony to all nations, and then the end will come" (Matthew 24:14).

Taking Jesus at His Word

People who don't believe in missions have not read the New Testament. Right from the beginning, Jesus said the field is the world. The early church took Him at His word and went East, West, North and South.[10]

—J. Howard Edington, pastor

Even though it took Peter time to embrace what Jesus said about going to all peoples, it was clear that he had heard the message. In a sermon he preached in the Temple not long after the Day of Pentecost, Peter looks back to the Abrahamic covenant, "You are heirs of the prophets and of the covenant God made with your fathers. He said to Abraham, 'Through your offspring all peoples on earth will be blessed'" (Acts 3:25). Although Peter did not travel as extensively as Paul, the Holy Spirit used him in some key cross-cultural preaching. On the Day of Pentecost, it was Peter who preached to the cosmopolitan crowd in Jerusalem. Later, Peter was pushed out of his Jewish comfort zone when he was sent to preach in a Roman army officer's house (Acts 10).

After his own conversion, Paul came to see that, from the beginning, the Abrahamic covenant was meant to include the Gentiles. To the churches of Galatia, Paul wrote, "Scripture foresaw that God would justify the Gentiles by faith, and announced the gospel in advance to Abraham: 'All nations will be blessed through you'" (Galatians 3:8).

The Gospels

As has been noted, Matthew 1 places Jesus within the lineage of Abraham, the man to whom God had said, "All peoples on earth will be blessed through you" (Genesis 12:3). The genealogy Matthew gives for Jesus has an intriguing non-Abrahamic feature: four women, two of whom were not Hebrews. Because names of Hebrew male ancestors would have sufficed to show the authenticity of the Messiah's lineage, the inclusion of non-Hebrew women in this most-Jewish of the Gospels clearly signals that Matthew saw Jesus as a Messiah for all peoples.

> There is no gospel without mission, and there is no mission without the gospel.[11] —Alex Deasley, Nazarene Theological Seminary professor

Matthew tells how the infant Jesus was sought out by Gentiles, magi from the East (Matthew 2:1-11). The area where Jesus grew up was called "Galilee of the Gentiles" (4:15; cf. Isaiah 9:1). The Gospels recount significant ministry encounters Jesus had with Gentiles. Among those was the encounter with the Syro-Phoenician woman (Mark 7:24-30), an episode in which Jesus was likely showing His disciples the absurdity of their narrow, prejudicial ethnocentrism. A man Jesus delivered from demonic possession in the area of the Gerasenes may have been a Gentile (Mark 5; Luke 8). After healing a Roman centurion's servant, Jesus said that Gentiles would one day join Jewish patriarchs at the feast (Matthew 8:11, likely a reference to Isaiah 25:6-12).

The episode in which Jesus cleansed the Temple is full of global mission implications. People are inclined to think Jesus got upset because of commerce going on in the Temple, but that does not seem to be the trigger point for Jesus' anger. What Jesus said that day was: "Is it not written, 'My house shall be called a house of prayer for all the nations'? But you have made it a den of robbers" (Matthew 21:13, NRSV, quoting Isaiah 56:7). The disturbing thing, therefore, for Jesus was not currency exchange or the selling of sacrificial birds. The main issue was that because an area of the Temple (most likely the Court of the Gentiles) was occupied by commerce, the Temple was being kept from being "a house of prayer for all the nations."

The first time Jesus sent His followers on a preaching mission, it was to their fellow Jews (Matthew 10). However, His best-known "go" command is His post-Resurrection restatement of the "all nations will be blessed" part of the Abrahamic covenant. That restatement, found in Matthew 28:19-20, launched Jesus' followers into a vocation to create a global fellowship spanning all clan and cultural boundaries. It has been rightly said that this Great Commission of Jesus is not the Great Suggestion. Missionary Hudson Taylor said the same thing in a slightly different way, "The Great Commission is not an option to be considered; it is a command to be obeyed."[12] Those who take Scripture seriously understand that this Great Commission, also found in Mark 16:15, is the Church's Kingdom calling.

The 153 Fish

To most of us the number of "a hundred and fifty-three," which was the number of fish caught in the net along the shores of Galilee after the resurrection (John 21:4-14), seems incredibly trifling. We might be inclined to wonder why the writer had any interest in giving the number. When, however, we realize that in ancient times the number 153 was given as the total number of all the tribes and nations of the earth, it is no wonder that the early church interpreted this passage as the assurance of success in fulfilling the Great Commission to bear the Good News to all men everywhere.[13]

—Eugene Nida, linguist and Bible translator

The Gospel of John repeatedly emphasizes how central mission is in the heart of God. Throughout John's Gospel, Jesus is referred to as being "sent" (see sidebar "Sending"). Indeed, a strong rationale for the Church's mission involvement can be based on the sending of the Son by the Father. In the Gospels, **apostle** or "sent one" always refers to one of Jesus' followers. However, Hebrews 3:1 calls Jesus an "apostle" or "sent one." The writer of Hebrews uses that language because the Father sent the Son to all the world (John 3:16). The Son responded to His own sending by saying to His followers: "As the Father has sent me, I am sending you" (20:21). Scripture makes clear that this divine sending/going has a **soteriological** purpose, the salvation of the world (3:17; 6:38, 57; 17:3, 21). Jesus tells His disciples that the Holy Spirit who has already been active in their ministry will soon empower them in fresh ways for mission (14:26; 16:7). In Jesus' high-priestly prayer for His followers the night before His crucifixion, He said the disciples would be commissioned for a missionary task, that is, they were being *sent* into the world (17:18).

Sending

Almost every page of the Gospel of John speaks of mission as sending, with regard to Jesus and with regard to us as well. Jesus did not come on His own, but His Father sent Him (John 8:42). He did not speak His own words but the words of the Father who sent Him (3:34; 7:16; 12:49). He did not do His own works but the works of the Father who sent Him (5:36; 9:4). These works were His miracles. He did not come to do His own will but the will of His Father who sent Him (5:30; 6:38). Like Jesus, we must receive a supernatural message, a supernatural ministry and a supernatural motivation to enable us to fulfill our mission.[14]

—Paul R. Orjala, missionary to Haiti

Acts

Acts shows how the Early Church realized it had a global mission. In Acts 1:8 Luke uses Jesus' own words to outline how his compact account of church history will unfold: "You will receive power when the Holy Spirit comes on you; and you will be my witnesses in Jerusalem, and in all Judea and Samaria, and to the ends of the earth." Following that geographical progression, Acts 1—7 describes the proclamation of the gospel in Jerusalem. Chapters 8—9 recount the spreading of the Good News into Judea and Samaria. The remainder of Acts describes church planting and discipling in the Gentile world around the northern rim of the Mediterranean Sea.

The diverse crowd to which Peter preached on the Day of Pentecost included people from across the Roman Empire. Acts 2:8-11 lists 15 different language groups who heard the gospel that day from Peter and others of the 120 who had been in the Upper Room. Peter interpreted the events of that particular Pentecost morning as fulfilling Old Testament prophecies involving all peoples. The miracle of languages occurring prior to Peter's sermon further indicated God's desire that the gospel be understandable to peoples of all nations. In 2:39, Peter says that *everyone,* and not just Hebrew-speaking Jews, who calls on the name of the Lord will be saved.

James' Speech to the Jerusalem Council

James spoke up: "Brothers, . . . listen to me. Simon has described to us how God first intervened to choose a people for his name from the Gentiles. The words of the prophets are in agreement with this, as it is written:

"'After this I will return
    and rebuild David's fallen tent.
Its ruins I will rebuild,
    and I will restore it,
that the rest of humanity may seek the Lord,
    even all the Gentiles who bear my name,
says the Lord, who does these things'—
    things known from long ago."

—Acts 15:13-18, quoting from Amos 9:11-12

Acts 10 tells how the circle of believers widens beyond Jewish culture when Peter visits the house of a Roman centurion in the coastal city of Caesarea and the Holy Spirit comes upon Gentiles there. A bigger breach into the Gentile world opened in chapter 11 when the gospel was preached to some Greeks in Antioch. Not long afterward, the Holy Spirit directed the church in Antioch to commission its first cross-cultural missionaries: "So after they had fasted and prayed, they placed their hands on them and sent them off" (13:3). The last half of Acts tells how missionaries originating from the church in Antioch took the gospel northward to Turkey and westward to Macedonia, Greece, Cyprus, Malta, and even to the Italian peninsula.

Paul's Life and Writings

Paul of Tarsus, whom many consider the greatest missionary of all time, set the pattern for missionary strategy in his willingness to:

- Suffer for Christ's sake
- Learn the local culture
- Look for receptive people
- Contextualize the gospel
- Plant churches rapidly
- Immediately empower local leadership
- Expect new churches to be self-sustaining
- Infuse churches with his own missionary vision

In his first letter to Timothy, Paul repeated Peter's thought about God wanting "all people to be saved" (1 Timothy 2:4). Paul felt specifically called to the cross-cultural missionary task that most Israelites had ignored (Ephesians 3:1-8). As was noted earlier, Paul reminded the Galatians that global mission had been God's plan all along (Galatians 3:8).

Spreading Fire

Where there is no mission, there is no Church, and where there is neither Church nor mission, there is no faith. . . . Mission, Gospel Preaching, is the spreading out of the fire which Christ has thrown upon the earth. He who does not propagate this fire shows that he is not burning. He who burns propagates the fire.[15]

—Emil Brunner, theologian

Romans is often thought of as the major theological treatise of the New Testament. Paul began that letter by saying he had been asked "to call all the Gentiles to faith and obedience" (Romans 1:5). Galatians 2:7-8 echoes the same thought. In 2 Corinthians 10:15-16 Paul announced his desire to preach to the "regions beyond." As Paul took the Good News into the Gentile world, he told those non-Jewish believers that they, too, had become children of Abraham (Romans 9:22-24; 15:27-28; Galatians 3:7, 28). This would imply that because they were being blessed, they had a responsibility to be a blessing.

Both Old and New Testaments portray Yahweh as a missionary God who seeks and sends to seek. That picture emerged immediately after the Fall and was intensified when God made His covenant with Abraham. If God's people today want to be covenant partakers, they must view global mission as something more than optional or tangential. Passages like Romans 1:14-16 put mission at the very core of what the Church is and does. If the Church is to be truly the Church, it must operate, as Paul said to the Romans, "by the command of the eternal God, so that all nations might believe and obey him" (16:26, NIV).

Questions for Reflection

1. Why can it be said that the biblical basis of mission can be defined as the search for the heart of God?
2. What significance does God's covenant with Abraham have for the entire world?
3. What are the implications of Israel being a chosen people?
4. What does *gôyim* mean and what makes this often-used Hebrew word critical to understanding what the Bible says about mission?
5. In what way does Jonah's attitude toward Nineveh mirror Israel's reluctance to engage in mission?
6. How does Jesus reveal the missionary character of God?
7. How does the Gospel of John explain mission as sending?
8. What statements by Peter and Paul show their understanding of the missionary character of the Abrahamic covenant?

3
CHRISTIAN MISSION
A BRIEF HISTORY

Objectives

Your study of this chapter should help you:

- See the key events in the history of mission from the time of Paul to the beginning of the 20th century
- Recognize how conditions at the beginning of the New Testament period aided the formation of Christian mission
- Define *Diaspora* and explain its significance for mission
- Evaluate the importance of early Christian missionaries (e.g., Patrick, Augustine, and Boniface)
- Identify important moments in the rise of Islam
- Understand the roles of the Pietists and of William Carey in the development of the modern era of mission

Key Words to Understand

Diaspora
monotheism
Qur'an (Koran)
Pax Romana
Patrick
Augustine
Alopen
Muhammad
ethnocentrism
Pietists
Nicholas von Zinzendorf
Moravians
John Wesley
William Carey
Robert Morrison
Robert Moffat
Samuel Mills
Haystack Prayer Meeting
Adoniram Judson
J. Hudson Taylor
Student Volunteer Movement

Getting from where Christianity was on the day of Jesus' ascension to where it is today has made for an interesting journey. Along the way the faith has been battered by internal and external persecution. It has found itself outlawed by government decrees in some places and embraced as the state religion in others. Through the rise and fall of nations and empires and the emergence and collapse of cultural systems, the Christian faith has done more than survive; it has thrived, spreading across every continent and to the islands of the seven seas.

No other religious faith has taken root and become indigenized in as many places as has Christianity. Believers in Jesus Christ can now be found within every one of the world's 238 politically organized nations. Michael Jaffarian, former missionary to India and Singapore, has asserted that Christians can communicate in more than 90 percent of the world's spoken languages and dialects.[1] What began 2,000 years ago as a small movement within Judaism has clearly blossomed into a global religion.

Laying the Groundwork: Between the Testaments

Synagogue Worship

After the Babylonians destroyed the Jerusalem Temple in 586/7 B.C., the Jews went for the better part of a century without a Temple. Forced to come up with new patterns of worship, they developed the infinitely reproducible local synagogue. Synagogues, which did not use animal sacrifices, could be organized anywhere there were at least 10 male Jews. This new style of worship involved significant lay participation with male Jews in good standing allowed to publicly read and comment on Scripture. During the first half century of Christianity, these synagogue meetings served as centers for spreading the Good News. In addition, synagogue services became a pattern for Christian worship events.

Diaspora

In the aftermath of Jerusalem's destruction, the Babylonians forced large numbers of Jews to move to Babylon. To escape that forced deportation, a significant number of Jews fled southward to Egypt. Over the next five centuries, Jews from these two population centers—Egypt and Babylon—spread far and wide. This dispersion, or **Diaspora,** of Jews created a network through which first-century Christian mission could flow. After all, Jesus was the Messiah whose advent had been prophesied by the Hebrew Scriptures. Having people sprinkled all around the Mediterranean who were versed in those Scriptures gave the Holy Spirit a perfect foundation on which to work!

That the Jews of the Diaspora became skilled in cross-cultural communication was also a plus for the spread of the gospel. Living as a minority among polytheistic peoples, they developed an apologetic or rational defense for their **monotheism.** They translated the Hebrew Scriptures (the Old Testament) into Greek, the lingua franca or trade language of the Greco-Roman world. That the Jewish holy books could be translated and remain authoritative Scripture is different from the situation with some other religious texts. For example, most Muslims view the **Qur'an** as the word of Allah only when it is in Arabic. Translations of the Islamic holy book are considered commentaries rather than the actual Qur'an (formerly spelled "Koran" in English). For Hellenistic Jews, the Septuagint version of the Old Testament was authentic Holy Scripture even though it was in Greek rather than Hebrew. While the Council of Jamnia in A.D. 90 would move Jews back to using the Old Testament in Hebrew, the way the Greek Septuagint was viewed paved the way for early Christians to embrace that widely used language as one through which God could speak. Having the Hebrew Bible in Greek made it easy for Greek New Testament documents to be accepted as Holy Scripture. For many in Christian mission, this translation of the Old Testament into a lingua franca also laid the groundwork for translation work to seem a normal part of the missionary enterprise.

The God-fearers

The monotheism of the Hebrew Bible and its high ethical standards attracted numerous Gentiles, and by the first century B.C., Gentiles were associated with Jewish synagogues all around the Mediterranean. However, while they financially supported the synagogues, attended services, and studied the Hebrew Scriptures, those Gentiles did not heartily embrace Jewish identity markers such as circumcision and dietary laws. Because of that reluctance, they frequently failed to follow through on conversion to Judaism. These God-fearers, as they were called, would be a receptive audience for Christian missionaries who preached from the Old Testament but did not see circumcision and Jewish dietary restrictions as part of God's plan for all peoples.

The Empire's Positive Effects

The military and cultural rule of the Greek and Roman empires also aided Christian mission. Roman rule brought 150 years of peaceful stability, the **Pax Romana,** to the Mediterranean basin. The Pax Romana fostered economic and cultural growth that made it easier for people to consider new religious ideas. To maintain their rule, the Romans built roads that facilitated the travel of Christian missionaries. Then, when localized cultures were overwhelmed by more dominant ones (such as the Greco-Roman culture), confidence in local gods and traditional religious beliefs was undermined. That created an openness to other religions. Thus, although several Roman emperors actively persecuted Christians, the political unity these emperors gave to the Mediterranean world, the roads they built, and the doubts their cultural dominance induced about local religions spread the very faith those emperors tried to stamp out.

The First 500 Years

In July of the year 180 a number of very insignificant people, led by a man named Speratus, coming from the small, now unidentifiable townlet of Scillium, were brought before the proconsul Saturninus in Carthage and charged with the practice of an illicit religion. The proconsul was reluctant to order their execution and begged them to "return to a right mind," or, at least, think it over for 30 days, but they remained adamant in adherence to "the religious rites of the Christians." They insisted that they lived in the most moral way, abhorred murder, theft, and bearing false witness. They willingly paid tax but absolutely refused to do as the proconsul required and "swear by the genius of our Lord the Emperor" because they did not recognize "the empire of this world" but served instead the "God whom no man has seen nor can see." Such are the simple words of Speratus. Donata, one of his companions, added "Give honour to Caesar as unto Caesar, but fear to God," while Secunda remarked that "I wish to be none other than I am." Speratus had brought with him a bag containing letters of St. Paul, in case, perhaps, they might need to refer to them, but there was no need. As they persisted in their obduracy, Saturninus read out a sentence of execution and the twelve of them, seven men and five women, were immediately beheaded. They reign, concluded the undoubtedly authentic account of their martyrdom, "with the Father and Son and Holy Spirit."

It may seem surprising that already in the year 180 one could find a little group of highly committed Christians in some obscure corner of North Africa. . . . [This] demonstrates how fast this new religion was spreading across the Roman world and, in fact, already beyond it.[2]

—Adrian Hastings

One way of dividing up Christian history is to think of A.D. 1 to 500 as a period of expansion, 500 to 1500 as a period of uncertainty, 1500 to 1800 as a renewal of expansion, and 1800 to 1914 as the great century of Christian missions. At the beginning of that first period, not long after Christ's resurrection and ascension, Paul of Tarsus became one of Christianity's chief persecutors. A transforming encounter on the Damascus road turned Paul (then called Saul) into the most visible cross-cultural missionary of the New Testament. Paul and others masterfully contextualized the gospel into Greco-Roman culture, using principles many consider timeless. Roland Allen's classic book *Missionary Methods: St. Paul's or Ours?* urged mission leaders to adopt Paul's ministry as a pattern for today's missionary endeavors.

By A.D. 200, Christianity had infected every province of the Roman Empire. The gospel had also reached eastward to Mesopotamia, Persia, and India. An imperial declaration issued in A.D. 313 by Emperor Constantine giving Christianity legal protection reflected how widespread the faith had become. A century or so later, an English slave in his 20s named **Patrick** escaped from slavery in Ireland. Some time later, he felt called to return to Ireland as a missionary. His vibrant Christian witness turned Irish hearts from belief in spirits living in the rocks and trees to belief in the Lord Jesus. In 30 years of missionary ministry Patrick was so successful that he was able to plant about 700 churches in Ireland.

No Shortcut to Understanding People

The fact that Patrick understood the people and their language, their issues, and their ways, serves as the most strategically significant, single insight that was to drive the wider expansion of Celtic Christianity, and stands as perhaps our greatest single learning from this movement. There is no shortcut to understanding the people. When you understand the people, you will often know what to say and do, and how. When the people know that the Christians understand them, they infer that maybe the High God understands them too.[3]

—George G. Hunter III

By A.D. 500, Christianity had enveloped the Roman Empire and had begun penetrating the Gothic and Slavic areas of Central and Northern Europe. The faith also continued spreading eastward and southward. However, after more than four centuries of nearly continuous expansion, some difficult days, even days of retrenchment, lay ahead.

500 to 1500

The first part of the thousand years from 500 to 1500 saw continued mission expansion. In 596, Gregory the Great, bishop of Rome, sent 40 Benedictine missionaries to Britain. En route to their assignment, the group became frightened about dangers they might face. They sent their leader, **Augustine,** back to Rome to ask for permission to abort the mission. Gregory would not hear of it and ordered them on.

At about the same time, the fruits of Patrick's missionary ministry in Ireland began multiplying. The Celts, the people group evangelized by Patrick, launched out as missionaries themselves. One such endeavor came in 563, when Columba took a large group on a mission to the Picts in Scotland. That resulted in the establishment of a missionary training center on Iona, an island off Scotland's west coast. By 633, Iona had spawned a mission led by Aidan to England's northeast coast. Both of these group missions demonstrated what Craig Sheppard, missionary to Kosovo, has called "the power of the critical mass."[4] Within 100 years, the majority of the Picts of Scotland had become Christian and thousands of pagan Angles and Saxons had been converted. These people groups were soon sending missionaries to northern Europe.

By the 7th century A.D., Christianity had been taken across Asia to China. A 10-foot tall limestone stele discovered in China in 1625 tells of the arrival around A.D. 635 of **Alopen**, a Christian missionary. Among other things, that monument, which archaeologists think was erected in A.D. 781, says, "Bishop Alopen of the Kingdom of Ta-Ch'in (Syria) . . . has come from afar. . . . Having examined the scope of his teaching . . . having observed its principal and most essential points, we reached the conclusion that they cover all that is most important in life."[5] By 638 a church building had been constructed in China with imperial financial support. Alopen and his Chinese coworkers had also completed the first Christian book in Chinese: *The Sutra of Jesus the Messiah.*

400-Year Epochs

One way of visualizing the spread of Christianity is to use Ralph Winter's 400-year Christian history epochs where each supercentury has a cultural basin into which Christianity flowed during that time:

- 0-400—Romans
- 400-800—Central Europe (Goths, Visigoths, Slavs, and Vandals)
- 800-1200—Vikings
- 1200-1600—Muslim world and global coastlands
- 1600 to present—Ends of the earth

Winter's list can seem simplistic and too Western in focus. There are things it does not account for, such as the missionary thrust into China in the 600s. It does, however, give a good idea of the timing and direction of Christianity's flow into several key cultural groups.

Even with such advances, the years from 500 to 1500 held some disheartening periods for the Christian Church. In 845 government-sponsored persecution against Christians broke out in China. Within a few decades, all traces of Christianity disappeared from that country, except for one limestone monument. At about the same time devastating losses occurred in North Africa and the Middle East, causing historian Kenneth Scott Latourette to note that by 950, "Christianity was far less prominent in the total human scene than it had been in A.D. 500."[6] Two events caused this loss of prominence: One was the sapping of the vitality of the Christian movement by repercussions from the Roman Empire's collapse and the other was the rise of Islam whose militancy dealt Christianity some hard blows.

Filling the Power Vacuum

When the Roman Empire disintegrated under the weight of repeated Barbarian invasions, the consequent collapse of civil institutions created a power vacuum. The part of Christianity led by the bishop of Rome moved to fill that vacuum. The church thus began wielding political as well as religious authority. Sadly, in assuming political power, the church traded its prophetic voice for the tasks of administering cities, collecting taxes, running prisons, defending borders, and maintaining armies.

The Rise of Islam

In the sixth and seventh centuries A.D., Christians and Jews could be found in trading caravans that traversed the Arabian peninsula. Through these travelers, fragmentary information about the gospel reached a man in Mecca named **Muhammad.** Muhammad was born in A.D. 570 and began having visions at the age of 40. His "revelations," which included snatches of biblical stories, were eventually written down, becoming what is called the Qur'an. While the holy books of Islam and Christianity appear to contain some of the same stories, the narratives common to the Bible and the Qur'an differ in fundamental details. For instance, in the Qur'an, Abraham's chosen offspring is Ishmael rather than Isaac. The Qur'an says it was Pharaoh's wife who adopted Moses rather than Pharaoh's daughter (Sura 28:7-9). The Qur'an says that the Hebrews made a golden calf at Mount Sinai at the suggestion of a mysterious Samaritan rather than Aaron (Sura 20:85-87, 95-97). In the Qur'anic Sodom and Gomorrah narrative, Abraham does not bargain with God about the number of righteous people in the city; God simply tells Abraham what He is going to do (al-Hijr 15:15-60; Hud 11:74-75; al-'Ankabut 29:31-32). While the Qur'an calls Jesus a prophet born of a virgin, it emphatically states that Jesus (or Isa) is not God incarnate who is the Savior of the world (Sura 5:75-76; 4:171).

When Muhammad began preaching his new ideas to the animistic people of Mecca, persecution broke out against him and those who had accepted him as a prophet. In what Muslims call the *Hijra* (withdrawal), Muhammad escaped to nearby Medina. After accumulating converts in Medina, Muhammad returned to Mecca with a military force, conquering it and making it his base. After his death in 632, Muhammad's followers continued military campaigns across the Middle East and North Africa. In fairly quick succession they conquered Damascus, Antioch, Jerusalem, Caesarea, and Alexandria. Not much later, in 650, the Persian Empire fell to them. Muslim armies swept across North Africa, taking Carthage in 697. By 715, Islamic military forces had crossed the straits of Gibraltar and occupied most of Spain. Only when they attempted to cross the Pyrenees into France in 732 were they finally stopped.

While Christians were not evicted from countries taken over by Muslim armies, religious conversion was a one-way street. Jews or Christians could become Muslim, but Muslims were not allowed to become Christians. A **Law of Apostasy** even permitted the killing of Muslims who converted to Christianity. As can be imagined, this death threat based on the *Hadith* (a work containing eyewitness accounts of Muhammad's life and quotes attributed to him) greatly hindered evangelism in Muslim-dominated areas. Thus, by 950, though Christianity was moving northward into Viking Scandinavia, no longer was it the dominant religion in its former heartland of the Middle East and North Africa.

The church-sponsored Crusades of the 12th and 13th centuries in which Christian armies attempted to retake areas of the Middle East were a dark blot of misconceived mission rooted in a geographic, terrestrial understanding of the kingdom of God. It was a dark period not only in terms of losses but also in terms of attempts to militarily reevangelize areas that had been Christian before the appearance of Islam. The result was that by 1500 the Western church had not only lost great geographic areas but had also besmirched its reputation for centuries to come.

Missionary Orders

Even with considerable unchristian activity going on in Christ's name, there was a "remnant" of believers (in the words of Jeremiah 23) whose reflection of God's missionary character and purpose caused a resurgence of the faith. One example was Francis of Assisi. When Francis went to Egypt preaching the gospel, the Sultan reportedly said, "If I would meet more Christians like you, I would be tempted to become one."[7] Francis turned his followers into a missionary organization: the Order of the Little Brothers. Not long after Francis's death, the Franciscans, as they came to be called, were in China preaching the gospel.

In the late 1200s, a well-to-do Spaniard named Ramon Llull spent time, energy, and family fortune establishing a missionary training center on the west Mediterranean island of Majorca. Its purpose was to prepare missionaries for Muslim North Africa. Llull himself made evangelistic forays into Tunisia and some reports say he died there.

In the 1300s Franciscan and Dominican missionaries were sent to India and southeast Asia. In the 1400s the western coast of sub-Saharan Africa saw the arrival of Roman Catholic missionaries.

1500 to 1799

The years from 1500 to 1799 saw fresh expansion of the Christian faith, the spirit of which is exemplified in Martin de Valencia. In 1511, Martin came to believe that Psalm 57 prophesied the conversion of all peoples. Among the words of that psalm are:

> Be exalted, O God, above the heavens;
> let your glory be over all the earth. . . .
> I will praise you, Lord, among the nations;
> I will sing of you among the peoples *(vv. 5, 9).*

Martin asked, "When will this be? When will this prophecy be filled?"[8] Not long afterward, he had a vision of multitudes being converted and baptized and began to pray that he would be the one sent to convert them. Martin died 20 years later as a Franciscan missionary in Mexico.

Missionaries and Colonial Adventurers

European exploration thrusts provided sea lanes and overland paths for colonization enterprises. These transportation routes facilitated Christian missionary outreach in the same ways as had the Roman Empire's roads of the first century. Because Christian missionaries and colonial adventurers of the 16th and 17th centuries sometimes traveled together, they occasionally are assumed to have been basically one and the same. They were not. The life of Bartolomé de las Casas shows how diametrically opposed they could be. Around 1500, Las Casas went to the New World as a slave-owning colonial settler. Eight years later he had a change of heart, set his slaves free, entered the priesthood, and began a fight against slavery and the mistreatment of indigenous peoples.

Of course, even though missionaries did not share all the aims of the colonizers, they were still "children of their times." It was difficult for their judgment not to be colored by the **ethnocentrism** of colonialism. For their part, colonial authorities tried to control and even curtail missionary activity because the preaching of the gospel was deemed "unsettling" to people in subjugated lands.

Protestant Foot-Dragging

Although the Protestant Reformation brought renewal to the Western European Church in the 1500s, Reformed churches did not immediately follow the missionary-sending model of the first-century Antioch church. To be sure, in 1523 Martin Luther did write a hymn based on these words from Psalm 67:

May God be gracious to us and bless us
and make his face shine upon us—
so that your ways may be known on earth,
your salvation among all nations. . . .
May the nations be glad and sing for joy . . .
May the peoples praise you, O God;
may all the peoples praise you *(vv. 1-5).*

Titled "May God Bestow on Us His Grace," that hymn has been called "the first missionary hymn of Protestantism." However, Gustav Warneck and other scholars noted that Luther almost always interpreted the Great Commission as simply meaning that believers should share their faith with their next-door neighbors.

About 150 years after the Reformation began, Lutheran layman Count Truchess of Wetzhausen asked the theological faculty of Wittenberg why his church had not sent out missionaries in obedience to the Great Commission. Their response was that Jesus' Great Commission had been directed only to the original apostles who had fulfilled it. Fortunately, the Holy Spirit was still at work and, within a decade, Justinian von Welz was pelting European Christians with tracts calling on the Church to send missionaries to evangelize the world.

While the Reformed state churches of Northern Europe were tardy to mobilize for world mission, a zeal for global evangelization enveloped Pietist groups whose intense devotional lives led them to embrace God's heart for all the world. Under the leadership of Philip Spener and August Hermann Francke, the **Pietists** founded the University of Halle. That school soon became what Canadian missionary to China J. Herbert Kane called the "fountainhead of the missionary enterprise in the 18th century."[9] Out of Halle came the first Protestant mission organization whose first two missionaries, Bartholomew Ziegenbalg and Henry Plutschau, arrived in India in 1706.

A bit later, Pietist missionary ventures came to center in the Moravian refugees who had settled on the estate of Count **Nicholas von Zinzendorf**. His fervor sparked the Moravian missionary outreach to the New World and to India. The depth of the count's passion was noted by historian Frederick Klees, who wrote: "At one time Zinzendorf went so far as to decide that it was more important [for the **Moravians**] to convert the heathen than to sow grain to keep themselves alive."[10]

After pointing out that **John Wesley** had in 1740 translated one of Zinzendorf's hymns into English, Mark Noll commented:

> Evangelicals . . . responded to unique possibilities of their age by being much more active in cross-cultural evangelism than any Protestants had

> been before their time. The missionary efforts of Spener, Francke, and the Moravians were major Protestant innovations. The zeal displayed by the Wesleys, Whitefield and a host of unsung Methodist itinerants for carrying the gospel message to Britain's miners, soldiers, industrial workers and others whom the established church ignored was the beginning of massive evangelical efforts at carrying the gospel to the unreached. . . . By the end of the eighteenth century, evangelicals in the English-speaking regions would be imitating their Pietist colleagues from Germany and Scandinavia in beginning to send representatives overseas to preach the gospel.[11]

As Europeans became aware that indigenous peoples inhabited what was often called the New World, the Roman Catholics, Moravians, and others began trying to evangelize them. Two important mission societies were founded in Britain in the 17th century: the Society for the Propagation of the Gospel in New England (1649) and the Society for Promoting Christian Knowledge (1698).

In 1784 Methodist leader Thomas Coke submitted a "Plan for the Society for the Establishment of Missions Among the Heathen." Methodist missions began two years later when Coke set sail for Nova Scotia. Driven far southward by a storm, Coke's ship landed on Antigua in the eastern Caribbean. Undeterred, Coke set to work developing mission outreach to both slaves and landowners. Within a few years almost every colony in the West Indies had been reached by the Methodists. Under Coke's instigation, a mission to West Africa was undertaken in 1811. Coke also promoted mission ventures in Canada and on Gibraltar. Hoping to start Methodist missions in India, he set sail for Ceylon in 1814 but died on the way.

> I never made a sacrifice. We ought not to talk of "sacrifice" when we remember the great sacrifice that He made, who left His Father's throne on high to give Himself for us.[12]
>
> —David Livingstone, missionary to Africa

William Carey's Role

It was a bivocational Baptist pastor named William Carey who played such a pivotal missions mobilization role that he is often called the father of the modern missionary movement. Carey's burden for global mission began in the early 1790s after reading explorer Captain Cook's writings. Carey started talking with Baptist church leaders about the need to send missionaries to indigenous peoples like those Cook had described in *Voyages Around the World.* The response Carey got was less than enthusiastic. When he proposed to fellow ministers that they discuss fulfilling Christ's Great Commission, one said, "Young man, sit down. When God chooses to convert the heathen, He will do it without your help or ours."[13] Carey did sit down that day, but he continued to lift up God's imperative to mission. On May 30, 1792, he preached a mission sermon to the Baptist Ministers' Association using Isaiah 54:2-3: "Enlarge the place of your tent, stretch your tent curtains wide, do not hold back; lengthen your cords, strengthen your stakes. For you will spread out to the right and to the left." The passage is very similar to the prayer of Jabez in 1 Chronicles 4:10, which has been seen in recent years as concerned with personal advancement. Carey saw the similar words in Isaiah as an encouragement for the church to launch into global mission. In that 1792 sermon Carey used a phrase that had become a famous mission slogan: "Expect great things from God; attempt great things for God."

Five months after preaching that sermon, Carey was still trying to persuade his colleagues to mobilize themselves for world evangelism. Finally, at one meeting, he pulled out a booklet titled *Periodical Accounts Relating to Moravian Missions.* Holding it up, Carey said, "See what the Moravians have done! Can we not follow their example, and in obedience to our heavenly Master, go out into the world and preach the Gospel to the heathen?"[14] That day, Carey's zeal and the accomplishments of the Pietist Moravians aroused his listeners to action. They formed the Particular Baptist Society for Propagation of the Gospel Among the Heathen and set things in motion to send out Carey as their first missionary.

Other mission societies soon sprang up, in many cases through the direct influence of Carey's letters and booklets. Carey's most famous writing was his 87-page *Enquiry into the Obligation of Christians to Use Means for the Conversion of the Heathen.* Kenneth Mulholland, former missionary to Honduras and Costa Rica, said that Carey's *Enquiry* was "the Magna Carta of the Protestant missionary movement, and it is probably as significant in the history of the church as Luther's Ninety-Five Theses."[15]

1800 to 1914

After Carey set sail for India, the number of missionaries going out from Britain increased from what had been a trickle to a torrent. Indeed, the 120 years following William Carey's 1793 arrival in India saw such intense Protestant mission activity that Kenneth Scott Latourette and others have called it the great century of Christian missions. One of the British missionaries following Carey's example was **Robert Morrison,** who in 1807 went to China as that country's first Protestant missionary. When an owner of the ship on which

Morrison was traveling found out why Morrison was going to China, he asked, "Now, Mr. Morrison, do you really expect that you will make an impression on the idolatry of the Chinese Empire?"

"No, sir," replied Morrison, "but I expect God will."[16]

The London Missionary Society, which had been founded in 1795, sent Robert Moffat to Africa in 1816. It was Moffat's report of seeing "the smoke of a thousand villages where no missionary has ever been" that inspired David Livingstone to go to Africa in 1840.

Across the Atlantic, **Samuel Mills** of Connecticut felt a call to missionary service. In 1806, Mills enrolled in Williams College in western Massachusetts. One day he and five other students who had gathered for an outdoor prayer meeting took refuge from a rainstorm in the lee of a haystack. While that group normally prayed for the spiritual renewal of their campus, during that **Haystack Prayer Meeting** they found themselves praying for the spiritual needs of people around the world. That prayer meeting ignited a missions passion in their souls that never dissipated. On June 28, 1810, Mills, joined by **Adoniram Judson** and others, pleaded with the "Reverend Fathers" of Congregationalism to do something about fulfilling the Great Commission among the unreached. Thus, the American Board of Commissioners for Foreign Missions was born and by February of 1812 it had sent out its first eight missionaries, including Adoniram and Ann Judson.

In the mid-1800s, with Christian missionary work taking root in coastal cities around the globe, young missionary **J. Hudson Taylor** began feeling drawn to the unreached interior of China. In 1865 he resigned from his mission board and formed the China Inland Mission. Taylor's passion and his mobilizing skills made the China Inland Mission (now known as OMF International) the largest missionary sending agency in the world and sparked the formation of other mission boards focused on inland areas.

Being a missionary during the great century was not the easiest of vocations. Missionaries of that era frequently had their lives cut short by disease or hostile people groups. In some areas of Africa, the average life span of Western missionaries in the 1800s after arriving on the field was only nine months. During that period, some missionaries used coffins as shipping crates in order to spare others the trouble of constructing burial boxes for them.

No Sacrifice Too Great

If Jesus Christ be God and died for me, then no sacrifice can be too great for me to make for Him.[17]

—C. T. Studd, missionary to Africa

The gospel was also island-hopping in the Pacific as missionaries laid down their lives there. It is believed that John Williams of the London Missionary Society visited almost every inhabited Pacific island within a radius of 2,000 miles. In 1839, as Williams moved on to yet one more island, he was martyred. James Chalmers went to Papua New Guinea and was instrumental in bringing peace to several warring people groups. In 1901, during an effort to reach one more group, he was killed. The London Missionary Society sent Robert J. Thomas to Korea. In 1866, while his ship was marooned on a sandbar, Thomas was seen kneeling on the beach and handing a Bible to a man who then speared him to death. Later the man who had speared Thomas became a Christian and church leader. The man's nephew, Lee Yeung-Tai, also became a Christian and wound up working to update the Bible in Korean.

As the 19th century drew to a close, the devotion of such missionaries sparked the start of the **Student Volunteer Movement.** Under John R. Mott's leadership, the SVM adopted the slogan, "The evangelization of the world in this generation." Mott turned out to be a superb mobilizer of youthful volunteers. Two of his most widely circulated books were *The Pastor and Modern Missions: A Plea for Leadership in World Evangelization* (1905) and *The Decisive Hour of Christian Missions* (1911). The enthusiasm and passion of the Student Volunteer Movement resulted in more than 20,000 young people becoming foreign missionaries.

By the early 1900s tremendous global mission advance had occurred. Ralph Winter has calculated, for example, that in 1500 only 1 out of 70 people on earth was "a committed Christian," someone who knows and truly believes the God of the Bible. Four hundred years later, that ratio had improved to 1 committed Christian for every 28 people on earth.[18] Bible translation work surged forward during this period. In 1705 portions of Scripture were available in 60 languages. Two hundred years later, printed Scripture was available in 537 languages. By 1900, 62,000 foreign missionaries were being sponsored by 600 Protestant missions organizations in Europe and the Americas.

The spirit of this period of mission is exemplified by the electric atmosphere of the 1910 Edinburgh Missionary Conference. Participants at that 10-day conference in Scotland anticipated "the speedy completion of the Great Commission."[19] Because of the mission advances of the great century of the 1800s, there was great optimism about how quickly the task of world evangelism could be achieved.

Questions for Reflection

1. In what ways did the Jewish Diaspora and the Pax Romana contribute to the expansion of Christianity?
2. What are some important facets of Patrick's ministry in Ireland?

3. What led to the decline of Christianity in the period A.D. 500-950?
4. What factors ignited the great expansion of mission in the period 1800-1914?
5. Why might one say the Crusades were a failure on the part of the Church? What ramifications might this have for mission in the 21st century?
6. Why did the Pietists, who initially seemed focused on personal spiritual deepening, become leaders in mission?
7. What would you describe as key moments in the great century of missions?
8. What are some common elements in successful mission through the ages?

4

DOING MISSION *TOGETHER*

Objectives

Your study of this chapter should help you to:

- Understand the strategic usefulness of organizational bodies specifically charged with doing global mission
- Reflect on various organizational models used for doing mission
- See various ways in which finances for world mission have been raised
- Examine various models of eventual mission/church relationships
- Research how mission is done within your church or a parachurch organization

Key Words to Understand

sodality
modality
missionary orders
parachurch organizations
faith missions
paternalism
dependency
Theological Education by Extension

The Italian language has a wonderful idiom or figure of speech that says, *fare un buco nell'acqua.* In English that phrase means "to make a hole in water." Imagine sticking a finger in a pool of water. In a manner of speaking, the finger will make a hole in the water. Of course, when that finger is taken out of the water, the hole is no longer there. That image is exactly the point the Italians make with that phrase. They use *fare un buco nell'acqua* to describe something or someone that is very visible at one point but then leaves no lasting results, no permanent mark.

Through the centuries, Christian mission efforts have been much more than making holes in water. The local congregations in cities, towns, and villages around the globe are evidence of the widespread, long-lasting impact the missions enterprise has had.

More Intensely Missionary

The spirit of Christ is the spirit of missions. The nearer we get to him, the more intensely missionary we become.[1]

—Henry Martyn, missionary to India and Persia

To answer the question of what those involved in mission have done to ensure permanency for the fruit of their ministries, one must take a look at the ways the world mission enterprise has been organized, how resources are gathered, and the eventual relationships of parent churches or mission agencies to their clusters of daughter and granddaughter churches. This chapter will lay a foundation for individualized study of mission structures to which the reader's church is connected. The Case Study Appendix has an example of what such research can produce.

The reason this chapter calls for individualized research is that Christian mission efforts have been done with a variety of structures and systems. The sending and supporting structures of various organizations have been diverse with all of them having positive features and all having their drawbacks. Many mission organizations have developed because of the slowness or reluctance of official church structures to respond to global mission challenges and opportunities. Thus, an in-depth study of a mission organization needs to look at the why as well as the how.

Modality/Sodality Structures

Two things contributed to William Carey being called the father of modern missions. One was his prolific letter and pamphlet writing in support of world mission outreach. The second was his development of a functional and reproducible structure for missionary deployment and support by believers. Carey at first tried to mobilize the existing structure of his denomination for world evangelism. When that did not happen, he and some friends organized a Baptist mission society focused on foreign missions. Carey's missionary society found a place alongside the official structure of his church just as the Roman Catholic orders had, although Carey's organization did not have the degree of denominational accountability that Roman Catholic orders have to their official church structure. Carey did not dream up this structure on his own. Justinian von Welz had proposed something similar more than a century earlier. It was, however, Carey that made it a working reality that could be replicated.

The Protestant mission agencies begun in Europe and America as the result of William Carey's influence were organized and operated in a variety of ways. Some agencies were nondenominational or interdenominational, such as the London Missionary Society organized by John Ryland just two years after Carey left for India. Some were denominational, such as the Church of England's Church Missionary Society (CMS), whose founding in 1799 was inspired by Carey. Its missionaries included people like Alexander McKay (Africa) and Samuel Zwemer (Muslim world). Marcus Whitman, missionary to Native Americans, was one of the better-known missionaries of the American Board of Commissioners for Foreign Missions, founded in 1810 also as a result of Carey's inspiration. Well-known names like those are part of the universal Church's mission history. In addition, every mission board will have key people who should be known by the supporters of that particular board.

Ralph Winter has noted that specific mission-focused organizations like Carey's have been present when the Church did its most aggressive global outreach. Winter gave the name *sodality* to such task-oriented groups of committed people focused on evangelizing the world. Sodalities focus on a limited set of goals and tasks within the larger framework of all that the church does. Winter used the word *modality* to refer to the larger, all-inclusive church organization that gathers nominal as well as committed members under the same umbrella. During those periods when global mission was left to the modality or larger group, cross-cultural outreach has usually waned.[2]

The mission sodality is a structure that Roman Catholicism has also used. Protestants sometimes think of Roman Catholic orders as people living in isolated monasteries where they give themselves to prayer and meditation, with some even having taken a vow of silence. While there are a few cloistered religious orders, most Roman Catholic orders were started as mission arms. Indeed, it was the founding of those orders as missionary sodalities that launched the Western Church into aggressive global outreach. Two **missionary orders**, the Dominicans and the Franciscans, came into being in the 1200s. The Jesuits, who have been among the most determined of the missionary orders, were founded in the 1500s.

One question a person needs to ask is: What are the mission sodalities in the community of which I am a part? If there are none, there may not be much involvement in global mission. If there is a mission sodality in your church, why did it come into being and how does it relate to the church today?

Specialized Agencies

While some sodalities have been integrated into church structures, others have been very independent. Among the independent ones are **parachurch organizations** like Wycliffe Bible Translators, Gospel Recordings, and Greater Europe Mission. Although most specialized support agencies that have sprung up focusing on one particular area of ministry—literature, medical work, or missionary aviation—are independent, a lot of networking with denominational agencies goes on. These independent agencies are often called parachurch organizations because they see themselves as coming alongside churches to aid them. Thus a denominational mission board may use Missionary Aviation Fellowship for transportation into remote areas while it enlists the help of Scripture Gift Mission or Bibles for the World to provide Bibles and Scripture portions for evangelism and discipleship. At the same time, it may be partnering with Trans-World Radio to follow up on listeners who respond to broadcasts as well as using Campus Crusade's *JESUS* film and Evange-Cubes from E3 Resources. A denominational mission working in impoverished areas may cooperate with Compassion International to provide meal programs for at-risk children and with World Vision in village health-care programs. That resulting health-care ministry may get medical supplies through MAP International, formerly Medical Assistance Programs. The denominational board might interface with World Neighbors in community development projects. In the wake of natural disasters, mission boards often partner with groups like Heart to Heart and World Relief to give help to devastated areas. A study of one's mission board should include a look at the organizations with which it networks and which may even be supported by people in one's own church.

Financing

Coupled to the structure issue is the question of financial resources and how those are raised and spent. Fund-raising and administration of finances differs from mission board to mission board. A thorough study of one's own mission organization will find out the means of raising funds and look at how the support system for missionaries is structured. Using diverse sources of funding has been a characteristic of global mission from the beginning. The apostle Paul put together a mobile missionary team that was partially funded by existing local churches. For instance, in Romans 15:24, when Paul said he hoped to have the Roman Christians "assist me on my journey there," he seemed to be asking for material help for a planned trip to Spain. However, according to Acts 18:3, the missionary journeys of Paul and his group were funded in part by their own tentmaking work.

Some of the first Protestant missionaries were sent out by government money. In the early 1700s the Danish Halle mission was initiated and paid for by the King of Denmark. That was not an infinitely reproducible model. While Danish government sponsorship did get Ziegenbalg and Plutschau and others to India, government funding had obvious limitations and would today be unthinkable for Christian missionary work.

The Moravians did things differently. Most of the early Moravian missionaries went out as tentmaker missionaries, earning much of their livelihood with their own hands with limited dependence on the brotherhood back home. It was a system that enabled the Moravians to send as much as 10 percent of their total membership into missionary service. The word *tentmaking* is used because the apostle Paul, as has been noted, earned some of his living making tents on his church-planting missionary trips. Using that tentmaking model to finance world mission ventures reflected Moravian ecclesiology because that movement did not have a professional paid ministry even in its home churches.

The 1800s saw a wave of start-ups of faith mission agencies, many of them taking inspiration from Hudson Taylor's China Inland Mission. These were independent mission organizations not tied to a denomination or group of churches. Though *faith mission* is a bit of a misnomer since all mission groups plan and run by faith, the name has endured. In almost all **faith missions**, individual missionaries and often even headquarters personnel have to marshal their own financial support. Very few actually follow Taylor's principle of never asking anyone for money, something he picked up from his contemporary George Mueller. Mueller is famous for praying in support for his orphanages in England. Believing that mission is ultimately God's work, Taylor's support principle became: "God's work done in God's way will never lack God's supply."[3] Those faith groups that follow Taylor's principle never mention their financial needs; they talk about their work but leave it to the Holy Spirit to touch people's hearts to fund their ministry.

Denominational missionary organizations generally fund their operations in one of two ways: individual support raising or a cooperative central fund. Those that use individual support raising follow variations of models used by faith missions in which individual missionaries raise their own support. In one variation, friends and family members commit so much per month or year to that missionary. Other missionaries trying to raise support concentrate on cultivating a group of supporting churches, each of which pledges annual financial support to particular missionaries. Usually a minimal support level is set by a mission agency for all its missionaries with newly appointed missionaries having to secure pledges or commitments that total at least that much before they leave for the field. In the individual support system, the missionary's home office sometimes takes out an administrative overhead percentage of what each missionary raises. Often new appointees are given two years or so to raise their support. If they are unable to do so within the specified time period, their appointment expires or is rescinded. If the monthly or yearly income of missionaries being supported in this system falls below a set minimum, those missionaries often must return to their home country to raise additional pledges or commitments. While being supported by particular individuals and local churches does create special bonds between missionaries and their supporters, fall-off in support for a missionary in this system can occur when a supporting church changes pastors or has a significant turnover in membership and new leaders have a different set of missionaries they want to support.

In other denominational mission agencies, missionaries do not raise their own individual support but are instead supported from a cooperative central fund that cares for all the missionaries of that agency or board. To create that centralized fund, local churches in such denominations commit to giving a percentage of their total income to world evangelism, in some cases "a tithe of the tithe." During periods of home assignment, missionaries from these denominations generally speak in many more local churches than do those trying to raise their own support. One reason for this is the need for local churches to encounter individual missionaries face-to-face since their funding is not tied to particular missionaries but is going to support all of that denomination's mission force. As such missionaries travel around speaking, they may have special projects for which they will receive offerings. However, their major objective in speaking in churches is to promote the entire missionary force of their denomination or board.

For needs other than personnel support, mission organizations will often take special offerings that appeal to a variety of motives. In her denomination Elizabeth Vennum began an annual offering for global construction projects with the slogan "Giving up a want to meet a need." Using that slogan, she asked women to put off buying a new dress or a bottle of perfume in order to give money to the construction offering. In one December compassionate ministry offering promotion, people are urged to give based on how many pairs of shoes they own, how many light bulbs they have in their home, and how many trips to the grocery store they make in an average week.

Structure Issues

Gathering the Harvest

Another reason Christian mission efforts have been more than making holes in water is that they have generally been done in the context of a sending community seeking to create other communities. To be sure, there are stories of resolute individuals who have valiantly set out to try to bring God's justice and *shalom* to the world all by themselves. However, in missionary deployment, God's call is only one ingredient of the recipe. Other ingredients include the sending church making sure there are supporting supply lines in place, systems of accountability, and structures to guarantee long-term continuity.

The difference that working within a structure can make in long-term results can be seen in the ministry of two men in Great Britain in the 1700s. John Wesley and George Whitefield were two well-known evangelists of that era. While Wesley is widely talked about today, George Whitefield is little remembered although it is said that during his lifetime he preached to more people face-to-face than did John Wesley. Accounting for the difference between the residual effects of Wesley's ministry and those of George Whitefield may be Wesley's creation of a follow-up system within the context of a faith community. Though Whitefield was seemingly more successful in attracting crowds than Wesley, Whitefield did not provide for long-term follow-up of converts. He preached and called for decisions but left follow-up to other people. After Wesley's death, the Methodist movement he began and organized lived on. After Whitefield's death, it soon became hard to point to any discernible long-term impact of his ministry.

Research on a mission board or agency should ask what is done to guarantee long-term continuity of the work of that board or agency. It is very risky to gauge the effectiveness of evangelism by raw numbers of conversions without taking into account the structures being organized to carry on outreach and discipleship ministries. Indeed, in the first few centuries of Christianity, benchmarks other than raw numbers of conversions were often used for gauging mission success. One marker of successful mission work in Early Church history was the appointing of an indigenous bishop. The appointment of a local leader as a bishop was a signal that evangelistic outreach had been fruitful and leaders were emerging who could oversee churches.

End Result

Although missionaries are one of the most visible elements of global mission efforts, they are not the most important element of the mission enterprise. The key issue is not even the number of converts or their quality. The most important bottom line involves the clusters of churches that result from the mission enterprise. A person doing research on a particular mission board or agency needs to find out how that board tries to relate to the clusters of churches emerging from its work. The end result that some mission teams are working toward is the spinning off of independent churches or groups of churches. In their exit strategies, such mission agencies fully embrace a scaffolding metaphor in which any structure related to the parent mission group is to be dismantled and taken away. Some mission agencies, such as the Methodists, have opted for loose international fellowships of various national associations. The Anglicans have put together a little tighter organization, using words such as *federation* or *federalism* to talk about how their global communion is structured. Still others, such as the Presbyterians, become global partners (usually in terms of financial aid) with groups that may not even have roots in their tradition. A handful of denominations are trying to create global, organically unified associations of churches.

Paternalism and Dependency

Missionaries are always children of their times. So, paternalistic attitudes lingering from colonialistic times have had to be faced. Students doing research on their mission board need to ask how its mission policies have been shaped by **paternalism** in the past and how the board is dealing with that problem in the present. Questions such as "Who ultimately calls the shots?" and "Who makes the final decisions?" can help reveal the degree of paternalism tainting a mission agency.

The relationship between a national church and the international body that gave birth to it usually goes through a series of stages that have been called pioneer, parent, partner, and participant.[4] These stages define not only attitudes but structural relationships as well. Missionaries infected by paternalism often are satisfied with progress at a snail's pace through these stages.

While the problems of paternalism and dependency are often intertwined, they deal with different issues. Paternalism has to do with decision-making power. Dependency relates to who is expected to provide financial resources. In earlier centuries it was often the gospel being shared between equals or even from poorer to richer. Then, beginning with the Age of Exploration in the 1500s, a reversal occurred and world evangelism became largely a going from well-off Christian areas of the globe to the poorer, unevangelized areas. That reversal in terms of economic levels has too often produced unhealthy dependencies on the financial resources of parent organizations. Funding came to be accorded such a determining role that many assumed evangelism or compassionate ministry work was possible only when outside funds were available. Any study of a mission organization should ask questions about dependency problems it has encountered and take a look at how it is dealing with them.

Individualized Research

Among the projects students can do when this book is used as a classroom text:

1. Prepare a comprehensive report over one mission board.
2. Research a parachurch organization.
3. As part of a small study group, explore one specific area (finances, history, structure) of a mission organization more fully.

The research can be done locally by interviewing a pastor and local mission leaders and using whatever library and Internet resources can be found. Or, students can be encouraged to go global in their research by contacting denominational headquarters, mission leaders, and even field missionaries.

Projects can be turned in individually, or the results can be shared and pooled together in a classroom setting.

Leadership Training

Leadership development is a key factor in the progress of a cluster of churches on the journey from pioneer to participant. Thus, knowing how leadership preparation is done is part of understanding the mission organization of which one is a part. How leaders are recruited, trained, and mentored varies from group to group. In pioneering situations, training has often been done one-on-one or in very small groups. Faith groups have tended to set up Bible institutes or schools that copied the residential Bible institute model that sprang into existence in the U.S. with Moody Bible Institute in the late 1800s. Denominations with institutions of higher learning in their sending base usually tried to marshal the resources to set up similar training institutions on their mission fields. Then, in the 1970s creative Presbyterian missionaries in Guatemala revolutionized theological education by shutting down their residential seminary and giving birth to an educational delivery system called Theological Education by Extension. In some ways, TEE was a precursor of online studies because it is a schooling that goes to the students instead of vice versa. Theological Education by Extension students are not uprooted and moved to a residential campus. Instead, they gather at a central location one day a week or for two days at a time twice a month and the professor comes to them. In the early years of the TEE movement, emphasis was placed on developing programmed learning texts with the thought that printed texts developed by experts would be the primary vehicle for delivering course content. Textbooks using that specialized teaching technique are no longer seen as an essential component of a TEE program. In its initial days TEE was seen primarily as a way of preparing pastors for rural churches. Extension programs have expanded far beyond that one focus and are now even being used to deliver graduate theological education.

Your Mission Board's Story

To fully achieve the objectives of this chapter, readers must do some research on their own. Due to readers' differing church backgrounds, the directions that will take may vary. The way the Southern Baptists do global mission will be somewhat different, for instance, from what the Church of God (Holiness) does. Here are some questions to consider and to research:

1. How did the missionary work of your church or organization come into being?
2. Did mission happen as a part of original vision or did that come later?
3. What are the sodalities of your organization?
4. What are some key events or turning points in the history of your group's missionary outreach?
5. Who are the important people in your missions organization's history?
6. What are the key historical periods into which your group's mission outreach can be divided?
7. What emphases or programs are trademarks of your group?
8. What are the chief goals for missionaries of your group?
9. How have concepts like contextualization and indigenization been evidenced and dealt with in your organization?
10. What solutions has the mission board come up with to erase paternalism?
11. What accountability structures have been put in place?
12. How are funds raised and spent?
13. With which parachurch organizations are the churches you are connected with the most familiar?
14. Do the missionaries of your organization have an exit strategy, a plan to *leave* a field?
15. How is leadership development done?
16. In terms of raw statistics, what does the work look like now compared to what it was 10 and 20 years ago? Some statistics to track over the 20-year period would include the number of world areas in which your mission organization is working, church membership figures, and the number of expatriate missionaries.

5
A GLOBAL CHURCH

Objectives

Your study of this chapter should help you to:

- Glimpse important trends in the contemporary global church, including the tremendous growth in China
- Observe the southward shift of Christianity's center of gravity
- Define *contextualization* and *syncretism*
- Understand the principles of reciprocity, mutuality, and identification
- Reflect on the Church's role in global justice

Key Words to Understand

majority world	reciprocity
non-Western	mutuality
contextualization	identification
animism	partnership

Sometimes it has taken a long time for the gospel to take root in an area. The reasons are many. Sociological factors have kept some groups from being receptive to the gospel. In other situations, outside forms introduced by missionaries produced churches with an air of foreignness about them. Once in a while, as happened in China in the 800s and again in the 1300s, a nascent church has been crushed by government opposition. At other times expatriate missionaries remained in charge too long, stunting the development of indigenous leadership.

Over the long run, however, Christian missionary efforts have paid enormous dividends with clusters of churches springing up all around the globe. As prophesied in Isaiah 9:2, 42:6, and 49:6, the light did come to the Gentiles. The *gôyim* or nations have heard the Good News and have responded to it. David Livingstone may not have had more than a couple of converts during his 30 years in Africa. His life, however, inspired generations of missionaries to go to Africa. As a result, sub-Saharan Africa is today more than 50 percent Christian.[1] In the early 1800s Robert Morrison worked in China for 7 years before seeing his first convert to Christianity. In the last 50 years the Church in China has grown in unbelievable ways.

Significant church growth is occurring in parts of the Muslim world. Though Indonesia is earth's largest Muslim country, 1.5 million Indonesians have been baptized since Dutch colonialism ended in 1949. The iron curtain that separated Europe for half a century fell apart in 1989. In former Eastern Bloc countries where atheism was a suffocating state religion, Christian believers can now freely gather. On the day after the Berlin Wall came down, a Methodist church in Prague that had suffered under Communist rule put up a sign proclaiming: "The Lamb wins!"[2]

The Church has recently experienced growth in several parts of the **majority world,** that 80 percent of the world that is not part of the North Atlantic system. The Church in Africa, for example, is increasing by more than 24,000 people a day. Such growth has caused Stephen Bevans, former missionary to the Philippines, and Roger Schroeder, professor of mission theology at Catholic Theological Union in Chicago, to say that Africa is becoming "the most Christian continent" in the world.[3] Evangelical churches in Latin America, an area already considered at least nominally Christian, have grown tremendously. *The Economist* reported that 400 people an hour join evangelical churches in Latin America.[4] As a result, evangelicals in Latin America have grown from under 250,000 in 1900 to more than 60 million.[5] In the last half century rapid church growth in Korea has produced some huge Christian churches. Indeed, recent research indicated that 6 of the 10 largest evangelical churches in the world are in South Korea, the world's 28th largest country.[6]

The growth of the Church in China is a special story. During the rule of

Mao Zedong and the Gang of Four in the tumultuous 1960s and 1970s, mission researchers wondered if there were any Christians left in China. Some bemoaned Christianity's "loss" of the world's most populous country and offered opinions on how missionary work there should have been done differently. Then, the bamboo curtain opened slightly and reports filtered out that, even though the Church in China had been driven underground, it had survived. Word came that the persecuted Chinese Church had grown beyond the 700,000 to 800,000 members it had in 1949 when Mao came to power. Initial speculation was that there might be a million or more Christians in China. Against a background of fears that the Church in China had completely disappeared, that was an incredibly positive report. As word got out that Christianity was alive and well in China, Christians elsewhere in the world rejoiced and reminded each other of Jesus' words, "I will build my church; and the gates of hell shall not prevail against it" (Matthew 16:18, KJV).

Amid the rejoicing, one Chinese pastor stepped forward to say, "We have at least 5 million Christians in my province alone." That was electrifying news, because the People's Republic of China has 22 provinces and five autonomous regions. In Wenzhou, a city of 7.5 million in the coastal Zhejian province, 15 to 20 percent of the population is reported to be Christian.[7] With reports still filtering out, missions researchers now say it appears there are between 30 and 100 million Christians in China.[8] Such growth led *TIME* magazine to conclude, "The revival of the Christian church in China is by far the biggest and most significant in the history of Christianity."[9]

Shifting Center

West to East/North to South

The growth of the Church in the majority world has significantly outstripped Christianity's growth in the Western world. The result, Philip Jenkins has said in *The Next Christendom,* is that "the center of gravity in the Christian world has shifted . . . to Africa, Asia and Latin America."[10] As startling as that may seem, a movement like this of Christianity's center from one place to another has happened before. Andrew Walls, former missionary to Sierra Leone and Nigeria, has noted that Christianity's expansion has tended to be serial rather than progressive.[11] By that, he meant that the growth of Christianity has not been a spreading of the faith in ever larger circles from a single center that remained the place of authority and energy. Christianity instead has had several centers of gravity. It began when the Roman army destroyed Jerusalem in A.D. 70, and Christianity's mother church vanished. From several points in Syria and North Africa as well as Rome, Hellenistic (Greek-speaking) Christianity became the hub of the faith. When Hellenistic society collapsed, Christianity's center of gravity moved northward. Now, the growth of churches in the majority world of Africa, Latin America, and Asia has pushed Christianity's center of gravity into the Southern Hemisphere.

Plate 5.1 shows that in 1800, 99 percent of all evangelical Christians lived in Western Europe, the U.S.A., and Canada. A hundred years later, the percentage of evangelical Christians living in the **non-Western** or majority world had jumped to 9 percent. Then, within an 80-year period, the demographics of evangelical Christianity so changed that by 1980 more evangelical Christians lived in the majority world than did in Western Europe, the U.S.A., and Canada.

What has happened since 1980 is really amazing. As plate 5.2 clearly shows, evangelical Christians in the non-Western world now outnumber those in the West by four to one. Thus, said Jenkins, the mass media need to learn not to say "what Christians believe" when they have only interviewed *Western* Christians. One further reason these figures are so astounding is that a significant portion of the growth has come in areas that formerly seemed resistant to Christianity, countries such as China and India.

The map shown in plate 5.3 depicts the growth rate and population percentage of evangelicals in various parts of the world. As can be seen, the fastest growth is occurring in the non-Western areas of the world. Jenkins and others say this trend will continue. If it does and it is healthy growth unfettered by paternalism, the face of the Church will change even more.

The Face of Today's Church

What does it mean for the Church to be global? Is the Church global because the same songs are translated and sung worldwide? Is the Church global because believers are all reading the same books (translated, of course) and being enamored by the same evangelists who use interpreters? While the story of God's relationship with His people does transcend cultural barriers, singing the same songs and reading the same books is not what being a global church means. Though the various parts of today's global church are very much interconnected, they are quite diverse and, in most cases, very indigenized.

Diverse

Of course, just because particular denominations describe themselves as worldwide does not mean they are truly global. In some instances, they are simply paternalistic Western churches with lots of international affiliates. Another side of the story, however, is that the global growth of the Church does not always mean more Southern Baptist churches, more Methodist churches, more Assembly of God churches, or more Nazarene churches. As gospel proclamation has borne fruit in the world's cultural mosaic, great diversity has ensued with indigenous churches springing up that are quite different from Western churches. David Barrett reminded a *Newsweek* reporter that a significant part of Christian growth in Africa and Latin America was in independent movements "which have no ties to historic Christianity."[12] Some of those movements have beliefs, worship styles, and practices that Christians from historic churches find questionable and even heretical. Some, for example, allow polygamy, practice veneration of ancestors, have rigorous dietary laws, and believe that all disease has spiritual origins. Many wear distinctive costumes and emblems.

Contextualized

Some missionary outreach efforts of the 18th and 19th centuries used extractionism strategies. When people came to faith one by one, they were praised for their courageous willingness to break with or extract themselves from their past and from unbelieving family and friends. Extractionism usually involved the setting up of a mission compound or station that contrasted with the surrounding culture. These settlements ran the gamut from Praying Towns of converted Native Americans set up by John Eliot to mission compounds in Africa where 25 or more missionaries would live and run a clinic, elementary and secondary schools, a printing plant, a church, a Bible college, and even economic development projects providing employment for national Christians living near or on the mission station. Such mission stations engendered the development of a Christian subculture very different from that of nearby towns and villages. In *Bridges of God,* Donald McGavran argued that these subcultures made most mission compounds counterproductive. Almost no mission group uses the mission station strategy today or appeals to new converts to "come out from them" (2 Corinthians 6:17) and sever their relationships with friends and family. Instead, the focus is now on the need for believers and their churches to be salt and light within a culture.

Instead of wrestling over issues of maintaining and administering mission compounds, mission leaders now talk about contextualization and its destructive mutation, **syncretism**, that combines elements from different religions into new hybrid religions. In contextualization, the context in which the Good News is being announced is allowed to shape how the gospel is proclaimed and practiced. There is careful reflection on how the Church can fit within a particular culture while also filling pastoral and prophetic roles. One of missionary anthropologist Paul Hiebert's illustrations for explaining contextualization is the plea of Indian evangelist R. K. Murthi, "Do not bring us the gospel as a potted plant. Bring us the seed of the gospel and plant it in our soil."[13]

Framing the Gospel Message

The idea of contextualization is to frame the gospel message in language and communication forms appropriate and meaningful to the local culture and to focus the message upon crucial issues in the lives of the people. The contextualized indigenous church is built upon culturally appropriate methods of evangelism; the process of discipling draws upon methods of instruction that are familiar . . . The structural and political aspects of leadership are adopted from patterns inherent in national cultures rather than imported.[14]

—Sherwood Lingenfelter, consultant with Wycliffe Bible Translators

Even though *contextualization* as a word was not coined by Taiwanese Shoki Coe until 1972, the process has been going on for centuries. Contextualization began in the Book of Acts. The key question facing the Jerusalem Council in Acts 15 was about whether the gospel could be contextualized in the Gentile world and still retain its core essentials. In the early 1800s, Adoniram Judson's adoption of the Burmese coffeehouse or *zayat* as an evangelistic meeting place was a contextualization breakthrough. Hudson Taylor's embracing of Chinese clothing and hairstyles were attempts to aid contextualization. In the 1800s, Mary Slessor so identified with the people she served in Calabar that she could be described as more African than some Africans. Because of Slessor's willingness to contextualize her ministry, she was instrumental in stamping out the custom of killing infant twins.

Contextualization shapes preaching styles. It affects how invitations to accept Jesus as Lord are expressed. In the U.S.A., individuals are often asked to "take a stand" and come forward in a public service. Not so in Haiti, for example. There, people will likely declare their faith by joining a new believers' Bible study class much as happened in the 18th-century Wesleyan revival in England. Contextualization affects forms of church government and decision-making processes. In good contextualization, church governing procedures will feel at home to believers. In some cultures, decisions are made on the basis of whether an idea can get 51 percent or more of the people to vote for it. In that situation, decisions have winning and losing sides. In other cultures, arriving at a consensus acceptable to everyone takes priority over marshaling yes and no votes. Good contextualization will affect the kinds of people chosen as leaders. Some cultures prize the wisdom that comes with age; others greatly value the energy levels and idealism of younger people.

Power to Penetrate

True contextualization accords to the gospel its rightful primacy, its power to penetrate every culture and to speak within each culture, in its own speech and symbol, the word which is both No and Yes, both judgment and grace.[15]

—Lesslie Newbigin

Contextualization shapes Christian music styles. The quarter tones of some Asian church music sound off-key to Westerners, and the joyous songs of groups like the Canela of Brazil can seem like funeral dirges to American ears. Contextualization will affect the way buildings are built and even the clothing considered appropriate for believers. Good contextualization affects the length of worship services and how they are conducted. For example, the Native American Wiconi movement is trying to get American Indian churches to consider using their people's indigenous powwow format rather than following the lecture hall church service style of Euro-America.

Contextualization affects the way theology is expressed. During the 19th and 20th centuries the theological center of Protestantism seemed to be in North America and Europe, with Germany being the nexus or center for theological scholarship. However, the issues German theologians talk about are not always the issues being wrestled with in other parts of the world. In this regard Korean Bong Bin Rho has written:

> Western evangelical theological schools have emphasized the inerrancy of the Scriptures and orthodox theology versus liberal and neo-orthodox theologies. But these are not major issues in Asia. Rather, the prevalent areas of concern here are poverty, suffering, justice, Communism, and non-Christian religions.[16]

Thirty years ago Andrae and Sandra Crouch wrote a song titled "Jesus Is the Answer." That is true. Jesus is indeed the answer in every context; nonetheless, the gospel does speak in unique ways to each cultural context. One hears talk of Asian theology, African theology, and Latin American theology. That need not mean a different gospel is being preached on each continent. Actually, it might be better to say theology in an Asian context, theology in an African context, and theology in a Latin American context because what is meant is that there are different emphases being highlighted in each context, just as happens with varying age-groups in the same culture. For example, those in the **persecuted church** find what the Bible has to say about suffering to be extremely relevant to their daily lives. In parts of the affluent and pragmatic West, people want to know what the Bible has to say about God's plan for their lives. Immigrant and refugee populations will be attracted to biblical passages that speak about God's righteousness extending to "strangers and aliens" (Ephesians 2:19, NRSV). An honor/shame continuum based on God's redemptive acts is attractive to Muslims and those from the Far East. For them to hear that Jesus honored His Father by dying for humanity's shameful acts is very powerful. Liberation theology, which in many people's minds focuses too narrowly on economic and political issues, grew out of the realization in Latin America that Yahweh is a God of justice who takes the side of the oppressed. In this regard Joon-Sik Park wrote in an article about John Howard Yoder, "God is not indifferent to exploitation, pain and poverty and his presence is clearly linked with their elimination."[17]

Contextualizing theology does not mean that theology simply responds to questions posed by the culture. Theology has its own questions to pose to cultures. For instance, some Asian cultures need to hear the biblical affirmation that Yahweh is a God of mercy as well as holiness, while many in the West need to hear that He is a God of holiness as well as mercy. People living in areas where **animism** is widespread need to see the biblical portrayal of God as transcendent but not remote, since animistic cultures often think of the Creator as remote and uninvolved with the world.

Being a Change Agent

As the gospel has moved into different cultures, it has confronted sinful practices and issues of injustice. That, too, is a part of contextualization since a truly contextualized church will have a strong prophetic voice. All believers live in "a warped and crooked generation" (Philippians 2:15). Mention has already been made of Bartolomé de las Casas and his denunciation of the enslavement practices of European colonists. William Carey pushed to outlaw *sati,* the Hindu practice of burning widows alive on their husbands' funeral pyres. In the early 20th century, Gladys Aylward fought against foot binding in China, a practice that crippled women for life. Amy Carmichael gave her life to rescuing children from temple prostitution in India. The work of Mark and Gloria Zook, missionaries with New Tribes Mission, was made famous by the *EE-Taow* film. As the Zooks worked among the Mouk people of Papua New Guinea, the gospel changed that group's pattern of deceit and ill-treatment of women. Internal revenge killings were wiping out the Waodani people in Ecuador when Rachel Saint and Elisabeth Elliot went to live among them. As the Waodani came to faith in Jesus, they emerged as a healthy, viable people group.

Churches in Central and Eastern Europe were active participants in the events that brought down the iron curtain. On December 22, 1989, Baptist pastor Peter Dugulescu led 100,000 people in reciting the Lord's Prayer in a Romanian city square. That prayer was an act of defiance culminating a week of protests against Romania's atheistic and despotic dictatorship. Within days of that public prayer, the Communist regime was gone. "We did not have machine guns," Dugulescu said. "We had only songs, prayers and candles. And we won."[18]

Doing Justice

Conflict between cultures has had a long history in South Africa. Some people believed that the best way to avoid cultural clashes was to separate the different groups. To that end, a system called apartheid (separation of peoples) was set up after World War II. Based on the concept of race, which anthropologists have discarded as invalid, apartheid fostered hatred and social stress.

Then, during a relatively peaceful transition, the evil system of apartheid was swept away. Institutionalized discrimination was dismantled with all South Africans now having the right to vote. In a nation as deeply divided as South Africa had been, this was nothing short of a miracle.

Christians were crucial players in South Africa's healing. At a critical point in the negotiations to abolish apartheid, Michael Cassidy, founder of an evangelistic organization called African Enterprise, intervened when hope for a peaceful transition seemed to be vanishing. American Secretary of State Henry Kissinger and Lord Carrington from Britain had already boarded their planes when Cassidy urged the mediator from Kenya, Washington Okumu, to continue negotiations. Then, Chief Mangosuthu Gatsha Buthelezi, founder of the Inkatha Freedom Party who had already threatened to boycott the election, gave up and boarded his plane. After takeoff, however, the chief's plane developed a mechanical problem, forcing it to return to the airport. Cassidy took this as a sign from the Lord, and after prayer, got the three main leaders to forge an agreement opening the way for the birth of a reconstituted nation.

On Sunday, April 17, 1994, the three leaders joined hands and raised them together at a Jesus Peace Rally organized by African Enterprise. On the following Tuesday, the chief minister stated, "God has saved South Africa from civil war." Just days later, the newly reborn nation officially began life almost without incident. For his contribution to the process, Archbishop Desmond Tutu was the first sub-Saharan African to be awarded the Nobel Peace Prize.

Not long ago, George Otis produced two widely shown "Transformations" videos. These videos electrified viewers by pointing to social changes ascribed to Christian revival and renewal movements in cities around the world. Although criticized for hyping or overplaying the effects, Otis's videos did point to the longing that believers have for seeing spiritual changes eventuate in social changes. Today, groups like the International Justice Mission partner with global church leaders to fight specific acts of injustice, release people from slavery, rescue children from forced prostitution, and bring relief from the oppressive brutality of the powerful.

Fears of Straying

The shift of Christianity's numerical center of gravity southward and away from Euro-America has unleashed what Harvey Cox called a "tidal wave of religious change."[19] One change has to do with control. For the last few centuries, Westerners have dominated the Church's theological thinking, strategic planning, and missionary-sending in ways that made believers in the West start thinking of themselves as the mother church. Now that Westerners are a minority in the global church, some are worried that leaders from other parts of the world will make changes in the beliefs and practices of their beloved churches and organizations.

This fear of straying from orthodoxy is a topic Jenkins addressed in *The Next Christendom.* He argued that Westerners have little reason to fear, noting that majority world Christians tend to be more theologically conservative than their counterparts in the West. Jenkins pointed out that Southern Hemisphere delegates at some recent denominational gatherings were the ones who kept their churches from straying from orthodoxy.[20] Forty years ago, in anticipation of this, Paul Orjala wrote, "Some people are worried about the doctrine deteriorating in the hands of the nationals." Acknowledging that effective mission work must include a theological education component, Orjala went on to say, "There is more hope theologically for a newly literate mountain Indian in Mexico with his Bible than for an over-sophisticated American pastor who has a weak devotional life."[21]

Listening as Well as Telling

As the center of gravity of the Church moves away from the West to the majority world and from the north to the south, Western church leaders must learn to receive spiritual insights from wherever the fresh wind of God's Spirit is blowing. Christians in the West will be blessed if they will listen as well as talk. Mission leaders must become sensitive to biases in their ways of thinking and speaking and eliminate them. In their book *Choosing a Future for U.S. Missions,* Paul McKaughan and Dellanna and William O'Brien said:

> Churches in the West, and especially in the United States, must work on enhancing their "receivers." We have overworked our "transmitters." The arrogance reflected in one-way communication of the gospel ultimately creates a deafness to what the Spirit is saying through other parts of the body . . . We desperately need to assume a humble, learning posture.[22]

A Global Blessing

One of the most remarkable blessings I have ever experienced in a classroom came through a young man from China. Jon (not his real name) had been under the tanks in the Tiananmen Square uprising. His two companions had been killed by tank treads. Jon, however, fell under the raised middle portion of the tank. Although his back was torn open, he survived and escaped. Under the ministry of another Chinese Christian, Jon heard about Jesus and accepted Him as Savior. God called Jon into the ministry, and he enrolled at the seminary where I taught.

Life was not easy for Jon. To pay his school bill, he worked long hours in the kitchen of a Chinese restaurant. At one point, lacking money to enroll for the following semester, Jon came to my office to say that he would have to leave school. A few days later, I shared his plight with a class. As we prayed for Jon, a remarkable thing happened. Some students began to weep and pray, others confessed to shallow spirituality. One young man said he needed to be sanctified wholly. We gathered around him as he found victory. Revival came. It was the most memorable day of my teaching career. God came to bless and encourage because of the life and ministry of a young man from China. Later, when I told Jon what had happened, he, too, began to cry. What had seemed a trial became a triumph because God's people listened and received the blessing of God through Jon's life. We had learned that mission really is a two-way street. Revival may come as we learn to listen to fellow Christians from around the world.[23]

—Charles Gailey

The Curse of Dependency

During the last two or three centuries, the Church has struggled with issues of financial dependency. While Peter could say "silver or gold I do not have" to a lame beggar (Acts 3:6), churches in more wealthy areas of the world cannot say that today. On occasion that wealth has been more of a curse than a blessing. Western mission organizations have set up structures that were relatively expensive to maintain, causing national churches to struggle when they attempted to take over those obligations. Other things that foster dependency include a failure to teach about stewardship and the regular subsidizing of pastors and evangelists with outside funds. "We've ruined a lot of good leaders by teaching them to rely on foreign funds," missionary Terry Barker has lamented.[24]

When outside funding is used in global mission work, it must be disbursed in restricted and strategic ways. As mission leaders set up administrative structures, start new programs, and plan construction projects, they must be continually asking, "Is this sustainable?" and "Is this reproducible?"

Edward Dayton and David Fraser have said that "mission has its source in the Triune God."[25] Within the divine Trinity of the Father, Son, and Spirit there is a continual giving and receiving. Mission that truly reflects God and is grounded in and shaped by Trinitarian theology will be done in that same attitude of **reciprocity.** Such reciprocity is not primarily something financial (e.g., "I'll buy our lunch today; you pay for it tomorrow"). Reciprocity means people seeing each other as equals with a willingness and even eagerness to learn from each other. It means never giving the impression that the Holy Spirit speaks through some people and not others. Reciprocity means sitting under each other's ministry.

In terms of money, reciprocity means that everyone will contribute financially in a proportionate measure of giving reflective of Luke 12:48 ("from the one who has been entrusted with much, much more will be asked"). Churches in the less affluent parts of the world need to experience the blessedness that comes with giving. To foster the growth of healthy churches that can be mature global partners, leaders must enable churches and believers to internalize a lesson about giving that Paul attributed to Jesus, "It is more blessed to give than to receive" (Acts 20:35). A Navajo Indian believer once lamented how the paternalism of missionaries robbed them of divine blessing, "The missionaries did not teach us to tithe because they thought we were too poor. They did not know that we were poor because we did not tithe."[26]

The embracing of Reuben Welch's book title *We Really Do Need Each Other* as a theme for cross-cultural relationships will foster a sense of **mutuality** that creates an authentic interdependence. Purposefully cultivating mutuality will help church leaders resist paternalistic temptations to use their global outreach programs as bragging points. One example of mutuality in action was noted by historian Frederick Klees when he said, "Much of the success of the Moravians in converting the Indians [in America] was due to the fact that they looked upon the Indians as fellow human beings."[27]

Identification is the process in which an outsider gains a sense of belonging and is able to feel empathy with those of a different culture. Identification does not mean exuberantly "going native" and abandoning one's own cultural identity in order to uncritically embrace a new one. Good identification leads to a **bonding** of expatriate missionaries with their adopted culture. Bible translator William Reyburn tells of a visit to the Kaka people that taught him a significant lesson about identification. During Reyburn's visit, a young Kaka man read aloud from Acts 10 where Peter was instructed to kill and eat animals considered inedible by the Jews. When the young man finished reading, he looked up at Reyburn and said:

> "Missionaries don't believe this because they don't eat some of our foods either."
>
> I quite confidently assured him that a missionary would eat anything he does. That evening I was called to the young man's father's doorway where an old man sat on the ground in the dirt. In front of him were two clean white enamel pans. . . . I caught a glimpse of the contents [of one of the pans]. Then my eyes lifted and met the unsmiling stare of the young man who had read about the vision of Peter earlier in the afternoon. The pan was filled with singed caterpillars. I swallowed hard, thinking that now I either swallow these caterpillars or I swallow my words and thereby prove again that Europeans have merely adapted Christianity to fit their own selfish way of life.

Reyburn ate the caterpillars that day and wrote in his journal that evening: "An emptied pan of caterpillars is more convincing than all the empty metaphors of love which missionaries are prone to expend on the heathen."[28]

Being a Global Church

Paternalism or Partnership

The fiction writers referred to in this book's opening pages have portrayed missionaries as paternalistic outsiders who often attempted to act for the good of others without their consent. As with most stereotypes, that image has some basis in reality. Western missionaries have not always been free from paternalistic biases. Such paternalism is destructive because even when its goal is benevolent, the means can seem coercive. Honestly answering "Who feels the most ownership for this?" and "Whose words carry the most weight?" can uncover vestiges of paternalism. To be truly a global church is to live in ways that erase even the most unconscious remnants of paternalism. On the other hand, equal privileges and opportunities as well as shared authority are cornerstones of **partnership** in the global church.

No Longer Foreigners

Worldwide unity in the Body of Christ has nothing to do with speaking the same language or singing the same tunes in church or following a particular order of service (as much as those actions make Christians of different cultures feel "at home" with each other). The *koinonia* in the Holy Spirit that is real Christian unity is not rooted in shared human culture. In a sense of identification with each other and with an attitude of mutuality uncolored by ethnocentrism or paternalism, believers around the world must together affirm the words of Paul:

> Consequently, you are no longer foreigners and aliens, but fellow citizens with God's people and also members of his household . . . with Christ Jesus himself as the chief cornerstone. In him the whole building is joined together and rises to become a holy temple in the Lord *(Ephesians 2:19-21).*

Questions for Reflection

1. How does the story of God transcend all cultural barriers? Explain and give examples.
2. In what ways is the Church different from what it was 100 years ago? What are the ways the Church is (or should be) the same?
3. What is paternalism? How might it impact attempts at global church development?
4. In what different ways might Christians and non-Christians explain "global togetherness"?
5. How will the shifting of the geographic center of Christianity affect the Church?
6. Why are reciprocity, mutuality, and identification so important when cultural boundaries are being crossed?
7. What is the importance of partnership in the contemporary world?

6
FROM EVERY NATION

Objectives

Your study of this chapter should help you to:

- See that mission is flowing from wells all over the world
- Define *majority world mission*
- Evaluate the importance of missionaries who are non-Western in origin
- Define *creative access nation*
- Decide how you can participate in this new era of mission

Key Words to Understand

Lausanne Covenant
majority world mission
non-Western missionaries
native missionaries
barefoot evangelists
regular missions
frontier missions

About A.D. 1400 Christianity became identified as the religion of the Western world. At that point, lines crystallized in many people's minds between which countries were the ones that sent out missionaries and which countries were the ones that received those missionaries. Following World War II, American GIs who returned home burdened for Europe found fellow church members puzzled when they spoke about Europe's need for missionary work. Europe was, those church members thought, a Christian continent! Years later church members were puzzled again when they heard that Korean and Brazilian churches were sending out foreign missionaries. Those two nations, thought many people, were supposed to be *receiving* countries, not *sending* countries.

When Westerners who are passionate about global outreach have talked about taking the gospel "to every nation" they have often fixated on the *to* of that phrase. They have not seen that God desires to call people *from* every nation to engage in the world missions enterprise. It is time for the Church in the West to see that the *from* part of God's design must be promoted just as strongly as the *to* part. Being a global church means more than being present everywhere. Being global means more than believers of different ethnic groups warmly hugging each other. Being global means that the Church everywhere has become a center of missionary outreach.

Throughout Church history, God has followed a pattern of calling missionaries from people groups soon after they have been evangelized. One of the earliest missionaries to India was likely Pantaenus from North Africa. An Italian named Denis planted the first church in Paris. A Cappodocian named Ulfilas took the gospel to the Goths. Nubia (southern Egypt and northern Sudan) heard the Good News from Julian, a Turk. A Syrian named Alopen may have been the first to take the gospel to China. An Englishman named Boniface helped turn the peoples of what is now Germany to Christ. A Frenchman named Anskar took the gospel to Denmark. A Belgian named William of Rubruck went on missionary journeys to the Mongols. A Spaniard named Francis Xavier, one of the pioneer Jesuits, was one of the first to preach the Good News in Japan. George Mueller from Prussia went as a missionary to the Jews in England.

Italy, which Paul reached toward the end of his missionary travels, sent out wave after wave of missionaries. Spain has been a significant source of missionary personnel. The Celts evangelized a great deal of northern Europe and the first Protestant missionary movements came from Viking descendants through the Danish-Halle Mission. Then that cycle of the evangelized turning into the evangelizers seemed to slow down and almost stop. During the Great Century of missionary outreach, it appeared to many people that missionaries were being sent out solely by European and North American churches. Indeed, as has been noted, the missionary-sending paradigm of recent centuries was that Christians from *have* nations went as missionaries to *have not* nations. There is now a move back to the pattern of Christianity's first millennium in which it was expected that the receivers would quickly turn into senders. Indeed, the **Lausanne Covenant,** which was signed by representatives from all over the world, talked about the urgent need to get missionaries flowing "ever more freely from and to all six continents."[1]

The church is not primarily an institution; it is an expedition.[2]

—Honorato T. Reza

Fortunately, "from every nation" is not just an unrealized ideal. Those mental lists people still have of sending and receiving countries are completely outdated with churches in many countries doing both. There are now more than 2,500 missionary sending agencies in the world, of which only about a thousand are based in Europe and North America. That means authentic cross-cultural global missionary outreach is being done by believers from many countries as vibrant churches from Africa, Asia, and Latin America step forward to accept the Great Commission as their marching orders. "Missionaries," Rob Moll has written, "are going from just about every country to every other country."[3] The participant list for the mission conference that ratified the Lausanne Covenant is evidence of that trend. Those signing that covenant in Switzerland represented more than 150 nations, a dramatic increase from the 20 nationalities present at the 1910 Edinburgh World Missionary Conference.

Majority World Mission

In order to track the missionary activity of denominations and mission agencies in what were formerly labeled as receiving countries, many missiologists use a category called majority world mission. Among the cross-cultural missionary efforts in this category are those from areas of the world where per capita income statistics would make one wonder how there could be enough money to effectively support any kind of world evangelism effort. Astoundingly, Rob Moll of *Christianity Today* has estimated that the number of Protestant missionaries from the majority world now equals and may well be greater than those from the Western world, with something over 100,000 coming from each of those two global groupings. That number of majority world missionaries represents a recent explosion because in 1973 there were only 3,400 non-

Western missionaries[4] (see plate 6.1). Some majority world missionaries are supported by funds from the West, but many are not. Amazingly, churches in poorer areas of the world have found ways to send out missionaries. While the U.S. is still number one in the list of missionary-sending countries, that will likely change in the not-too-distant future. That is because the Protestant missionary force from non-Western churches is increasing by a phenomenal 13 percent annually while the number of Protestant missionaries coming from the West is growing at just over 3 percent annually.

Global Missionary Team

When we were in Swaziland, my wife and I worked with three missionaries who had come from Asia. God had called them from successful medical practices in the Philippines to serve in Africa. Those doctors are prime examples of a mission team being internationalized. Such internationalization or globalization is beginning to extend to leadership levels. My denomination's work in Africa is directed by a man born in the Cape Verde islands. A Guatemalan directs the work across Eurasia. Our missionary outreach in Mexico and Central America is led by a Panamanian. The work in South America is supervised by a Colombian.

Various church planting thrusts into Eastern Europe and countries of the former Soviet Union and some Asian countries were spearheaded by a German. Missionaries from South Korea have founded churches in Uzbekistan and Kazakhstan. In Bangladesh, churches were begun by members of my church from Western Samoa and from Ireland.

—Charles Gailey

Thousands of majority world missionaries are from Latin America. As churches in Mexico and Central and South America began looking at the least-evangelized parts of the world, they focused attention on Islamic areas with the thought that their missionaries would carry less political baggage there than did typical Western missionaries. In Bible schools in the Middle East, Christian Arab young people are preparing to be missionaries in the Muslim world. Not to be outdone, churches in Nigeria have sent hundreds of missionaries to other cultural groups within their country as well as into neighboring nations. Significant numbers of majority world missionaries are also coming out of Asia. The mission zeal of churches in Singapore, Nigeria, Korea, and India is reminiscent of the fervor of the Moravians in the early 1700s. Building on European and American examples from the past, evangelicals in Singapore now send out 1.5 missionaries per congregation.[5] The first Protestant missionaries entered Korea a little more than 100 years ago. South Korea is now a leading missionary-sending nation, supporting more than 13,000 foreign missionaries. *Operation World* says that with large numbers of missionaries from India being sent cross-culturally within the borders of their own country, that country rather than South Korea could claim the title of the world's second-largest missionary-sending country.[6]

Phill Butler of InterDev reports that non-Western Christians now account for as much as 80 percent of the personnel in various **strategic partnerships.**[7] Some people have been tempted to take this and other statistics as a sign of declining spirituality in the West. Butler came to a different conclusion, saying, "This should be seen as amazing good news, a striking return on investment from mission efforts over the last years"[8] (see "Global Missionary Team" sidebar). In Butler's evaluation, the sacrifices of previous decades by churches in the West are bearing wonderful fruit.

Plate 6.2 indicates how global the missionary force has become with missionaries now coming from most of the countries of the world. Because the Church cannot truly be the Church unless it fully embraces global mission, then the missionary zeal of majority world churches should be celebrated and further encouraged.

The mention of non-Western missionaries may bring to mind names from the first half of the 20th century, such as Santos Elizondo, Hiroshi Kitagawa, Samuel Krikorian, Rochunga Pudaite, and David Ramirez—all of whom went back to their own people in Mexico, Japan, the Middle East, India, and Nicaragua. However, immigrants like these people who went back home to evangelize are not what majority world mission is about. To be sure, God has used people like those mentioned in extraordinary ways. Though the Kingdom accomplishments of these immigrants going back home to preach the gospel need to be celebrated, they are not the temporary scaffolding of the missionary enterprise.

Rochunga Pudaite would be, of course, the one exception on this list. To be sure, the first dozen or so years of his ministry were spent in Bible translation work among his own people, the Hmar of northeast India. That part of Pudaite's life story is told in the film *Beyond the Next Mountain.* Later, however, Pudaite broadened his ministry to found an organization called Bibles for the World, a global mission ministry that uses Scripture distribution as an evangelistic tool.

More than "Warm Bodies"

Some have rejoiced in thinking that one of the best uses of majority world missionaries would be for them to go to countries where Westerners might have difficulty getting visas or resident permits. One must be careful, however, not to view the majority world missionary force primarily as a source of surrogates for Western missionaries. Majority world mission movements also should not be seen as a cheap source of warm bodies that can be deployed for less money than personnel from the more affluent West.

With mission leaders and organizations having arisen in the majority world, the non-Western world missionary movement provides leadership and creative thinking as well as needed personnel. Mission strategist Luis Bush, who coined the term *10/40 Window* to describe the area of the globe where many of today's unreached peoples live, grew up in Argentina. Samuel Escobar, whose most recent book is titled *The New Global Mission,* is from Peru. Missiologist David Bosch, mentioned earlier, is from South Africa. Gottfried Osei-Mensah, chairman of African Enterprise and former executive secretary of the Lausanne Committee for World Evangelization, is from Ghana. Theodore Williams, author of *The Local Church and Mission,* has been a key mobilizer for global missionary outreach in India. Through his writings, Puerto Rican Orlando Costas has echoed many majority world theologians and missiologists in calling the Church to be holistic in its ministries. Tite Tienou, a native of Burkina Faso, is a respected authority on missions, theology, and the church in Africa. Vinoth Ramachandra from Sri Lanka has helped believers think about and respond to the social, cultural, and political challenges they face in contexts throughout Asia.

One challenge for the global church is to make sure prospective missionaries from countries around the world get adequate cross-cultural training. That is a goal of mission associations springing up around the world. Several denominations and mission agencies in Asia have formed the Asia Missions Association. Representatives from 20 countries in Africa, Latin America, and Asia founded the Third-World Missions Association with David Yonggi Cho, pastor of the 800,000-member Yoido Full Gospel Church in South Korea, as one of its leaders. The Nigerian Evangelical Missions Association (NEMA) has drawn together more than 100 churches and mission agencies from that African nation. The India Missions Association does a similar thing as an umbrella organization for about 175 denominations and mission agencies in India.

Reprise: Who Is a Missionary?

Sometimes American believers who are discouraged about low rates of church growth in their country get excited when someone says that missionaries are arriving in the U.S.A. from other countries. To these Americans, unreached peoples on the other side of the globe seem far away while their nearby neighbors who do not have a relationship with Jesus loom large in their consciousness. So, the American Christians rejoice when they think that evangelists from abroad are coming to try to lead their neighbors to the Lord. What they may not understand is that most of those reports about missionaries are actually about pastors who have immigrated to the U.S.A. to lead churches of fellow immigrants. That is not what the "being sent" part of missionary service means. Colombians immigrating to the U.S. to pastor churches of Colombians (or Koreans pastoring Korean immigrants) are evangelists or pastors in the sense of Ephesians 4, but they are not missionaries who have been specifically gifted by the Holy Spirit for cross-cultural ministry. Such pastors and evangelists are almost never sent with the prayer and sacrificial financial backing of partners in the churches of their home country. On the contrary, believers in their countries of origin often bemoan the losses of key church leaders who emigrate elsewhere. These pastors are even envied in their home country because of their good fortune in getting to a place where they can improve their standard of living.

To be sure, in relation to their place of residence, these Christian workers have crossed some cultural and language barriers. Such immigrant pastors may have had to learn a new language to get a driver's license. However, on Sundays, they preach in their mother tongue, and when they pray with parishioners during the week, it is in that shared **heart language** they learned as children. Pastors and parishioners are living together in the same strange land and together share the struggles of being an immigrant. Hesitating to put these people in the missionary category does not belittle their service for the Lord. However, referring to them as missionaries muddies the picture of what they are doing or, in Donald McGavran's analogy, becomes a fog that keeps leaders from having a clear understanding of what is going on.[9] To be a missionary to another country, Christian workers need to be immigrating to that country for the purpose of evangelizing people of a different cultural and even language group.

How a person defines a missionary does depend somewhat on one's **pneumatology** or doctrine of the Holy Spirit. That is, does Ephesians 4 mean that the Holy Spirit calls specific individuals and gifts them for particular roles? If so, is there a particular giftedness associated with taking the gospel across cultural boundaries? If the answers to those questions are yes, then that makes a strong case for having a special missionary category rather than missionary being another title for all Christian workers or even all Christians.

Native Missionaries?

Majority world mission is not the same as the native missionaries mentioned in fund-raising advertisements in the pages of Christian magazines. Those advertisements are usually financial support appeals for village pastors or itinerant evangelists working among their own people in their home countries. Such appeals may grow out of good intentions, but that kind of financial subsidy will likely be as counterproductive under the native missionary label as it is when mission agencies do it under a national pastor label. The fact that these native missionaries are not working cross-culturally also raises the question: Is it honest to promote them in the West as missionaries? This is not to disparage the Kingdom work of such people. These barefoot evangelists, as Billy Graham and others have called them, are doing a remarkable work of evangelizing in their home countries. They need to be commended for their unique ministries rather than being lumped in with cross-cultural expatriate missionaries from those same countries.

African-American Missionary Outreach

"From Every Nation," the title of this chapter, needs to be understood in the sense of "From Every People." Because all sectors of the Church are supposed to embrace the global missionary enterprise, missiologists have puzzled over why some minority churches, such as African-American, Hispanic, and Native American ones in the U.S., have seemingly had only minimal involvement in world evangelism. Some hypotheses have been advanced to answer questions like these: Are there expectations that people from these minority backgrounds being called to missionary service will limit themselves to reaching only "their own people"? Do the models of global missionary outreach the minorities see in historic Western mission organizations seem too costly to implement? Sadly, American mission boards were as slow in racially integrating their global missionary force as the nation was in integrating its public institutions, its military, and its work force. Did the racism that made existing mission agencies reluctant to recruit Blacks, Hispanics, and other minorities discourage members of those minority groups from applying in the first place?

To be sure, stories of African-American missionaries do not get told very often. Adoniram and Ann Judson, who went to India in 1812, are often credited with being the first American Protestant missionaries. In reality, the title of "First Protestant missionary from the New World" may belong to John Marrant, a "free black" from New York City who in 1770 began preaching to Native Americans in Canada. Marrant went on to take the gospel to four tribal groups: Cherokee, Creek, Catawar, and Housaw. Or, if the title of "first American missionary" needs to be reserved for someone who actually boarded a ship, then it might be claimed by George Liele, a freed slave who went to Jamaica in 1783 to start a Baptist church. In 1790, former slave Prince Williams went from the U.S. to the Bahamas to plant Baptist churches. That work has borne so much long-term fruit that today the Baptists are the largest denominational group in the Bahamas. All three of these—Liele, Marrant, and Williams—were planting churches cross-culturally before the Judsons ever left New England.

Betsey Stockton, a former slave of the African Diaspora, was the first single female missionary in modern history. In 1882 Betsey was sent by the American Board of Commissioners to Hawaii partly as a missionary and partly as a servant for a missionary couple expecting a child. However, Betsey's contract with the American Board did make clear that she was to share in the mission's primary work.

African-American Christians may not have put a high priority on global evangelism because their own leaders have encouraged them to center their attention on Black America or at least look no further afield than the lands of their ancestors in sub-Saharan Africa. The story of Eliza Davis George illustrates the reactions that young African-Americans often got when they testified to a missionary call. In the early 1900s, Eliza taught at Central Texas College in Waco, Texas. During a morning devotional time on February 2, 1911, she had a vision of Africans passing before Christ's judgment seat. Weeping and moaning, those Africans in her vision were saying to Jesus, "No one ever told us You died for us."

The vision took her back to when she had been a student at Guadelupe College, a Black Baptist school near San Antonio, Texas. During the young lady's college years, the Guadelupe student body had been challenged to offer themselves as foreign missionaries and Eliza Davis George had responded affirmatively. Now, she felt this vision was prodding her to go to Africa. The college president tried to dissuade her by saying, "Don't let yourself get carried away by that foolishness. You don't have to go over there to be a missionary—we have enough Africa over here."

Two more years elapsed. Finally, Eliza got up the courage to leave her teaching position and head to Liberia. In her resignation speech at the college, she read an original poem with these lines, "My African brother is calling me. / Hark! Hark! I heard his voice. . . . / Would you have me stay when God said go?" On December 12, 1913, Eliza Davis George sailed from New York as a National Baptist missionary.

While these are great stories, they stand out because they are exceptions. Even with the excitement one might expect would be generated by the recounting of stories like these, global evangelism has never involved many African-Americans or other minorities. The amount of mission involvement that might be expected considering the numbers of minority churches around the world just has not been there. For instance, the word *missionary* in the name of the Missionary Baptist denomination does not have the world evangelism nuance that it does in A. B. Simpson's Christian and Missionary Alliance Church or the Missionary Church of Mennonite origins.

In recent years Marilyn Lewis tried to awaken Black American churches to their global mission responsibility. Marilyn, a schoolteacher in Pasadena, California, spoke often of her desire to go as a missionary to Brazil. Just prior to Marilyn's untimely death from a heart attack, she had written this call-to-action plea:

> Just look at an African-American church today and you can see testimony to our new era: richly decorated, air-conditioned sanctuaries with carpeted floors are now quite common. Many drive to church in the latest model cars. Today, instead of working tables at restaurants, many African-Americans own them. God has blessed us. Now it is time for the African-American to bless the world in evangelization efforts. In the past many African-Americans cried because they could not become involved in missionary work. But now the doors are wide open and we are without excuse.[10]

Hopefully, a new day of involvement in global mission is dawning for African-Americans and other minority churches around the world.

Telling Their Stories

Mission history published for Western consumption has focused on missionaries from the West. There is nothing unusual about that. However, by not telling the stories of missionaries from the majority world, the Western Church is in danger of letting those other missionary stories vanish from the Church's collective memory. For example, in the late 1940s Alice Khumalo from Swaziland obeyed God's call to go with American missionaries George and Jeanette Hayse to the Pedi people, a people group in South Africa. In an interview in Swaziland near the end of her life, Alice shared with gusto how she had learned the culture and language of the Pedi people. Suddenly, she bolted to her bedroom. Coming back holding a well-worn Bible in the Pedi language, she told how the Pedi people responded to her preaching from that very Bible.

In Papua New Guinea, the stories of Australian missionary Will Bromley's trek to the Jimi Valley are legendary. By his side, but virtually never mentioned, was a young man named Ap Tul who learned the language of the Jimi and served as Bromley's translator. Other names little known in the West include Semisi Nau from Fiji who was a missionary to the Solomon Islands and John Sung of China who ministered in half a dozen Asian countries. Their stories belong to more than one cultural group; those stories are the patrimony of the global Church. That they get overlooked in the telling of global missionary outreach can be illustrated by the experience of two of missiologist Andrew Walls' graduate students. Both students did their doctoral dissertations on Christian missions in southern Ethiopia. One drew primarily on missionary archives kept in Canada. The other student's research utilized oral history interviews among the Oromo (or Galla) people in Ethiopia. Relying on those different sources of information, the doctoral candidates' dissertations painted two different pictures of church development and expansion in southern Ethiopia. "Reading the [two] works," said Walls, "you could be forgiven for thinking these were two different places."[11]

Fortunately, Jonathan Bonk and a team at the Overseas Ministries Study

Center in New Haven, Connecticut, are attempting to track down and record the stories of non-Westerners who have served as cross-cultural missionaries. Some of their work is now available online within the "Dictionary of African Christian Biography."

Ramifications

Mission organizations face stiff challenges in globalizing their mission force. For example, there are financial issues to work through. When missionaries from different countries are sent out and supported by the same mission agency, the question must be faced: Should missionaries coming from Switzerland and Swaziland get the same level of financial support? If, in the name of fairness, it is decided that they should be supported at the same level, the Swazi will likely be paid more than any pastor or church leader in his home country while the Swiss will be seen by his countrymen as being forced to get by on a very low income. Mission boards will need to prayerfully think through such issues of financial support. Some majority world churches with their own mission boards utilize tentmaking strategies to get missionaries overseas where they work in service occupations. How do those missionaries, some of whom are working at low-paying jobs, interface with relatively well-supported Western missionaries?

A few organizations promote a system that brings to mind comity strategies from the past. In the 19th century, countries such as India were carved up among various mission boards with each agency or board having a particular geographic area assigned to it. Called comity agreements, these territorial assignments were an attempt to eliminate overlapping evangelism efforts and make sure all parts of a particular country heard the gospel. For a variety of reasons, the comity system fell apart. One problem was migration of believers. For example, when Baptist families moved to a Presbyterian area, they often dropped out of church or else tried to start a Baptist church on their own rather than adjust to Presbyterian worship styles, beliefs, and forms of church government. Another problem was that some groups were more zealous about evangelizing than others, so the comity strategy didn't really succeed in making certain all areas of a country were equally evangelized. The boundaries created for various mission boards also dampened the natural movement of the gospel through friendship, family, and clan networks stretching across areas assigned to different denominations or mission boards.

Today, some groups promote a world evangelism strategy in which the West is asked to provide the money with the majority world providing the personnel. That seems a little like a comity agreement in that it places limits on what each group will do. One problem is that it assumes God will quit calling North Americans and Europeans to missionary service. Stopping the flow of Euro-American missionaries would also damage the cultural exchange effects that are wonderful by-products of the global missionary enterprise. One must wonder as well whether churches in the West would maintain a high level of global mission zeal if they quit sending out their own members as missionaries.

Another question in globalizing a missionary force relates to how mission boards prepare their missionary candidates for service on multinational missionary teams. During a missionary ladies' retreat in Benin, for example, a German missionary said that while she had been well trained on how to work with Africans, she was having trouble knowing how to work alongside her American missionary colleagues. As multinational teams of missionaries have become common, intercultural communication with its challenges and opportunities has emerged as a critical issue. Mission leaders must find ways to lower the potential for misunderstandings between missionaries from different cultural groups. There are communication issues to be faced when missionaries come from different language groups. Does a mission board adopt one "official language" in which it will do all its communication with its missionaries? If so, is the mission board thereby favoring one language over another?

To help mission leaders understand cross-cultural communication issues, David Hesselgrave has used a three-culture model to illustrate how a variety of things affects cross-cultural communication of the gospel. Hesselgrave notes that missionaries must be aware that three cultures—the missionary's own culture, the target culture, and the biblical culture—affect communication of the gospel.[12] Ignoring the effects of any one of these three may mean the missionary will be communicating a distorted gospel. With a multinational missionary team, Hesselgrave's diagram becomes a four-culture (or even more) model in which missionaries from different cultural backgrounds must recognize that their missionary colleagues have cultural filters from their own background that color or shape understandings. Failure to realize this can quickly escalate small misunderstandings into big problems.

Among the positives of a multinational missionary team is that such a team is not likely to uncritically replicate aspects of one particular missionary's home church. Another positive aspect of multinational missionary teams is the flexibility they offer in approaching some visa and resident permit issues. Occasionally a door closed to missionaries coming from one country will be open for missionaries carrying passports from a different country. One majority world missionary who illustrates that was Honorato T. Reza who preached both in person and via radio across Latin America. Reza, a Mexican, was particularly instrumental in helping maintain relations with churches in Cuba after Fidel Castro came to power in 1959. Reza also impacted the English-speaking world by authoring *Our Task for Today*, a small volume on mission theology and strategy written for lay church members. Reza's story stands as a reminder that just because people share the same language does not mean they are the same culturally. As a Mexican, Reza was working cross-culturally when he went to Peru or Argentina or Panama. Bruno Radi, an Argentinean of Italian and Polish parents, was likewise working cross-culturally as he promoted evangelism and church planting in almost every country of South America.

Contributing to Closure

Much world evangelism work today goes on in cultures and people groups where the Church is already established. Continuing to do mission work in areas where churches already exist is not a bad thing in and of itself. However, in order to strategically distinguish such mission work from pioneer efforts to evangelize unreached people groups, it has been given the label of **regular missions.** Mission efforts within people groups where the Church has not yet been planted or is quite small are called **frontier missions.** As has been seen, God's purpose in giving the Abrahamic covenant and calling for its fulfillment in the Great Commission is to bring glory to himself through loving, caring relationships with people from every nation, tongue, and tribe. Obeying the Great Commission and working for closure, regardless of how that is measured, will not happen unless the Church puts a high priority on frontier missions. For the Great Commission to be fulfilled in the world's least-evangelized, the Church needs to zealously mobilize all its resources, including those in the majority world and in minority churches in the West.

Back to Jerusalem Movements

As has been noted, majority world mission groups are often very interested in frontier missions. Coming out of China and Nigeria are two vibrant Back to Jerusalem movements focused on unreached areas. House church leaders in China have committed to raising up missionaries to evangelize from China's borders westward through the 10/40 Window all the way to Jerusalem. The vision for that arose in the 1920s but then had to be put on hold in 1949 when the Chinese church was forced underground. Now, Chinese church leaders are once again talking about turning that dream into a reality. In Africa, the Nigerian Evangelical Missions Association (NEMA) has launched Vision 50:15 with the hopes of mobilizing 50,000 Nigerians over a 15-year period for the purpose of taking the gospel north and eastward from their country all the way to Jerusalem.

In talking about what Nigerian churches plan to do in Vision 50:15, Timothy Olonade, executive secretary of NEMA, has said some bold things:

We cannot get back to Jerusalem without—

- *Facing the enemy eye to eye.* This vision calls for holy confrontation. The nations between Nigeria and Jerusalem are known to have overtly set themselves against the Lord and His anointed.

- *Overrunning the enemy territory.* We must look into this vision "like a lamb in the midst of wolves."
- *Having a readiness to die.* This requires a reappraisal of our theology of suffering. This vision will query and question the laid-back theology of ease that has characterized the Nigerian Church over the last few years.[13]

Although more missionaries are needed around the world, world evangelism will not be accomplished just by mobilizing more British or Canadian missionaries or even more Korean missionaries. As has been noted, mission involvement is one reflection of the Church's spiritual health. From the Day of Pentecost on, the Christian Church has been the most healthy when its outreach was accomplished by an ethnically diverse team. While 11 of Jesus' original 12 disciples were Galilean, Paul, whom the Early Church considered an apostle, grew up in Gentile territory. Some of his key assistants, such as Titus, were not Jewish at all. The Early Church grew rapidly in the Middle East, North Africa, and Southern Europe as missionaries from a variety of cultures ministered there. That process is again occurring worldwide and has the promise of bearing much fruit.

Henry Venn, a mover and shaper of the 19th-century missionary movement, compared the planting of the Church in a new area to a construction project.[14] Venn said that missionaries and mission structures are the scaffolding, not the building itself. Expatriate workers and initial outreach structures are temporary and can be removed as the building moves toward completion. There are places around the world today where the scaffolding is going up as unreached people groups are being penetrated. In other areas, the scaffolding is coming down and the *ecclesia* or Church has become what God intended all along—a truly global community of "called-out ones."

Questions for Reflection

1. What factors might be contributing to the tremendous increase in the number of missionaries from the majority world?
2. Why are the old designations of sending and receiving countries no longer valid?
3. Why is it important to preserve the stories of majority world missionaries?
4. What advantage might a majority world missionary have in serving in some Islamic countries?
5. What are the Back to Jerusalem movements trying to do?

7

HOW CULTURE AFFECTS MISSION

Objectives

Your study of this chapter should help you to:

- Define *culture* and *cultural anthropology*
- See why it is said that culture is learned rather than being inborn
- Explain how important cultural awareness and sensitivity are to cross-cultural ministry
- Evaluate the validity of the term *race* as a label
- Understand the importance of symbols, form, and function
- Know how to adapt to a new culture
- Counter the statement that "Christian mission work destroys cultures"
- Reflect on what it means to say, "We are all one in Christ Jesus"

Key Words to Understand

culture
cultural universals
enculturation
acculturation
surface level
deep level of culture
cultural anthropology
fieldwork
ethnocentrism
racism
redemptive analogies
functional substitutes
appropriate technology
people blindness
cultural relativity
syncretism
form
function
culture shock
cultural adjustment
reverse culture shock
inverted homesickness
bicultural

In Christ there is no East or West,
In Him no South or North;
But one great fellowship of love
Thro'out the whole wide earth.[1]

What do the words of William Dunkerley's classic 1908 hymn really mean? Is it true that for those who are in Christ, there is no east or west or north or south? Paul clearly said that in Christ there was to be unity, "There is neither Jew nor Gentile, neither slave nor free, neither male nor female, for you are all one in Christ Jesus" (Galatians 3:28). While believers must affirm the truth of that biblical passage, there is danger that saying, "In Christ there is no east or west" really means, "Well, in the end, everybody is just like me." Clearly, everybody is not "just like me." To be sure, both science and the Bible say that the human family is one race, the human race. However, while human beings are one family biologically, they are very different culturally and linguistically.

Defining Culture

Definition

Culture can be used in a narrow sense to mean good manners and a taste for classical art and music. The word *culture* broadens in meaning when it refers to a people's way of life in phrases such as *Mexican culture* and *Indonesian culture.* Utilized in this way, *culture* means the customs, ways of thinking, and material products of individual societal groups. As missionary Bob Sjogren put it, culture is what makes people think of us as *us* and them as *them.*[2]

Englishman Sir Edward B. Tylor was a 19th-century pioneer in the scientific study of cultures. His 1871 definition of *culture* remains very usable, "Culture is that complex whole which includes knowledge, belief, art, law, morals, custom, and any other capabilities and habits acquired by man as a member of society."[3] Because none of these things are passed on biologically, the word *learned* is a key in defining culture. Take, for example, a Chinese newborn adopted by American parents of European origin. Because there is nothing inborn about language or culture, that child who is genetically Chinese will grow up speaking English rather than Mandarin and will eat with a knife and fork rather than with chopsticks.

To really know a culture, one must look at far more than how people dress and what they eat. Culture includes all of a society's material products from furniture to perfume and from art to toys. Culture includes ways of seeing and evaluating things. For example, what will be judged as unforgivably late by one culture may be seen as exactly on time in another. Culture determines the ways in which groups make decisions, and it shapes leadership styles. Roles and status are assigned to people within the framework of their culture. For instance, in some cultures there may be virtual equality between males and females while in others one gender is disadvantaged in significant ways.

Cultural Universals

1. Place and time
2. Family life
3. Economics
4. Food, clothing, and shelter
5. Communication
6. Government
7. Arts and recreation
8. Education
9. Quest for the supernatural

Culture is communicated to young children by **enculturation** while adults learn new cultures by a somewhat different process called **acculturation.** In both cases, culture is passed on by language ("use your fork," "say 'excuse me,'" "sit up straight," "be quiet," "don't forget to burp," "shake hands coming and going") and other physical phenomena to which meanings have been assigned. Such phenomena can be objects such as headgear (cowboy hats, turbans, *hijab,* and baseball caps) or colors such as those worn by urban gangs or used in national flags, or they can be sounds such as whistles, sirens, or the snapping of fingers (all of which signal different things in different contexts). The physical phenomena can be items with religious meaning, such as prayer beads or amulets or cornmeal drawings in the dust.

All the components of a culture can be divided into nine major categories (see **"Cultural Universals"** sidebar above). However, while the categories of what people do are universal, the particulars of how they do these things are not universal. For example, when people meet, Germans shake hands, Koreans bow, Mexicans embrace, the French kiss each other on the cheek, the Uduk snap fingers, and the Inuit rub noses. People from different cultures say "thank you" in different ways. In much of the Western world, people who receive a gift are expected to send a note right away and to say "thank you" the next time they see the person who gave it. In many African cultures, people do not mention a gift during casual encounters with the gift-giver. Instead, the recipients let time pass and then they go sit down with the giver and make a big thank-you speech.

While preparing and eating food is a cultural universal, American business etiquette manuals say it is polite for people sitting at a table to wait until everyone at that table has been served before anyone starts to eat. In Italy, people are expected to begin eating when they are served. To an Italian cook, letting a plate of food sit and cool down after it is served would be an affront. The Italians reason that the food was served at just the proper moment; therefore, eating must begin!

Surface and Deep Levels

External or surface manifestations of culture can be identified by simple observation. For example, the meanings cultures assign to colors can be quickly picked up by an outsider. In some cultures, black is the color of mourning while in others, white is the color of mourning. Many cultures now consider pink a girl color and blue a boy color, a reversal of what those colors represented in the 19th century. Another example of surface level cultural phenomena is how food is eaten. In some cultures that is done with a knife, fork, and spoon. In others, chopsticks are used and in still others, people pick up food with their fingers.

Noticing a culture's different customs, food, clothing, and language can be somewhat like seeing the tip of an iceberg. When people see a floating iceberg, they are looking at only about an eighth of it because the rest of it is below the waterline. Because so much of an iceberg is unseen, it makes a good analogy for understanding culture (see fig. 7.1). That is because, in addition to the external behavior and material objects that can be seen and even immediately understood, many significant cultural components exist only at an internal or deep level. At this below-the-waterline level are beliefs, values, and core identity thought patterns. They may be things based on kinship, gender roles, the idea of modesty, work ethic, social rules, ways of handling conflict, and decision-making processes. This deep level of culture shapes thoughts and behaviors without people even being aware that it is going on.

The academic discipline that studies culture is called cultural anthropology. It is one of the sciences, but instead of working in laboratories, cultural anthropologists do **fieldwork.** The term *anthropology* combines a Greek word, *anthropos,* which means "man or human," with the suffix *-ology,* which means "language about" or "the study of." Thus, anthropology means "the study of humanity." Cultural anthropology narrows that focus to human culture.

Commonalities and Differences

Anthropology is a word that is also used in theology to talk about commonalities of the human race. In terms of culture, however, anthropology looks at differences.

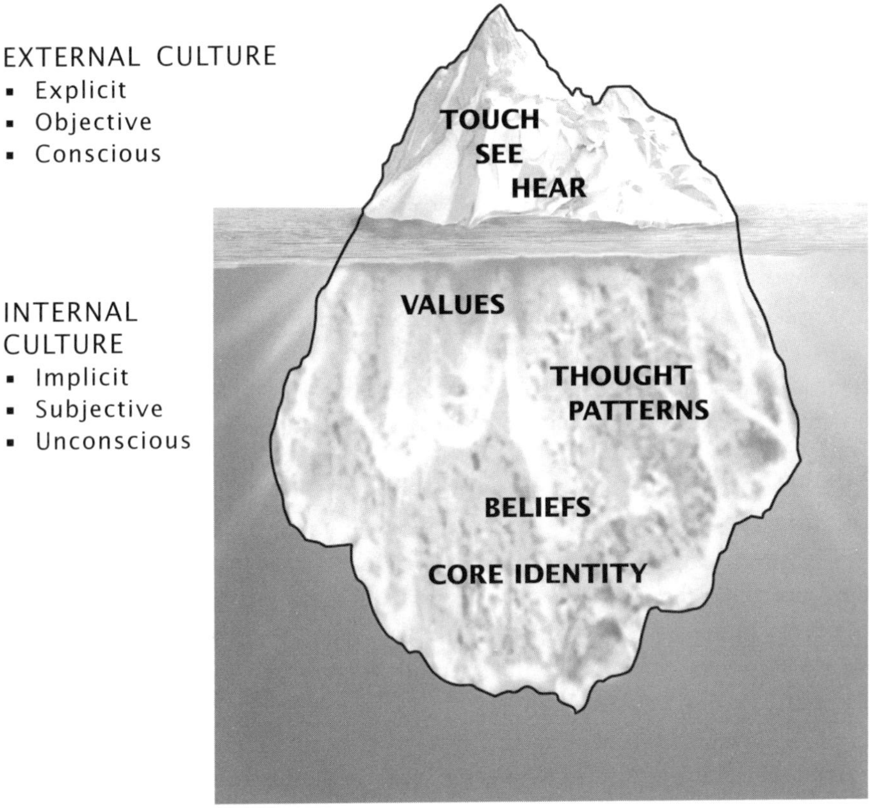

Fig. 7.1. Iceberg analogy of culture

Race and Culture

In recent centuries, there has been an erroneous tendency to see skin color or eyelid contour as differentiating marks determinant of culture. Skin color or eyelid contours do not determine culture any more than does height. People with very similar genetic makeup can differ widely in culture. Anglo-Americans have been caught off guard when people with dark skin from Trinidad or Jamaica speak English with a British accent and hold views different from African-Americans from Memphis. Those encounters make it clear that trying to differentiate people based solely on skin color sets up very faulty distinctions.

Indeed, many anthropologists today consider the concept of race to be meaningless and even misleading. Biologists note that all human beings have the same bone and muscle structure and even the same chemicals coloring the skin, where shading is caused simply by different amounts of those chemicals. Conrad Kottak has noted, "It is not possible to define races biologically. Only cultural constructions of race are possible—even though the average person conceptualizes 'race' in biological terms."[4] Indeed, there is no single gene that determines a person's race. Those physical characteristics that people think of when they say "race"—skin color, facial features, hair color, and texture—are determined by many different genes.

As British anthropologist Ashley Montagu looked at the "superior race" idea that the Nazis were promoting in the 1930s and 1940s, he saw the dangers of using racial labels. So, in his book *Man's Most Dangerous Myth: The Fallacy of Race,* Montagu called for discarding the word *race,* arguing that while there are physically distinguishable groupings of people, genetically determined physical characteristics such as skin color do not demarcate culture.[5]

Ethnocentrism

On what basis do people evaluate things in another culture that they find strange? In American culture, for example, used bathroom tissue is flushed down the toilet. In neighboring Mexico where the plumbing code allows smaller diameter sewer lines, used toilet paper is generally discarded in a wastebasket. When people encounter customs like this that are different from their own, they may express their dislike verbally or with body language. Such negative reactions come because of the human tendency to judge things on the basis of the values of one's own ethnic group. In almost everyone's eyes, what their own culture does is the best way and is therefore the standard for judging all other ways. Evaluating the values and motivations of other cultures by those of one's own group is called ethnocentrism. Unfortunately, ethnocentric attitudes have afflicted human beings since the human race broke up into different cultural groups after the Tower of Babel. Biblical examples of ethnocentrism include the way Jonah thought of the Ninevites or the way Jews looked down on Samaritans.

As people groups around the world encounter each other, ethnocentrism causes more than a few difficulties. In its mild form, ethnocentrism can keep missionaries from deciding that local leaders are ready to take over. In more severe forms, prejudiced and judgmental ethnocentrism gives birth to a **racism,** which provokes human beings to do horrendous things to each other.

Relevance for Global Mission

What importance does the need to understand culture have for Christian mission? With thousands of people going into eternity every day without Christ, should expatriate missionaries be spending time learning nursery rhymes or the intricate kinship relationships of their target culture? Unequivocally, yes. Missionaries must become amateur cultural anthropologists doing fieldwork in the name of Jesus. If missionaries want to be Christ-bearers who follow the **incarnational** model of Jesus, they must identify with the people they hope to reach. After all, Jesus did not appear out of the sky, spend a few days or even weeks on earth and then return to heaven. Jesus came to earth and participated fully in Jewish culture, eating its foods, learning and speaking its language, wearing its clothing, singing its songs, and participating in its cultural rituals.

There are at least three reasons for Christian workers to invest time in studying culture:

1. Missional Effectiveness

Two books by Don Richardson, *Peace Child* and *Eternity in Their Hearts,* got people talking about **redemptive analogies.** Such analogies are things in a culture that can bring the gospel into sharp focus for people of that culture. Several Chinese language characters, for example, can be used to talk about theological concepts. The Chinese character representing righteousness is a stylized drawing of a lamb superimposed over a man. Effective missionaries will continually look for such redemptive analogies in a culture.

A good understanding of culture will also help the church come up with **functional substitutes** to replace practices that are incompatible with Christianity but that have had great meaning for people within a culture and which would likely leave a void in converts' lives if they no longer can participate in them. A functional substitute is a practice that provides the same function as the original but in significantly different ways or forms. Thus, coming-of-age ceremonies that have unchristian content can sometimes be replaced by Christian coming-of-age ceremonies rather than simply being abolished.

A good understanding of culture can help the church make right leadership decisions as it ministers across cultural boundaries. Good cultural understanding can help expatriate leaders understand decision-making processes within a culture. It can help the church effectively exert its biblical roles of evangelist, prophet, and healer. Indeed, as missiologist Rod Spidahl has said, "You must become a prisoner of the culture in order to become a liberator of it."[6] When mission involves compassionate ministry activity, an understanding of culture will make leaders sensitive to using **appropriate technology,** methodology, and structure.

A good understanding of culture will go a long way toward curing churches of **people blindness.** A church has people blindness when it thinks of its ministry area as being monocultural when that area may really be a mosaic of different cultures or subcultures. People blindness keeps a church from seeing the unique challenges and opportunities posed by various societal groups within its ministry area. Thus, the Ivorian Christians in Abidjan need to see the Vietnamese immigrants in their country as people for whom Christ died. Churches in Portland, Maine, must recognize that the people of more than 70 nationalities living in their city are their evangelistic responsibility.

A Cross-Cultural Experience

It was a bumpy, rock-strewn trail, and we were traveling in four-wheel drive. Missionaries Bob and Lori Bracy were taking us to their rural house at Nondugl in the western highlands of Papua New Guinea. Down the dirt road, Nondugl eventually came into view. Brilliant red and white poinsettias splashed color around. Every part of the house where we were going to stay was constructed of bamboo—including the bed that we were to sleep on.

Pastor Yambe Sike and his wife, Marta, came out to welcome us. With evening shadows beginning their journey across the Highlands landscape, the Sikes invited us to have dinner with them. Their cookhouse was a large thatched structure with a friendly fire in the middle of the floor supplying warmth as well as light. Marta cooked our evening meal over the open fire. As we were eating, an early evening rainstorm blew up and soon sheets of water were lashing the bamboo cookhouse. But we were dry and cozy inside. The children of both families ventured out and returned decorated with mud.

Finally, Pastor Yambe picked up his Bible and announced that we would end the day with devotions. As we gathered around the fire, our host said he had selected Galatians 3 for the reading. In the flickering light of the cookhouse fire, Pastor Yambe read, "You are all children of God through faith . . . There is neither Jew nor Gentile, neither slave nor free, neither male nor female, for you are all one in Christ Jesus" (Galatians 3:26, 28).

I looked across the fading embers of the fire at the two families, one from Papua New Guinea and one from the United States. Some of the children were nearly asleep. *This is the truth: we are all one in Jesus Christ,* I thought. Jesus spans cultural and ethnic boundaries, binding us together in Him.[7]

—Charles Gailey

In the 1950s anthropologists began using the idea of **cultural relativity** to try to move people away from ethnocentrism and to abandon the **cultural evolution** paradigm of evaluating other cultures. That older cultural evolution model put cultures on a "progress" scale where some were categorized as backward and childlike and others were seen as enlightened and the standard toward which all other cultures should be moving. Cultural relativity insists that all cultures be judged on their own merits. Cultural relativity can, of course, be carried to an extreme with sinful prejudice, abuse, and injustice being glossed over because they are "part of that culture." Insights from cultural anthropology can help church leaders as they seek to discern where the Kingdom ethic should challenge, confront, and call for change. If that does not happen, an uncritical embracing of cultural practices can lead to syncretistic forms of faith with non-Christian beliefs and practices becoming intermingled with Christian ones. Ignoring a culture's deep elements can also result in a type of syncretism where Christianity becomes simply a thin coating of biblical material on top of other value systems.

2. Effectiveness and Emotional Well-being of Cross-cultural Missionaries

Cultural understanding is vital for ministry effectiveness and for the emotional health of cross-cultural workers. About 75 years ago missionary Lula Schmelzenbach wrote a biography of her husband who had died while they were serving in Africa. In telling Harmon's story, Lula revealed some of her own missionary philosophy and strategy, including how best to learn culture, "A missionary must live among the [local people] every day in the week and every week in the year if he would gain a knowledge of their language and customs, which one must have to win them for Christ."[8]

Missionaries will most effectively fulfill their call if they become ardent students of culture. Sometimes the burning desire to spread the Good News tempts new missionaries to spring into action before they have absorbed much of a culture or have had time to earn credibility within it. Too shallow of an understanding of culture is what led to the failure of Bruce Wilkerson's much-ballyhooed and well-financed Dream for Africa project. Julie Woolery, volunteer missionary to Guam, has said that she discovered being incarnational in mission meant "living with people, entering life together, building relationships."[9] As the Gospels make clear, Jesus lived as a first-century Jew for 30 years before beginning His ministry. Donald Larson, professor of anthropology and linguistics at Bethel College, wrote that an ideal entry model for the new missionary is that of being a learner and trader as opposed to trying immediately to be a teacher and seller.[10] Implied in all this is the thought that a missionary should have an insatiable curiosity. Anthropologist Miriam Adeney, who teaches at Seattle Pacific University, wrote that Mary Slessor's ministry as a Presbyterian missionary in Calabar in the late 1800s and early 1900s was effective because she was "awake, aware, curious, asking questions, categorizing information, applying it."[11]

Since missionary drop-out is often due in part to culture stress, proper acculturation may foster missionary longevity on the field. Tom and Elizabeth Brewster, specialists in language learning, wrote that early bonding with a culture is the best way to cultivate the sense of belonging and identification that is so crucial to effective communication.[12] If missionaries have bonded with a culture, they will do better at sorting through thorny issues that a shallow sense of cultural relativity would cause them to ignore. To aid the bonding process, the Brewsters urged new missionaries to consider living for a time in the home of a family of their host culture.

What do new missionaries need to learn about a culture? There is no detailed universal checklist although the ability to communicate is at the top. After that, individual items vary from culture to culture. For example, knowing how to ride subways would be important in Caracas, Venezuela, where there is a subway system; it would not be important in Dakar, Senegal, where there are no subways. The list of what one needs to learn will also vary depending on how closely the missionary's mother culture is related to the target culture. A Korean working in an Asian creative access area would not need to learn to eat with chopsticks; a European going to the same area would likely not have that skill and would need to acquire it. A good place into which to pour boundless curiosity is a list of cultural universals (see sidebar on p. 91). While such lists often have a handful of comprehensive categories, functionalist George Murdock listed 70 things he thought were cultural universals, including age grading, division of labor, property rights, status differences, body adornment, courtship, incest taboos, cleanliness training, personal names, gestures, hospitality, greetings, and jokes. Because learning a culture is a lifelong process, there is no master checklist that will ever be marked as completed.

3. Usefulness of Short-term Workers

Cultural anthropology will enable global mission strategists to make the best use of short-term mission teams and workers and to maximize the long-term impact of the experience upon team members themselves. Leaders on the receiving end as well as the participants themselves should be cognizant of cultural issues relating to the effective use of the short-term workers. Anthropological insights will help short-term mission teams with issues of communication, expectations, control, finances, gift-giving, and gender interaction as well as construction techniques and medical practices unique to their host culture. Both goers and receivers need to be aware of and at least somewhat sensitive to each other's cultures.

Form and Function

One anthropological concept helpful in the work of Christian mission is the distinction made between form and function. **Form** refers to the distinguishable characteristics of an object, sound; or custom. **Function** is the meaning or significance that those physical characteristics communicate in a given context. For example, to the Christian, the Cross is a form whose function is to evoke reflection about Christ's death. Jehovah's Witnesses argue that Christ died on an upright pole or stake rather than on a cross. In this case, the function is the same (both the cross and the stake were instruments of execution), but the form is different.

Sometimes form and function are closely related, sometimes not. For example, the relation between the form and function of a Styrofoam drinking cup is very obvious. Other relationships between form and function are not always so obvious, with many having been subjectively chosen, as is the case with the trademarked swoosh logo of the Nike company. Although that form or design is widely recognized, its relationship to the function it performs has been arbitrarily assigned. There is nothing inherent about the swoosh drawing that says "Nike" or even "footwear."

The different functions or meanings assigned to the same form can evoke different reactions in people of different cultures. For example, the hand gesture that signals "OK" or "superb" in the U.S.A. and Great Britain has vulgar and offensive meanings in Brazil and Russia. In southern Europe and Japan, that very same circle made with the thumb and forefinger means "zero." The form of the gesture is the same in all three cases, but the meaning or function varies greatly, producing very different reactions in different contexts. In many cultures, nodding one's head up and down is a nonverbal way of saying "yes." In Slavic countries like Bulgaria, a similar up and down head movement means "no." In some cultures, "picking up the check" (i.e., paying for someone's meal at a restaurant) is a magnanimous signal that says "I'm taking care of you." In some southern European cultures, the most important person at a table must never be the one to pay the tab.

How does a guest signal to the host that food at a meal has been good? In some cultures, the form of the signal is a completely empty plate. In Armenian culture, an empty plate signals that the quantity was insufficient. People in that culture must leave some food on their plates to signal that there was enough for them to be completely satisfied.

Do Missionaries Destroy Culture?

Some early cultural anthropologists such as Paul Erhard Eylmann claimed that missionaries were destructive to culture. They could point to things like the tragic burning of the Maya libraries in 1562 by Spanish priest Diego de Landa. They could point to the treatment a century ago of Native Americans in some mission boarding schools where American Indian children were forbidden to use their mother tongue. They could point to the imposition of

Western dress codes. Though such acts by a few missionaries created negative fallout for the whole mission enterprise, those few missionaries are not representative of all missionaries.

Generally, expatriate Christian missionaries have been insightful amateur anthropologists doing more to conserve cultures than destroy them. Missionaries tend to become excellent "participant observers," as anthropologist Bronislaw Malinowski started calling those who entered into a culture while studying and analyzing it. Bible translator Eugene Nida's classic *Customs and Cultures: Anthropology for Christian Missions* let the world know that Christian missionaries knew the value of cultural anthropology. Nida and some other missionary anthropologists also started a periodical for missionaries called *Practical Anthropology,* a journal that eventually merged with another publication to form what is now *Missiology.*

While most contemporary anthropologists understand that missionaries are less damaging to cultures than almost any other outsiders, missionaries currently find themselves needing to respond to fellow Christians who in a post-modern way ask, "What right do we have to try to change their beliefs?" One thing such criticisms of missionary work ignore is that cultures are always changing. Indeed, one aspect of culture that intrigues cultural anthropologists is the diffusion or movement of ideas and innovations across cultural boundaries, and the changes those imported items will bring about. Cultural anthropologists understand that the question is not whether a culture will change but what kind of changes that culture will undergo. The positive changes that Christianity has facilitated in cultures include leveling the playing field for females and other disadvantaged groups, such as twins, children, lepers, and AIDS sufferers.

Culture Shock

When missionaries move into a new culture, they usually experience a period of adjustment that includes attitudes and reactions labeled **culture shock.** The phrase *culture shock,* coined in 1951 by Cora DuBois and popularized by anthropologist Kalvero Oberg, describes the disorientation experienced when people move into an unfamiliar culture and have to learn a language and cope with new patterns of life as well as adjusting to different ways of thinking.

One way of looking at the **cultural adjustment** process is to see it as a series of progressive steps that can be labeled: (1) fascination, (2) distaste, (3) rejection, and (4) recovery and adjustment. The process begins when new missionaries arrive in their host culture and begin experiencing *fascination.* Goods sold in stores and open-air markets seem appealingly different from those back home. Enamored with new sights and sounds, the new missionary feels like a tourist. A second stage of cultural adjustment begins when feelings of *distaste* start crumbling that initial fascination. In the distaste stage, communication problems that had been only slightly annoying at first become frustrating. Traffic flow patterns, greeting rituals that initially seemed quaint, the way banking is done, and the absence of a favorite food begin to grate on the new missionary. Once-strange-now-familiar smells become annoying. The repetition of music that at first sounded clever becomes tiresome.

The distaste stage may lead to an even deeper phase of culture shock that has been labeled *rejection.* At that point, noise or the lack of it, order or disorder, the use or nonuse of certain colors, space or the lack of space, or the repetitive eating of some foods and the absence of other foods becomes overwhelming and a desire to escape wells up. Sometimes this escape takes the form of spending all one's time blogging or in e-mail communication with people back home. In this deep phase of culture shock, energy levels are usually low and irritability levels are high.

German mission leader Richard Zanner supervised outreach and church planting work all across Africa. He told the story of an American missionary whose fatigue in the cultural adjustment process brought acculturation to a standstill:

> I went to visit a missionary. I did not find him at home. When I asked where he might be, I was told that I would find him at his home country's embassy library. Everybody seemed to know that the brother was there twice a week. This made me curious, so I went there. Sure enough, there he sat, watching an American football game on television.
>
> Of course, there is nothing wrong in doing that except that in his case it was symptomatic of his lack of adaptation. I asked that particular missionary how many times he had watched an African soccer game in the maize fields. He did not know what I was talking about. He had never been to one.

Zanner concluded the story by saying, "It is quite acceptable to maintain your own personality and culture within reasonable bounds, but it is also wise to build bridges by developing interest in local enthusiasms as well."[13]

The convenience and low cost of global airline travel makes it possible for today's missionaries to make more frequent trips home. The downside is that frequent trips home can delay or stall out one's cultural adjustment. The ease and low cost of global communications also makes it possible for people to stay more connected to the culture and sports of their home society than was possible in the past. Culture fatigue tempts missionaries to listen to their home radio stations over the Internet rather than making the effort to listen to local broadcasts as an aid to acquiring the local culture and language.

So, when culture fatigue or shock wells up, new missionaries should be encouraged to hang in there, redouble efforts to learn the language, deepen relationships with people in the target culture, and strictly ration time they spend on instant messaging, e-mail, and blogging. People in various stages of cultural adjustment need to know that what they are feeling is natural. Generations of cross-cultural workers have experienced those same feelings and have gone on to thrive in incarnational cross-cultural ministry.

If missionaries can survive the shock, they will get to the fourth stage of *recovery and adjustment.* As new missionaries persevere in the bonding process, they will begin to appreciate many of the things that are different from what they grew up with. An embracing of new patterns of living will gradually displace homesickness. One day a once-rookie missionary will think, "Hey, this place no longer feels foreign to me; it's become 'home.'" That realization is a sign that cultural adjustment is well underway. Some have labeled this process of adjustment with an alliteration: *fun, fight, flight,* and *fit* with the stages culminating when it is obvious that the expatriate finally fits into the culture. To be sure, culture shock is not something that happens and then it is over. Cultural adjustment can take a very long time, as Linda Louw, missionary to Senegal, noted when she said, "I thought culture shock was something that you got through and it was done, but it just keeps coming."

Over the years, missionaries will get so acclimated to the new culture that when they return home, they may experience a package of reactions and feelings called **reverse culture shock** or reentry shock. Things in their mother culture that used to seem normal are now bothersome. Once again, the missionary feels disoriented and frustrated—only this time it is because of the way things are in the place thought of as home. Samuel Zwemer, missionary to the Muslim world, spoke approvingly of missionaries who had so "wedded their hearts" to the places where they served that when they returned to their countries of origin, they felt homesick for the mission field they served in. That feeling, said Zwemer, was **inverted homesickness.**[14]

As missionaries move back and forth from their home country and their country of ministry, they sometimes get beyond the settling-in stage to being comfortable with *both* ways of life. The people who are able to move from one culture to another and be seen as insiders rather than outsiders are called **bicultural.** Not all missionaries get to that point, but some will.

A Balance

In the opening of this chapter, the words of a classic hymn were quoted and the question was asked: Is there truly no east or west in Christ? The sense of oneness and unity proclaimed in Galatians 3 and other biblical passages must be balanced with the unity-in-diversity that John describes of people from every "nation, tribe, people and language, standing before the throne and in front of the Lamb" (Revelation 7:9).

Questions for Reflection

1. How would you define *culture*? What are some examples you would use to illustrate that definition?
2. Contrast external and internal levels of culture. In what way can external things of a culture be considered only the tip of the iceberg?
3. What is ethnocentrism? Why is it so difficult for people to recognize their own ethnocentrism?
4. Why can it be said that a missionary is sent to learn as well as to teach?
5. What is the difference between form and function or meaning?
6. What cultural universals are present in every culture on planet earth?
7. Why do many anthropologists say that *race* is a faulty concept?
8. Are there times you might have experienced something akin to culture shock? What things helped alleviate such shock or could do so in the future?
9. Why should missionaries try to move on beyond settling in to becoming bicultural?

8

INTERCULTURAL COMMUNICATION

Objectives

Your study of this chapter should help you to:

- Define language
- Identify the universal characteristics of languages
- Explain the importance of language—verbal and nonverbal—in communicating the gospel
- See the importance of language in fostering a global church
- Know some of the issues in Bible translation
- Understand how a new language is best acquired

Key Words to Understand

language
heart language
culture-bound
labels
code-switching
linguists
trade language
mother tongue
colporteur
dynamic equivalence
mimicry
informant
nonverbal communication

Language has powerfully affected the world since God spoke the universe into existence (Genesis 1). Christians talk about the Bible as God's Word and refer to its power. Acknowledging the power of language, John ends Revelation with a warning about adding to or subtracting words from that apocalyptic book (Revelation 22:19). Language was one dramatic sign of the Holy Spirit's coming at Pentecost. On that day, God moved in such a way that people from more than a dozen cultural backgrounds said they each heard the gospel spoken in their native language (Acts 2:5-11).

Language, whether vocal, written, or signed with the hands, is used to share ideas, cast visions, exchange information, express feelings, and deepen relationships. Because of how language serves human beings, one cannot overstate its importance in the study and practice of global mission.

Missionaries and Language

For almost everyone involved in Christian mission, language learning is a part of life. Not long after arriving on the field, one rookie missionary lamented the frustrations of language learning by saying, "I can't even communicate with a three-year-old on the train!" Because language is part of a culture, the sense of helplessness one feels in situations where a language is not understood is one trigger of culture shock. Once in awhile one will hear of rookie missionaries regularly attending an international church (often English-speaking) on their field of service because, they say, "We just cannot worship in _____ [language of their country of service]." In most cases, cutting back on participation in church services until one learns the language is a mistake. When language learning frustrations set in, missionaries must not cave in to the temptation to withdraw into enclaves of their own cultural group. This does not mean missionaries should refuse fellowship with people of their own nationality. If, however, they spend most of their free time with people from their home culture, they will miss out on things that facilitate language learning as well as cultural bonding. A frustrating downward spiral can set in that starts when discouragement in communicating leads to withdrawal and to spending more and more time with speakers of one's own heart language. Because of that withdrawal, language learning slows down, which in turn increases one's frustration level. That tempts the missionary to spend even more time with people who speak the language he or she knows. It is a discouraging cycle that prevents bonding and is counterproductive for language learning. Because the way people worship is an integral part of their culture, missionaries wanting to bond with a culture must learn to worship alongside people of that culture.

Whatever frustrations missionaries have with language learning, they must never think that using an interpreter means they have communicated perfectly with people. Being incarnational within a culture means being able to speak heart-to-heart with other human beings. That can be problematic to achieve when one goes to a country like Nigeria where scores of languages are spoken. If, however, missionaries want to be truly incarnational, they will remember that when Jesus came to earth, He did not speak some heavenly language that required an interpreter. He grew up speaking the languages the Jews would have spoken in that day (Aramaic, Hebrew, and Greek).

Language Landscape

Arbitrarily Assigned Meaning

One reason language learning is so challenging is that the meanings of the words and phrases of oral language have been arbitrarily assigned. There is nothing inherent, for example, in the sound of the English word *cat* that signals a small, domesticated feline. The act of translating will quickly highlight how arbitrary the assignments of meaning for oral and written symbols have been. Think about the English term *hot dog* or the phrase *fixing a sandwich.* Was there a canine that got overheated or was the sandwich broken?

Complexity

A second challenge to cross-cultural communication is that vocabulary lists from one language never match up exactly with the vocabulary lists of any other language. An English speaker uses the word *love* in both "I love pizza" and "I love you." Spanish speakers, however, use two different verbs to express those sentiments. Another challenge is that some words have multiple meanings that can only be sorted through by looking at the context in which the word has been used. The Italian word *piano* is an example. English has borrowed *piano* as a label for the instrument that Italians call *pianoforte.* That instrument is not what *piano* means in Italian. In Italian, *piano* can mean "soft volume" or "slowly," or it can mean the "floor of a building" (such as first floor or second floor). Which meaning is being used can only be determined from the context in which the word appears. To translate *piano* into English, one has to know which meaning is being used since no single English word carries all three of the meanings of the one Italian word.

A third thing that makes language learning so challenging is that grammar and syntax structures vary greatly from one language to another. Some languages use verb tenses or moods for which other languages have no exact counterparts. Greek, for example, has an aorist tense that Bible translators struggle to render into languages like English. Word order within sentences also varies greatly from one language to another. In English, adjectives usually go before the noun they modify. Romance languages do it differently, putting most adjectives after the noun. Verbs have complex conjugations in languages like Portuguese but no conjugations at all in languages such as Haitian Creole. Languages like French use double negatives in a sentence; English does not, except in slang expressions that schoolteachers decry.

These three things—arbitrarily assigned meanings, varying nuances in word meanings, and a variety of grammatical and syntactical structures—are reasons why no software program has been able to guarantee that sentences from one language fed into a computer will come out in well-formed, natural-sounding translations in another language. Sometimes such translation programs give decent results; at other times the results are abominable. For example, Babel Fish, one of the most popular online translation programs, took John 3:16 in Russian and rendered it in English in this puzzling fashion (including the two transliterated Russian words in brackets): "Since so [vozlyubil] god is peace, that he returned the son of its [Yedinorodnogo] that any believer in it, would not perish, but had a life eternal." This does not mean ideas cannot be translated meaningfully from Russian into English. It just demonstrates that machine translation has its limits.

Some words do not have equivalents in other languages because they are **culture-bound.** That means they refer to something that has meaning within only one culture and will thus necessitate an explanation when that idea is translated into another language. Pizza, for example, is a food that originated in Italy. While this baked, breadlike crust with various toppings is now eaten all around the world, people in most cultures have simply imported the culture-bound word *pizza* rather than trying to come up with an equivalent in their own language. The sport called American football has many culture-bound terms: *quarterback, tight end, bowl games, touchback,* and *first down.* None of those words have natural equivalents in other languages. Because that sport is uniquely American, its specialized terminology is culture-bound. An example from the legal field would be *mirandized,* which in U.S. culture means that as part of the arrest procedure a police officer will read to suspects a short paragraph of their legal rights ("You have the right to remain silent. . . . You have the right to an attorney"). Even though English is a native language for the people of several countries, the word *mirandized* has meaning only within U.S. culture because it comes out of a specific U.S. Supreme court decision in which the plaintiff's last name was Miranda. This does not mean that *mirandized* cannot be translated. It just means that an explanation rather than a single word will be needed (e.g., "The arresting officer read to the suspects a statement of their legal rights as outlined by the U.S. Supreme Court"). While Spanish is the official language of 21 countries, those countries also have words that are specific to them and are thus culture-bound. For instance, a special police force in Spain under the king's direct control is called the Guardia Civil.

Peru is about the only other Spanish-speaking country in which that phrase would be understood.

A Language Horror Story

When I was an inexperienced missionary, it was necessary for me to attend school discipline meetings. Teachers who were reporting infractions of students often showed intercepted notes to the committee. I looked at one note and, eager to learn the language, asked about the phrase *unesisu*. I was informed it meant "she is pregnant."

Several weeks later, new missionaries Robert and Peggy Perry arrived, and I was called upon to introduce them in church. Robert showed up at the last minute without Peggy. He explained that due to her pregnancy she was too ill to come. Utilizing my meager knowledge of the language, I introduced him. All went well until I explained that his wife was absent because *unesisu*. The congregation exploded into shocked laughter because I had implied that the missionary wife was *illegitimately* pregnant![1]

—Charles Gailey

Power and Beauty

Language is powerful. Winston Churchill's speeches bolstered British morale during the horrific bombing raids of World War II. The writings of William Carey awakened Protestantism to its responsibility for the Great Commission. John R. Mott's speeches on college campuses and his slogan "The evangelization of the world in this generation" inspired university students by the thousands to offer themselves as missionaries. Martin Luther King Jr.'s "I Have a Dream" speech energized the American Civil Rights Movement.

The powerful and the powerless of every culture use language to express themselves. The powerful use it to perpetuate their vision of the world while the powerless often use satirical proverbs to express their distaste of the powerful and to pass on survival mechanisms. One Haitian proverb, for example, says, "When the chicken is tied up, the cockroach can lecture him." Africans generally give descriptive names to expatriate missionaries, names that can express both tender feelings and satire. For instance, Lorraine Shultz was called *Dez Para Oito* ("Ten to Eight") because of her insistence that students at the Tavane Bible School in Mozambique be present in the dining area at 10 minutes before 8:00. William Esselstyn was called *Masithulele* ("Let us calm down") because that is what he said when discussions became heated. Elmer Schmelzenbach was called *Isisu Siyaduma* ("The stomach growls") because his stomach would rumble loudly. Amy Crofford was called "She who walks at noon" because of her habit of walking to her children's school at midday to pick them up for lunch (something people in Côte d'Ivoire thought strange in the heat of the day).

Good leaders will be sensitive to what language can do, not only in a positive way but also negatively since language issues can tear apart social groups such as a church. Sometimes language speaks powerfully through the use of **labels** that negatively identify people by their geographic or ethnic origins. Such labels are often an evaluative response expressing contempt and suspicion in contrast to an understanding response. Labels considered racist may evoke such powerful emotions that their usage can start riots. As mission workers learn a language, they must stay away from such labels and must call on believers not to use language that reinforces negative biases. A good principle to follow is to call people what they prefer to be called. Of course, even there, things can be complicated. For example, some Americans with ancestral roots in Africa want to be called African-American while others prefer Black. Generic words such as "people" should be used wherever possible, thus avoiding this issue.

Language enables people to express awesome ideas in picturesque ways. For example, in many cultures a person is said to love with the heart. Some African languages say that people love with the liver. In the Marshall Islands one loves with the throat. In Fongbe, a language of Southern Benin, one expresses loving tenderness by saying, "I accept your smell." In the U.S. a person with a great deal of courage can be said to have a lot of guts, while in Italy that person is described as having a strong liver. Such varied ways of expressing the same idea illustrate why language is more of an art form than something precise like 2+2=4.

Basic Principles

Some facts about language:

1. Natural languages used for ordinary communication differ from the formal languages constructed for use in logic and in computers. Unlike natural languages, those formal languages have finite vocabulary lists and limited grammatical constructions.
2. Natural language is a cultural universal that is used by even the most remote, cut-off-from-the-rest-of-the-world people group. Though languages vary greatly, they all are produced by the same biological mechanism and intellectual apparatus. This means the clicking sounds of some African languages are not made because Africans have a special click-producing mechanism in their mouths or throats. The same can be said for the rolled or trilled "r's" of Romance languages like Italian and Spanish.
3. Every natural language is complex. Cultural evolutionists of a century ago who divided the world into primitive people and civilized people thought that language development proceeded lockstep from simple to

complex along a single continuum with all other elements of civilization. According to the cultural evolution paradigm, the most civilized peoples would also be those speaking the most complex languages. Notwithstanding stereotypes nourished by movies such as *Tarzan,* those working in Bible translation have discovered that some so-called primitive peoples have extremely complex languages. Apart from an occasional trade language that no one speaks as a native tongue, there is no such thing as a simple language with a limited vocabulary and rudimentary grammar. Adding to the linguistic complexity are the separate registers or language variations used in differing contexts and social settings. For instance, a mother will use one way of speaking to her young child, while her vocabulary and grammar will be different when she speaks to her employer. When that mother switches her way of speaking, she is not changing languages or even dialects. She is code-switching within the same language.

4. Natural languages are tied to cultures. No natural language exists apart from a culture, except Esperanto, which originated in the 1880s with L. L. Zamenhof who hoped it would become an international language. The intertwining of language and culture caused **linguists** Edward Sapir and Benjamin Whorf to raise the question as to whether it is language that shapes culture or culture that shapes language. This discussion can be illustrated by the different points of view that cultures have on the past and the future. In many cultures people talk about the past as being behind them while the future lies in front of them. The Aymara culture of Peru sees the past and the future differently. Because the past can be seen, the Aymaras visualize the past as being in front of them. Since the future is unknown and therefore cannot be seen, they say the future lies behind them.

   Because languages are tied to culture, language learning and cultural acquisition can be thought of as two sides of the same coin. One cannot be done well without doing the other. With language being such an integral part of culture, various communication challenges must be overcome when the gospel is taken into cultures where it has not yet been preached. Discipling and leadership training are also challenging when scriptural and theological concepts have yet to be contextualized in a given language and cultural context.

5. Every language is sufficient for the use of the culture to which it belongs. Nomadic cowherds such as the Nuer in Africa may not have a lot of technical words and phrases about computers in their vocabulary, but in terms of talking about cows, the Nuer language is richer than

English. Because cultures are always undergoing change, languages are just as fluid and dynamic as the cultures to which they are tied. When the need arises for a new word, people will invent one or borrow one from another language. For instance, in Fongbe, automobile tires are called the feet of your car. Eugene Nida collected a lot of delightful examples of the challenges and richness that languages bring to Bible translation in his *God's Word in Man's Language.* Indeed, in what must be a sign of God's **prevenient grace**, each language is sufficient for initial gospel proclamation. That is certainly an implication of what happened on the Day of Pentecost. Don Richardson's work with redemptive analogies also implies that the proverbs and peculiarities of each language can be used to make the Good News clear within a culture.

Mother Tongue or Heart Language

The native language people are taught from birth is often referred to as their heart language. Even multilingual people use their heart language to give expression to their most profound thoughts. "Praying is best in the mother tongue," said a member of one German-speaking congregation outside of Germany.[2] Scripture recognizes the importance that language has for people, as can be seen by the report of Paul switching back and forth between Greek and Hebrew depending on his audience (Acts 21:37, 40) or when Eliakim asked to be spoken to in Aramaic rather than Hebrew (2 Kings 18:26).

Missionary Effectiveness

The effectiveness of a missionary depends to a large extent on his ability to communicate in the local language in a culturally relevant manner.[3]

—J. Herbert Kane

The human brain has the amazing capacity to learn a number of languages. Thus, in addition to their heart language, many people around the world use a national language or a **trade language** in business affairs and even education. In India that language may be Hindi or English while in many Pacific islands it will be a Pidgin. For indigenous peoples in Central and South America the trade language will be Spanish. Because English is widely known as a second or third language, people have sometimes made the assumption that world evangelism can now be done largely in English. The lack of literature for training in a language also tempts leaders to attempt theological training in another language such as English rather than in a people's mother tongue. It may seem faster and less troublesome for the communicator to use

English or Hindi to try to evangelize a country like India. However, while the use of a trade language can bear some evangelistic fruit, that fruit may not be the most lasting. Most lasting results in evangelism, discipleship, teaching, and training are produced when those are done in the mother tongue. Church leaders in areas where multiple languages are spoken have to weigh trade-offs about investments of time and finances when it comes to decisions about literature production for peoples who speak different languages but share a trade language. Into this decision must be factored the thought that the chances of syncretism will be greater if people are having to process the gospel in a language that is not their heart language.

When a trade language is used primarily for commerce, nonnative speakers of that language will likely not know how to use it effectively to communicate theological concepts. This is one reason mother-tongue churches are usually more healthy and vibrant than those using trade languages. As mission leaders try to decide which language or languages to use in evangelism and discipleship, the focus must be on the most effective way to communicate the gospel rather than on what seems quickest and easiest. Of course, what began as a trade language sometimes becomes the mother tongue of a group of people. This has happened, for example, with people in Côte d'Ivoire who have moved from rural villages into Abidjan, the capital city. The heart language or mother tongue of many children in the city is now French, which means they have trouble communicating with grandparents still living in villages where they speak the indigenous language of their ancestors.

This trade language/mother-tongue issue may also be one reason why trying to evangelize foreign university students has not produced abundant long-term fruit. Evangelizing someone in a language other than their heart language may be going down a path similar to that of the defective extractionist approach referred to earlier.

Potential for Misunderstanding

Learning to communicate in a culture involves more than learning words and grammar. It includes learning all the nuances being communicated by those sounds and written symbols. As pastors and evangelists can well attest, significant variations in the meaning of words and phrases can exist between groups using a common language. Navigating through language variants may be just as important in effective communication as knowing the major language. The diverse meanings applied to the same English words and phrases in various countries is a good example of what can happen. Picture this scenario: An American church leader participating in a church business meeting in London, England, hears someone ask to "table the measure." Interpreting that in their frame of reference, Americans would think the request is to postpone making a decision on something and move on to other matters. Actually, the British Parliament uses "to table" in an opposite manner. So, the Englishman in London is wanting to discuss the matter right away. When the American leader misses the point, as he or she likely will, confusion may occur.

Other examples can be found in French, Portuguese, and Spanish, which are all spoken in a variety of countries and cultural contexts. Sometimes a word or phrase in one of these languages will have harmless meanings in one country and crude or vulgar meanings in another. Another example is the word *tribal,* which has a pejorative sense for many Africans but is used with pride by Native Americans in the U.S. state of Oklahoma. Not realizing the nuances of a word in a particular culture has gotten traveling preachers in trouble. They have said things in sermons that provoked such strong negative reactions that they might as well have ended their sermon at that point.

Bible Translation

In 1917 William Cameron Townsend was in Guatemala as a young missionary selling Bibles. It was a good evangelistic strategy in an era when open evangelism was difficult for Protestants in Central America. One could, however, go to a village market as a **colporteur** or bookseller, set up a table, and sell books, including Bibles. Because they were booksellers, colporteurs could talk about the contents of what they were selling. One day in a mountain village marketplace Townsend was trying to sell a Spanish Bible to an older Kaqchikel Indian. The man asked Townsend a couple of times if he had any Bibles in his mother language. Townsend kept saying no and the Indian finally asked, "If your God is so smart, why doesn't He speak our language?"[4] That conversation sparked in Townsend a vision for Bible translation that led to the founding of SIL/Wycliffe Bible Translators, an organization whose translators have produced versions of the New Testament in 500 languages.

Never a Foreigner

The greatest missionary is the Bible in the mother tongue. It needs no furlough and is never considered a foreigner.[5]

—William Cameron Townsend, founder of SIL/Wycliffe Bible Translators

Many Protestant missionary pioneers used Bible translation as a key element of mission strategy. John Eliot, missionary to Native Americans in the 1700s, translated Scripture. In the early 1800s William Carey worked on more than 20 different Bible translations for languages spoken in India. Robert Morrison began Bible translation almost immediately after he arrived in China in 1807 even though it would take seven years for him to see his first convert.

American Board of Commissioners' missionaries reached Hawaii (then called the Sandwich Islands) in 1820. They so successfully planted and indigenized the church that they were able to withdraw after 50 years. Authorities in Hawaii still maintain memorials to these missionaries, including some of the original missionary homes. One element in those missionaries' indigenization strategy was that of devising a written form of the Hawaiian language so they could translate the Bible. In more recent times, medical missionary Evelyn Ramsey became so burdened to produce a Bible concordance for a language of Papua New Guinea that she reduced her hospital operating room schedule in order to have more time to work on the project.

Discussions over Bible translations often swirl around questions of dynamic equivalence. Dynamic equivalence translation attempts to capture the meaning of entire thoughts expressed in the source manuscript. Dynamic equivalence, also called functional equivalence, emphasizes readability while stopping short of being a paraphrase. Formal equivalence translation, on the other hand, translates a text word by word. Which kind of Bible translation is best? Does one aim for a word-for-word translation that stays as close to the Greek and Hebrew word order and grammar as the target language will allow? Or, does one seek to translate the meaning of larger units such as phrases and sentences? The answers one gives to those questions will be influenced by the translator's doctrine of inspiration of Scripture. For instance, someone who believes in verbal inspiration of Scripture (that the Holy Spirit dictated every word) will not be as comfortable with dynamic equivalence as will someone who believes that the Holy Spirit inspired the thoughts of the biblical writers and allowed them to use their own wording.

As has been noted, critics of Christian missionaries have sometimes accused them of destroying cultures. Bible translation does just the opposite. Small cultural groups whose language exists only in oral form are in danger of having their language fade away. Putting a language into written form and producing documents in it as significant as Scripture can give a language long-term viability as well as fueling healthy pride within a people group. Ironically, some Bible translators have been criticized for retarding the integration of cultural groups into the larger global culture because they have encouraged those people to hold on to their local language!

The Willowbank Report produced by the 1978 Consultation on Gospel and Culture held in Bermuda said that two formidable obstacles often hinder cross-cultural gospel communication. One is that of the gospel being viewed as a threat to a culture; the second is when the gospel is presented in alien forms.[6] The chances of either or both of these obstacles popping up are certainly greater if the Bible is not translated into people's heart languages.

It has been estimated that the people of earth speak about 7,000 distinct languages. Many of these are spoken by small numbers of people. Of the languages considered significant in terms of numbers of native speakers, Bible translators have said that 2,000 are still without the New Testament.[7] SIL/Wycliffe Bible Translators has adopted a vision for starting a Bible translation project in every one of those languages by 2025.

Language Learning

Wrong Order of Language Learning

1. Reading
2. Writing
3. Listening
4. Speaking

Occasionally people cringe at the idea of having to learn a new language. That may be because of frustrating experiences in which language learning was attempted as an academic exercise consuming a few hours each week rather than as a total immersion social activity. Often those who say they cannot learn another language are usually thinking about memorizing long lists of words and digesting complex grammatical rules. Language learning can also be frustrating when students are led through a historic but wrong order of learning by trying to read in their target language even before they can converse in it orally (see "Wrong Order of Language Learning" sidebar). The most natural order of language acquisition does not begin with reading. Because languages are primarily vocal, language learning is most effective when a learner becomes familiar with the sounds of the language before ever looking at written symbols or words. The most natural and productive order of language learning appears in the "Natural Order of Language Learning" sidebar.

Language learners should begin by mimicking the sounds of a native speaker. **Mimicry**, the most basic of language acquisition techniques, is the best way to learn the vocal or phonemic sounds of a language. Mimicry is how children begin learning their mother tongue. It involves observing the teeth, lips, and placement of the tongue as well as the speaker's tone and then attempting to closely copy all of that. Because children use so much mimicry, they get inflections and accents properly, something that is more difficult for adults. Part of that is because adults tend to try to reproduce what they hear without trying to copy what they saw.

Natural Order of Language Learning

1. Listening
2. Speaking
3. Reading
4. Writing

A second technique of language acquisition is repetition. One must listen to (and watch) an indigenous **informant** say things in the target language and then repeat, repeat, and repeat again. There is no way in language learning to bypass the need for repetitive practice. Along the way every language learner will make a lot of mistakes. Because making mistakes is an inescapable part of learning a language, learners must be prepared to laugh at themselves often, something that a missionary to the Xhosa people had to do when he confused *ngena* ("enter") and *phuma* ("leave") and thus testified that the Holy Spirit had left him! All language learners need to hear what one language teacher used to say, "You've got a million mistakes to make. So, let's get started!"

The third technique of good language learning is that of language usage. One does not learn to swim or play basketball by reading books about swimming or basketball even though some things about those sports can be learned that way. It is the same with language acquisition. To learn a language, one must use it in live-language situations. One must speak to people who know only that language, using whatever has been learned to that point, much as a child does. "Learn a little; use it a lot. Learn a bit; use it a bunch," Tom Brewster used to say.[8]

Most linguists say that total immersion is the best way to learn a language. In total immersion, the target language itself is used as the vehicle of instruction. In total immersion, English speakers learning Spanish never have Spanish explained to them in English. Everything is done in Spanish. To adult learners, total immersion learning may seem like it is going very slowly at the beginning, but in the end the actual acquisition of the language will be more rapid than with any other method.

Communicating Nonverbally

Communication is, of course, about more than just words, sentences, and even tone of voice. In fact, Albert Mehrabian, psychology professor at UCLA, asserted that 55 percent of face-to-face communication is done nonverbally through facial expression, gestures, eye contact, silence, posture, physical closeness or distance, and various other actions.[9] **Nonverbal communication** is more than body language; it can include other things in the context, such as seating arrangements, attire, and arrival times. Nonverbal communication both enriches and complicates communication. Indeed, what is expressed nonverbally can cause as many problems as things expressed by verbal language. As was noted in the chapter on culture, what is being communicated through particular actions will differ from culture to culture. The need to learn nonverbal communication is another reason why language learning is best done in live-language situations.

Using Words

Every Sunday, churches around the world worship in what could be a Day of Pentecost scene: "Praise be to the LORD," "Bendito sea Jehová," "Béni soit l'Éternel," "Binecuvîntat să fie Domnul," "Kia whakapaingia a Ihowa," "Ann fè lwanj Senyè a," and on and on in hundreds of different languages.[10] When God hears people praising Him in all of those languages, He understands perfectly and is delighted (Psalm 67:5; 117:1; Romans 15:11).

Francis of Assisi has often been quoted as saying, "Preach the gospel always; use words when necessary."[11] Believers do need to win credibility through actions demonstrating the presence of the transforming Christ. However, what Francis said must not be used to downplay how powerful words can be since language is the main tool humans use to communicate. Because the task of Christian mission is to communicate the gospel, those involved in it must be willing to pay the price to become incarnational enough to acquire fluency in people's heart languages.

Questions for Reflection

1. How, in your own words, would you define *language*?
2. What is a good principle to follow regarding the use of labels for people?
3. What would be some negatives for the use of an interpreter by a full-time missionary?
4. How does the embracing of the dynamic equivalence principles of Bible translation depend on one's doctrine of the inspiration of Scripture?
5. What is the most effective order of things to do in language learning?
6. From what you know about infants, how is mimicry a useful principle for adults in language learning?

9
VOLUNTEERISM IN MISSION

Objectives

Your study of this chapter should help you to:

- Define *short-term mission*
- Recognize the importance of volunteerism in the church
- Evaluate the benefits of volunteerism to both the individual and the church
- Identify what contributes to volunteer effectiveness

Key Words to Understand

short-term mission
volunteerism
reverse mission
Standards of Excellence
tentmakers
missional effectiveness

In the western United States, a layperson gave a missionary a ride to the airport after a local church's weekend missionary convention. The layman doing the driving had managed several successful business ventures, chaired a corporation, and been president of a bank. On the way to the airport, he talked about wanting to walk away from that part of his life and become a volunteer in overseas mission work. That layman had been a staunch supporter of missions through his prayers and financial giving. He now wanted to give a season of his life to global missions.

Volunteer opportunities in the global mission movement have attracted believers of all ages. Large numbers of young people go on **short-term mission** trips during times they are not in school. Adults of all ages who have prayed for and given money to missions efforts are jumping at chances to do hands-on mission work for brief periods. The modes of volunteer mission service are varied: weekend trips across a nearby border, one- to three-week trips, college students participating in spring break and summer-long events, people spending six months to two years or more serving as individuals or couples (rather than in large groups), and a hybrid kind of volunteer service called tentmaking. These short-term mission participants cross cultural and geographic boundaries to use God-given skills and talents to do construction, teach English, set up computer centers, work in orphanages, fit eyeglasses, tutor missionary children, and help with disaster relief, evangelism, leadership training, and medical work.

> In 1970, you could count the number of youth groups doing short-term missions on one hand. Now it has become a standard feature for thousands of youth groups.[1]
>
> —Seth Barnes

Involvement in volunteer short-term mission, as distinct from longer career service, began expanding just after the middle of the 20th century. Facilitating the growth of short-term mission have been global communication systems and the ease and speed of air travel. Short-term mission, regarded for a while with suspicion by mission professionals, is now a strategic component of world evangelism programs. Many mission agencies have **volunteerism** offices with career missionary teams often having someone assigned to supervise short-term mission groups and individuals coming to their field. Mission professionals have so fully embraced short-term mission that volunteer experience has virtually become a prerequisite for career missionary service.

Roger Peterson, longtime head of the Fellowship of Short-Term Mission

Leaders, has calculated that 1.5 million North Americans participate each year in various types of short-term mission.[2] Of that 1.5 million, roughly one-third are doing domestic trips, about one-third are going to Mexico, with the other third go elsewhere in the world.[3] Other estimates of short-term participants range as high as 4 million North Americans with a total annual investment of more than $4 billion U.S.[4] In terms of raw numbers, getting people to do short-term mission seems to have been hugely successful. Of course, participant numbers and money spent do not tell everything. There is more to short-term mission than numerical totals. Among the questions that will help evaluate the use of volunteers:

- Is mission volunteer activity moving the Church toward the fulfillment of the Great Commission or is it, in the words of Shakespeare's *Macbeth,* "full of sound and fury, signifying nothing"?
- In what ways do career missionaries see volunteers as a burden? In what ways do they see them as a blessing?
- Which specific long-term goals can short-term mission volunteers help accomplish?
- What are some positive and negative long-term effects of short-term mission activity on the participants and their sponsoring churches?
- In purely accounting terms, could money spent on travel and food and lodging be better spent by sending it straight to the mission field?

The Effectiveness of Volunteers

Short-term mission participants often receive minimal or even no cross-cultural training. Many do not speak the heart language of the people in the area where they go. Most participants are on-site for less than two weeks. Because of these and other issues, some have wondered whether it is possible that short-termers can be of lasting benefit to the world mission enterprise.

The verdict is now in on that question, and the answer is a resoundingly positive one. Parts of the global Church have been profoundly impacted by people doing short-term mission. The Kingdom effects of this huge number of people doing short-term mission are evidenced in three ways. The most visible and talked-about effect occurs in the places where short-term volunteers go. That receiving end is, after all, the focus of the trip. Still, even with all the things that are seen on the receiving end, mission professors John Nyquist and Paul Hiebert have concluded that those most affected by short-term mission involvement can be "the short-termers themselves and their sending churches."[5]

1. Effect on the Field

On the receiving end of a mission trip, the effects are both tangible and intangible. Given the obvious limitations of short-term volunteers, they still accomplish some very visible things. Construction work gets done on buildings; neighborhoods become aware of a church in their midst; people are drawn into events where the gospel is proclaimed; health-care needs are met and church leadership gets needed training. Some of these short-term mission accomplishments are quantifiable; other accomplishments are not easily expressed statistically.

Sometimes people look at the money being spent on transportation, housing, and food and wonder about cost-effectiveness. "Just send the money," they say, assuming that transferring financial resources is the most important result of short-term mission trips. Actually, some of the most significant effects of short-term mission have nothing to do with money or even hours of work on building projects. The relationships generated during short-term mission experiences may be more important for Kingdom purposes than the buying of concrete blocks or cement. Related to that is how short-termers help host congregations recognize their connection to the global Church. Believers whose congregations have hosted short-term volunteers frequently talk about how the arrival of a volunteer or a group from abroad confirmed to them that they belonged to the worldwide community of faith. A short-term team can also have energizing effects on the host church. When it sinks in to a host congregation that short-termers are giving of their time and paying for their own travel to work with them on a project, the effects can be both humbling and energizing.

In an ecclesiological sense, the short-term mission movement demonstrates that the Church is globally the Body of Christ where everyone's gifts and talents can be put to use, sometimes across great distances. Such volunteering of one's skills and talents for Kingdom work has been a fixture of Church history. While the Holy Spirit's gifting mentioned in Romans 12, 1 Corinthians 12, and Ephesians 4 does not specifically include construction skills, the recognition of craftsmanship skills as being from God is mentioned in the Old Testament when the Lord gave instructions to Moses concerning the construction of the Tabernacle: "I have given ability to all the skilled workers to make everything I have commanded you" (Exodus 31:6).

2. Effect on the Participants Themselves

The second set of effects of short-term mission concern the impact made on participants, or "goer-guests" as Roger Peterson calls them. On a strictly human level, short-term mission facilitates beneficial cultural exchanges. Another effect on participants confirms what the Bible says about the value of giving of oneself in service to others. During short-term mission trips, people experience firsthand the scriptural principle that it is more blessed to give than to receive. What frequently happens on mission trips is that those who have gone to minister wind up being on the receiving end of ministry in **reverse mission.** Social work educator Edward C. Lindeman noted how volunteer service often generates positive feelings of self-worth:

> The act of volunteering is an assertion of individual worth. The person who of his own free will decides to work . . . is in effect saying, I have gifts and talents which are needed. I am a person who accepts a responsibility, not because it is imposed upon me, but rather because I wish to be useful. My right to be thus used is a symbol of my personal dignity and worth![6]

One way that entering the ranks of mission volunteers enriches a person's life is through changed attitudes about prayer, mission giving, and mission education. This showed up in research that James Engel and Jerry Jones did on the attitudes of Christian baby boomers toward the missionary enterprise. Many of the Americans involved in short-term missions have been members of the boomer generation, that generation born in the 20 years following World War II. This generation began with the baby boom that resulted when hundreds of thousands of American soldiers returned home after World War II and started their families. After surveying professional baby boomers in several American evangelical churches, Engel and Jones concluded that going on a mission trip affects how members of that American generation view world evangelism. Engel and Jones said their research showed that "spreading the gospel overseas as a ministry is a high priority among those who have been onsite overseas, those who are financial contributors to missions, and those engaged in personal evangelism."[7]

Remedy for a Sick Church

The best remedy for a sick church is to put it on a missionary diet.[8]

—Unknown

Research by Roger Peterson and others has also shown that long-term shifts in attitudes and actions occurred among many short-term mission participants. Peterson's research indicated that mission trip participation generally resulted in a stoking of passion about global missions as evidenced by a doubling of prayer life and financial giving to mission causes. That same study also indicated a substantial increase in involvement in mission-related support activities.[9] Mission agencies say that significant numbers of new missionaries report receiving their missionary call during a short-term mission trip. All of this does not mean that every participant on a 10-day mission trip has been dramatically transformed. In that regard, going on a mission trip has some parallels in how a youth camp or a men's retreat affects people. For an occasional participant there will be striking positive changes; for most others who are positively impacted, the changes are smaller. The changes, however, are usually incremental; thus, the more short-term mission experiences people have, the more likely it is that they will experience noticeable changes.

3. Effect on the Sending Church

Kingdom Work Gets Done Too!

Short-term work, whether two weeks or two years, can indeed be effective and pleasing to God. Yes, it can cost a lot of money, disrupt nationals and missionaries, encourage short-term thinking, and inoculate some against career missions involvement. But done well, it can open participants' eyes to the sometimes gritty realities of the world, make them aware of their own ethnocentrism and the gifts and courage of non-Western believers, and spark a lifelong commitment to missions. In the best cases, some real kingdom work gets done, too.[10] —Stan Guthrie, *Christianity Today* news editor

How mission trips affect the sending church may be the least obvious of the three categories of short-term mission effects. Still, a lot of money comes out of local churches to transport short-term mission participants to and from a destination as well as feeding and housing them while there. The home church receives dividends from its investment when the spiritual fervor of returning participants ignites new passion within the local church. David Hayse, who coordinated hundreds of short-term mission teams, observed that short-term mission trips "have made an incredible impact on the sending church."[11] Many sending churches experience ripples of positive effects before and after having members participate in short-term mission trips. Excitement is generated within the local church as volunteers prepare to go and then after they come home. As trip stories are told and retold, sending congregations often gain a renewed sense of ownership for the world mission task. This can shift the focus of a congregation's concentration away from a maintenance mind-set toward the fulfillment of its global covenant responsibilities. As laypeople put their gifts and talents to use in world evangelism, there is often renewed recognition within the home church that believers need to function together as the Body of Christ. The mobilization of prayer support for the trip will often have positive side effects for the sending congregation. A burden and passion for lost people in another part of the world may get people thinking about the lost of their own city. As Engel and Jones noted, there is a link between involvement in personal evangelism and a passion for world evangelism. Churches that have people regularly going on short-term mission trips also often become leaders in overall financial support for world evangelism. As in the case of individuals, the changes in sending churches rarely are seismic shifts. More often the changes will be incremental with the impact increasing as more and more church members have short-term experiences. The effect that short-term mission has on sending churches is one answer to those wondering why all the money is spent on the trip rather than just being sent to the mission field. Of course, the question is a moot one anyway because money spent on mission trips is almost always "new" money for global mission.

The Downside

There is a downside to mission volunteerism. Because of the huge numbers of people involved, it should not be surprising that problems have occurred. Every mission organization has stories of disastrous volunteer experiences that include people not being adequately prepared, of groups destructively pushing their own agendas, and of inappropriate behavior that set back a church's witness. Volunteer mission can be done in ways that obscure key long-term mission goals. There is the danger of letting the desire to quickly accomplish something visible determine the overall mission agenda. Short-term mission programs risk amateurizing mission strategy with priorities and programs being determined by people with little training or cultural sensitivity and only limited experience on a given mission field. Some trips are overhyped in terms of what can be accomplished in one or two weeks. Short-term mission can mistakenly be presented as the primary way the Great Commission is being fulfilled. Sometimes, short-term mission participants do not really comprehend that they are just one more link in a chain of evangelism, discipleship, and church planting events.

It is not uncommon for short-termers to express disappointment that they did not accomplish more. What they have failed to see is that the changes in themselves and the accomplishments on the field need to be understood as small increments of bigger things going on rather than as paradigm-shifting revolutions. Sadly, there has sometimes been the artificial creation of a need so that volunteers will have something to do. Not infrequently, short-term mission activity creates dependency attitudes within the receiving church. Because there are new people continually coming in to short-term mission, the perpetual doing of very basic training can make it seem like the wheel is having to be reinvented every two weeks.

On occasion, self-centeredness, paternalism, or ethnocentrism cause short-term mission volunteers to do things without the knowledge of or against the wishes of the host church, necessitating damage control and even an occasional complete redoing of construction projects after the group leaves. Participants sometimes go on a trip just because a friend is going. Others have signed up thinking the trip they were going on was a sight-seeing one with only a small amount of spiritual flavoring. Some go on short-term trips seeking the emotional rewards of their own hands-on involvement rather than looking for ways to invest in long-term empowerment.

The participants of two-week mission trips must not be exalted as the superstars of world evangelism. While the overall impact of short-term mission has been significant, some participants come to think of themselves as excursion missionaries who feel that tremendous fulfillment of the Great Commission occurs whenever they make a two-week trip somewhere, an attitude that is a slap in the face to missionaries giving decades of their life to global mission.

For these and other reasons, going on a mission trip is not a positive experience for every participant or every group or team. Sadly, some short-termers even come home embittered by the experience. Sometimes there is bad team chemistry and people return home upset at each other. Sometimes clashes with field missionaries or national leaders occur that do not get satisfactorily resolved. Inappropriate behavior on the part of team members occasionally necessitates sending someone home early.

As the short-term movement gathered momentum, one concern was voiced that has turned out to be less of a problem than was feared. In those early years, there was concern that mission trips would drain money away from other world evangelism needs. That has not happened in the way people feared because most of the people going on short-term mission do not pay for trips with money they planned to give to missions; they use their own vacation money. So, people trying to conjecture how that $1 billion to $4 billion could be better spent need to realize that this is not money that would be given to global mission if all short-term mission opportunities were abolished. Rather than draining away funds, short-term mission has often increased mission giving.

Standards of Excellence

A few years ago short-term mission leaders in Great Britain and Canada drew up a list of characteristics of good short-term mission experiences. Building on what the British and Canadians had done, the U.S.A. Fellowship of Short-Term Mission Leaders created seven Standards of Excellence that it began promoting as marks of sound short-term mission. Those standards established benchmarks of God-centeredness, a partnership paradigm, mutually agreed-upon design, comprehensive administration, qualified leadership, appropriate training, and thorough follow-up. While many of the million or more short-term participants each year are going in groups, those standards are just as valid for individuals serving in short-term mission assignments. Trying to reach the benchmarks set by these seven standards will not guarantee a great experience for every participant, but it certainly moves things in that direction.

Standard 1: God-Centeredness

The first standard of excellence, God-centeredness, looks at how well short-term mission experiences follow the Matthew 6:33 principle of seeking first God's glory and His kingdom. In order to do this, short-term mission projects must be built on sound doctrinal foundations—ecclesiological and soteriological—rather than on the need to finish a construction project or give a youth group something to do. God-centeredness means that short-term participants will recognize and affirm that the primary focus is the triune God and not them or the experience. For mission trips to be truly God-centered, they must be enveloped in persistent prayer and seek to foster godliness in thoughts, words, and deeds.

Standard 2: Empowering Partnerships

The second standard of excellence calls for short-term mission to be done by an interdependent partnership of senders and receivers. In the best short-term mission experiences, short-termers recognize that they are primarily accountable to career missionaries and national partners on the field rather than to an individualistic sense that God has called them to accomplish something. Authentic partnerships can flourish only where there is mutual trust fortified by functional systems of accountability. Initiating, building, and nurturing partnerships can be a challenge in cross-cultural situations where communication problems cause frustration and misunderstanding. Then, even when the spotlight is on the receptors, the participants must never feel that they are going to *do* something *for* someone, whether that someone be a missionary, an indigenous pastor, or a congregation.

Standard 3: Mutually Agreed-Upon Design

The third standard of excellence judges whether goers and receivers have been equal partners in planning the experience. An excellent short-term trip never has one side announcing to the other, "Here is what we're going to do." Whatever methods and activities are done must contribute to the long-term health of the partnership and must fit within agreed-upon strategies. The experience must have a doable design. That is, it must ensure that participants can successfully implement their part of the plan while the expectations placed on the host receivers are within those people's capabilities. For example, it is probably unrealistic for a team to expect to do 10 days of one-on-one personal evangelism in a culture where none of its members knows the language. Likewise, it is probably unrealistic to expect that every member of a host congregation will give 40 hours to being with a mission team during the week they are on-site.

Standard 4: Comprehensive Administration

How short-term mission is set up and administered can make a difference in how successful it will be. This fourth standard calls on leaders of short-term mission programs to be above reproach in handling finances and to be truthful in pretrip promotion and in post-trip reporting. It expects that short-term mission programs will be of high quality and will be carried out with integrity, flexibility, and thoroughness. For example, in an area where there is little or no potable water, providing sufficient purified drinking water is a detail that must be on a priority list. Criminal activity on the field, an unstable political climate, or even just travel itself all have the potential for creating safety and security problems for short-term mission participants. Thus, good trip organization will set up appropriate risk management procedures. This includes formulating action plans for accident, natural disaster, or civil unrest scenarios.

Standard 5: Qualified Leadership

As with almost any venture, having leadership that is competent, organized, and accountable is important for successful short-term mission. This fifth standard calls on organizers of short-term mission programs to recruit and train capable leaders who are spiritually mature and who see themselves in a servanthood role. Such leaders must see their primary role to be that of empowering and equipping rather than of running the show.

Standard 6: Appropriate Training

A well-done short-term mission will train participants prior to their going to the field and continue that training while the volunteers are on the field. In addition to preparing participants for specific tasks, such training needs to foster in them a measure of cultural sensitivity. The training will also seek to prepare people for interpersonal and mission team dynamics and for handling individual behavior problems in biblical ways. One of the newest trends in short-term mission is that of putting groups together from two different nations or cultural groups to form a unified team to go to a third culture. In this case, participants will need cross-cultural training to enable them to successfully interact with other members of their team as well as with their site hosts.

Standard 7: Thorough Follow-Up

The seventh standard recognizes that good short-term mission programs provide debriefing and follow-up for participants. This should be done by on-field and post-field debriefing. It will be done with some on-field reentry preparation and through follow-up and evaluation after the volunteers return home. This standard recognizes that cementing long-term changes as a result of people's short-term experiences usually necessitates post-trip follow-up.

Longer-term Short-term Volunteers

As the numbers of participants on short-term mission trips have increased over the last few decades, remarkable things happened. One was that short-term volunteers began saying, "I don't want to go home after two weeks or a summer. I have a skill and time and money. I want to come back as soon as possible." Those short-termers began returning to mission fields to serve as volunteers for periods of up to two years. A positive thing for the career missionary is that midterm volunteers, as Miriam Adeney has called them, need less direct supervision than a team that will be on-site for only one week. The longer time frame gives more opportunities for the volunteer to learn culture and language. Thus, those midterm volunteers can usually assume more significant ministry roles than is possible for those who are on a field for only a few days.

Retirees

In many countries, people are able to retire from the work force while continuing to receive an income. Like the retiree previously mentioned who shared his dream with the missionary, other retirees are asking: "Is that all there is to life?" As people retire, they are faced with deciding what to do with the productive years they feel are still ahead of them. In an *Evangelical Missions Quarterly* article titled "Boomers, Busters, and Missions," Ken Baker noted that numbers of American evangelicals 50 years of age or older are giving themselves to a second career in missions.[12]

Precareer Volunteers

Spending a year or two in volunteer mission service has attracted college and university students wanting to do hands-on cross-cultural ministry before beginning their careers and families. The U.S. government fanned interest in volunteerism with its creation of the Peace Corps and Americorps. In Britain, taking a "gap year" during one's university years has been a long tradition. Those kinds of programs gave young adults a way to see the world while helping their fellow human beings. The government programs, plus the example provided by young Mormon volunteers, gave churches and mission agencies models for providing young adults in-depth mission experiences. Thus, in addition to those going to a mission field as volunteers for one to two years right after they graduate and before they launch into their career, some are taking a semester or even a year off during college to serve as mission volunteers.

There are pros and cons to sending young adult volunteers to serve along-

Illustrations

Plates

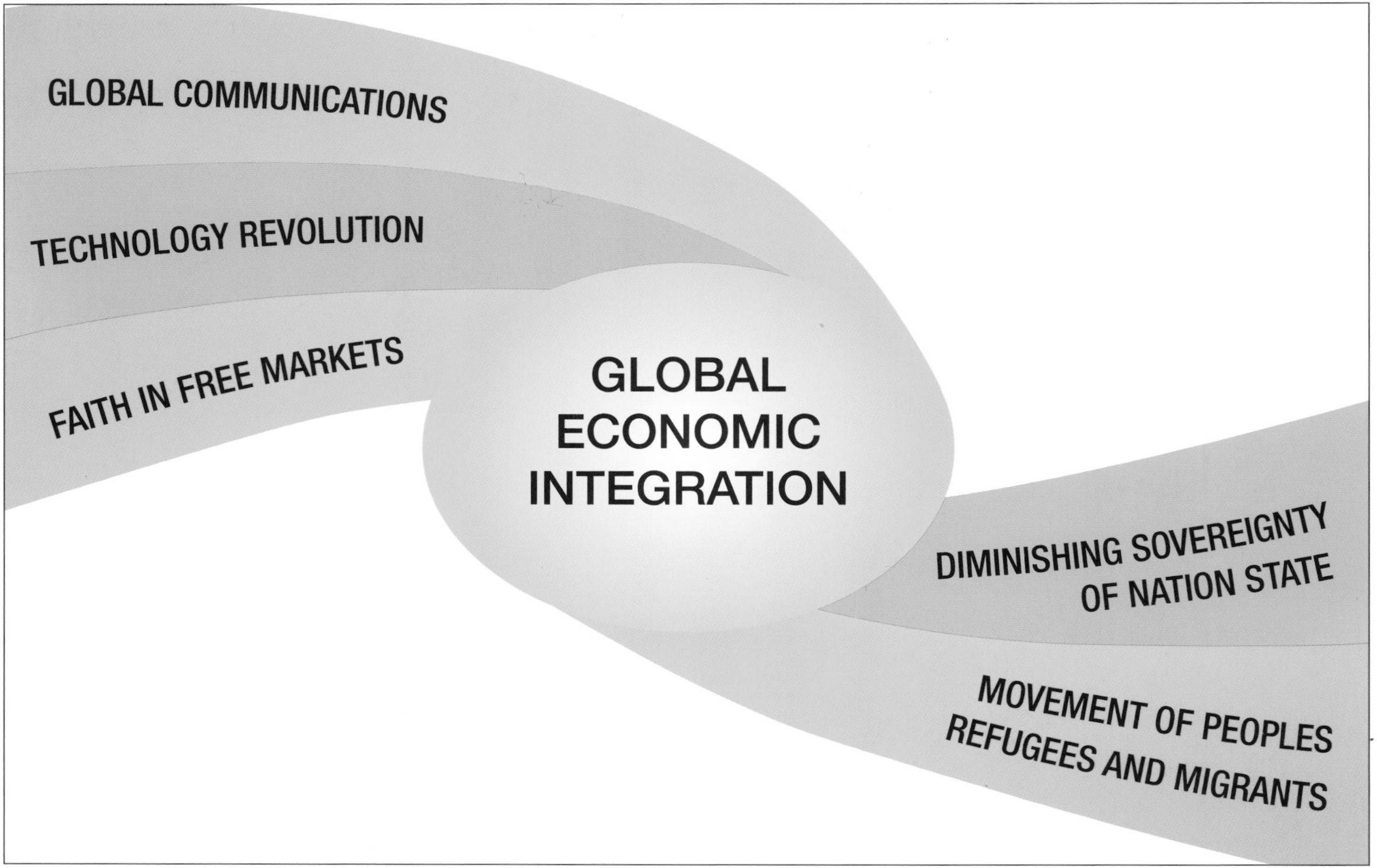

Plate 1.1. Global economic integration. (Source: Missions Advanced Research and Communications [MARC]. Used by permission.)

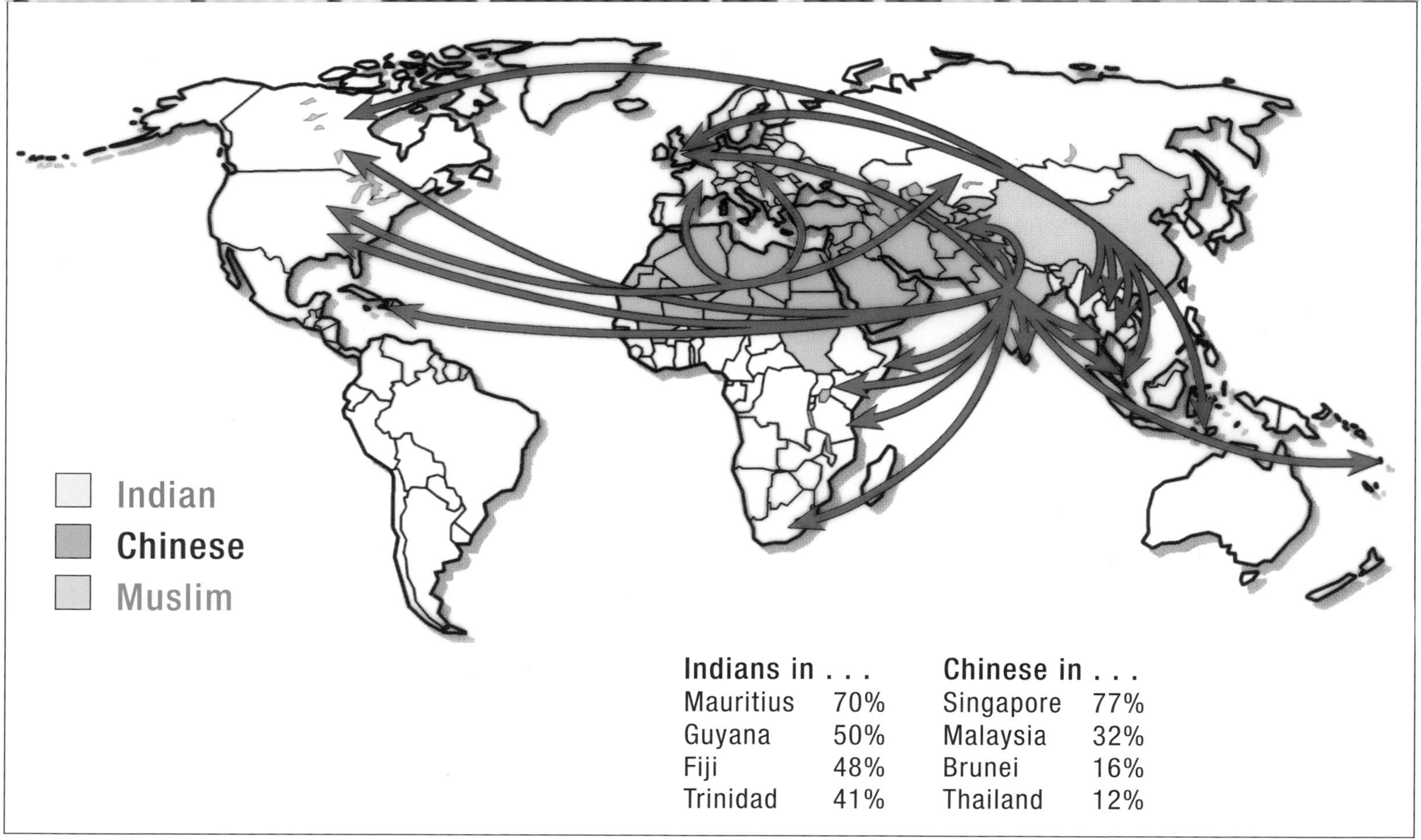

Plate 1.2. People without borders. (Source: MARC. Used by permission.)

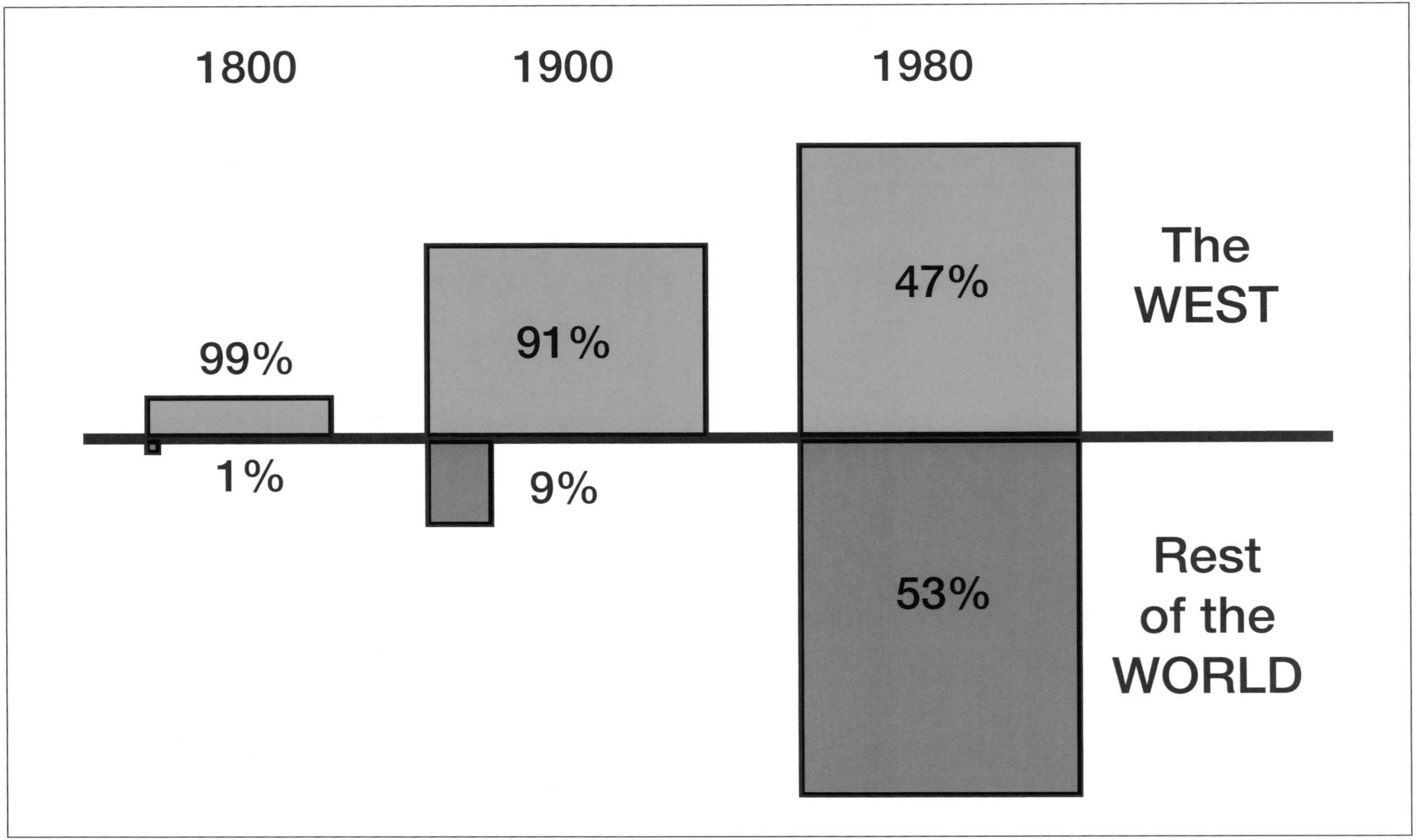

Plate 5.1. Evangelical Christians. (Source: WEC International. Used by permission.)

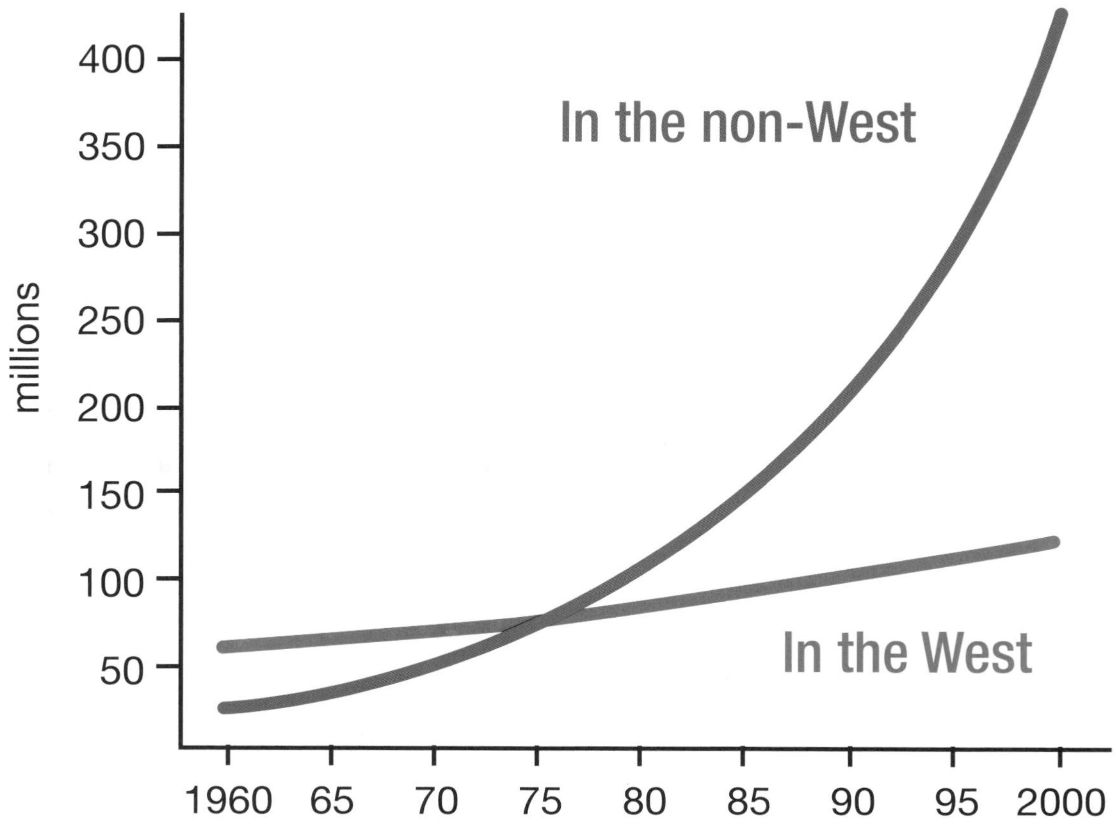

Plate 5.2. Number of Evangelicals in the West and the non-West. (Source: MARC. Used by permission.)

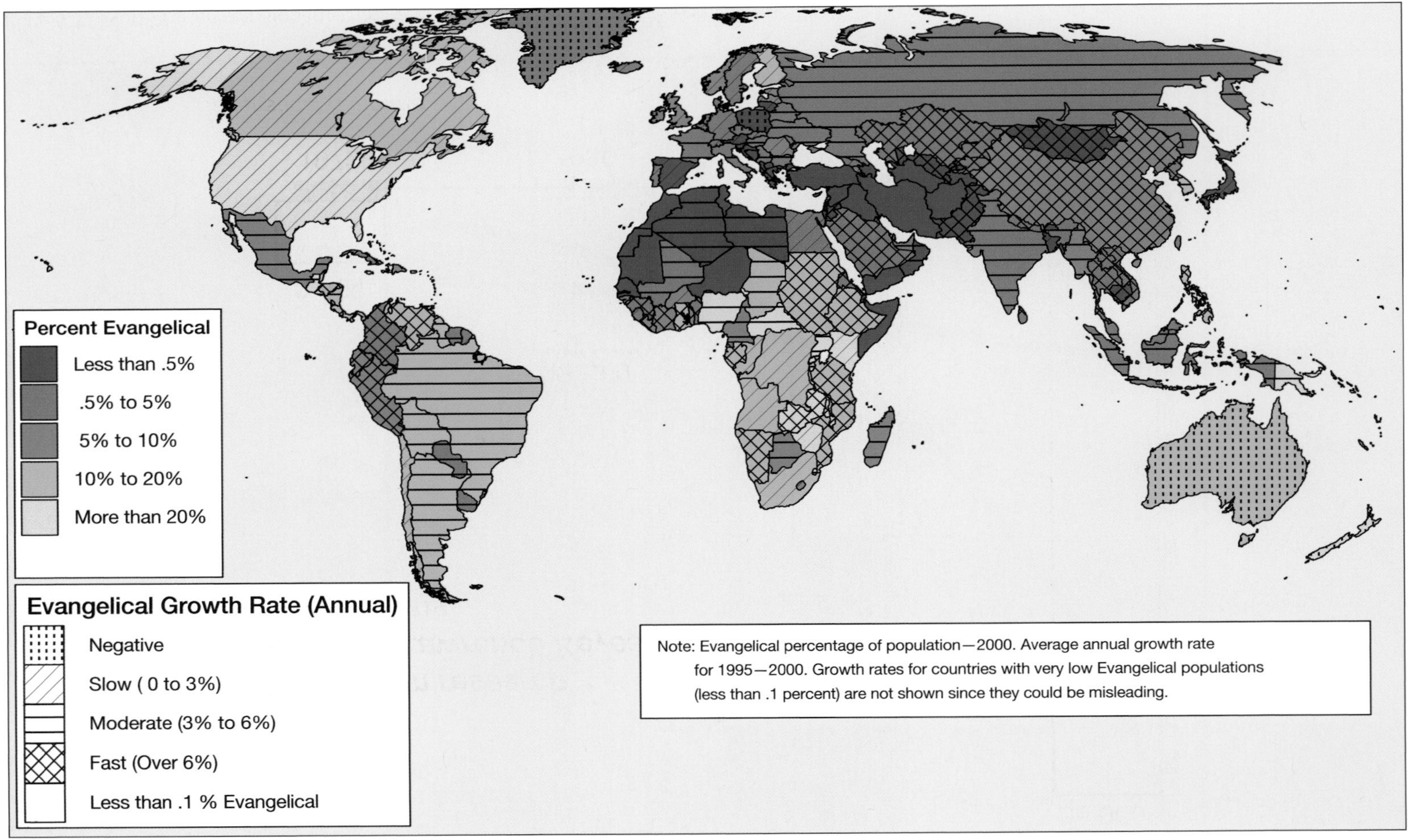

Plate 5.3. Evangelical growth rate. (Source: Global Mapping International. Used by permission.)

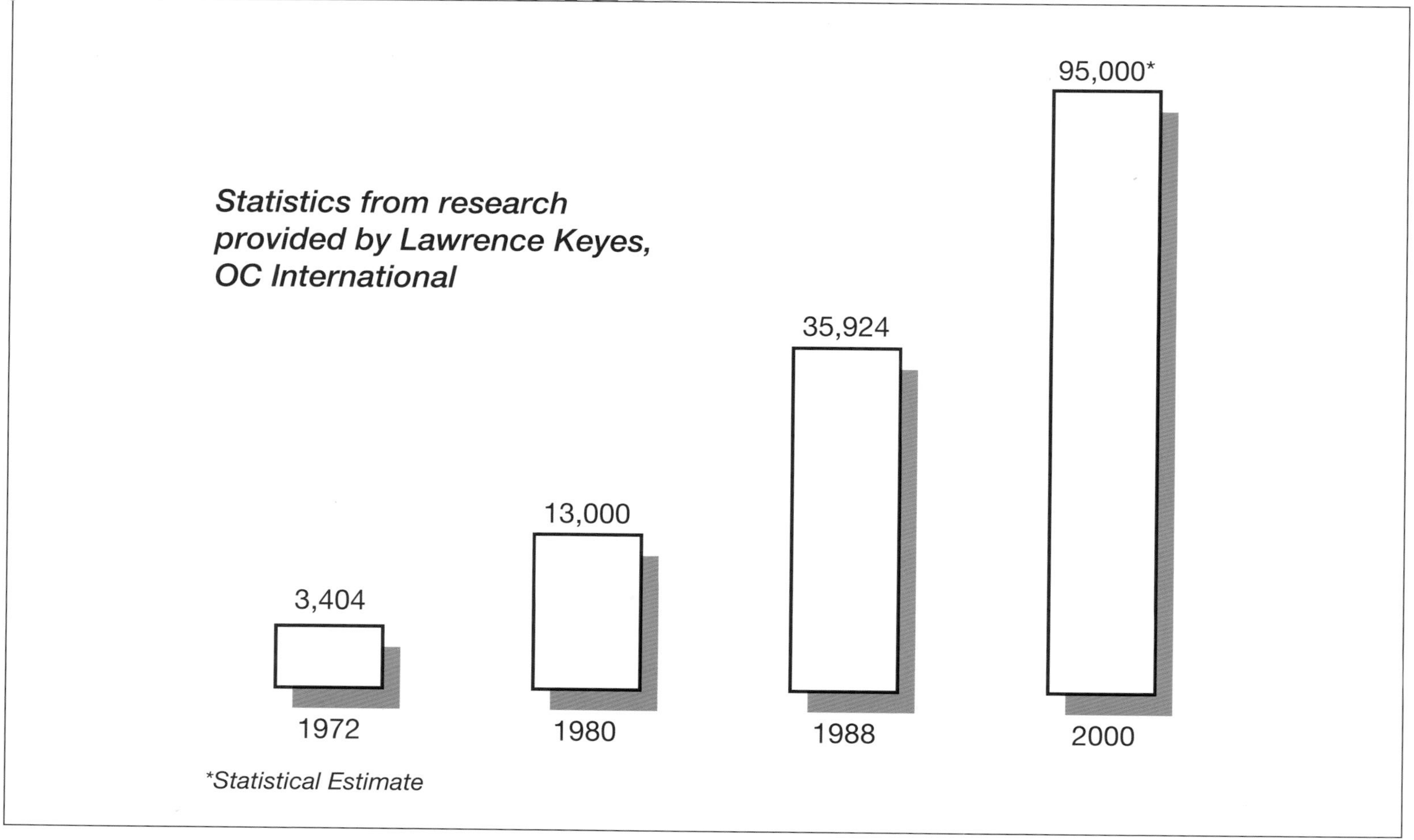

Plate 6.1. Non-Western missionaries. (Source: InterDev. Used by permission.)

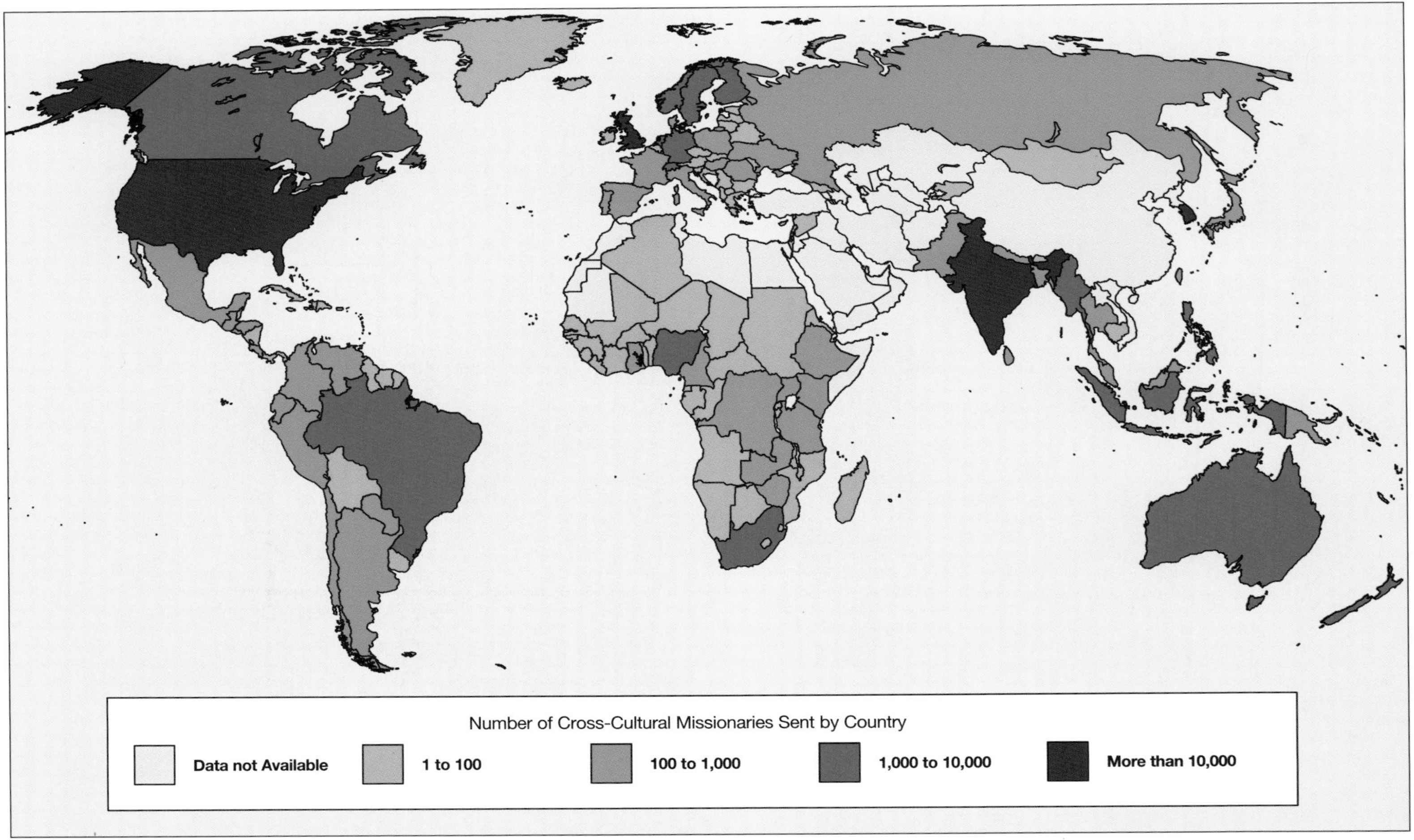

Plate 6.2. From where are missionaries sent? (Source: Global Mapping International. Used by permission.)

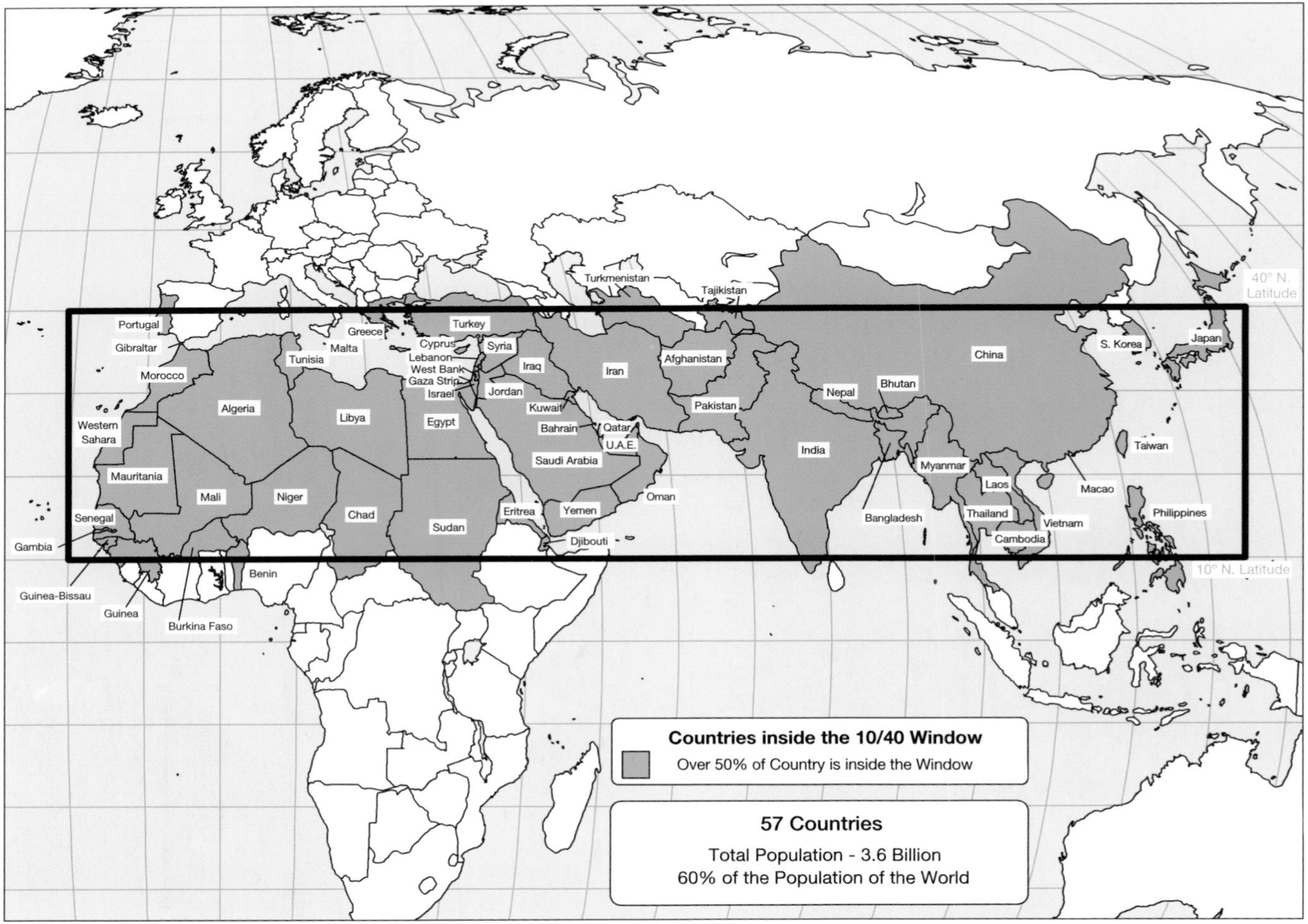

Plate 11.1. The 10/40 Window. (Source: Global Mapping International. Used by permission.)

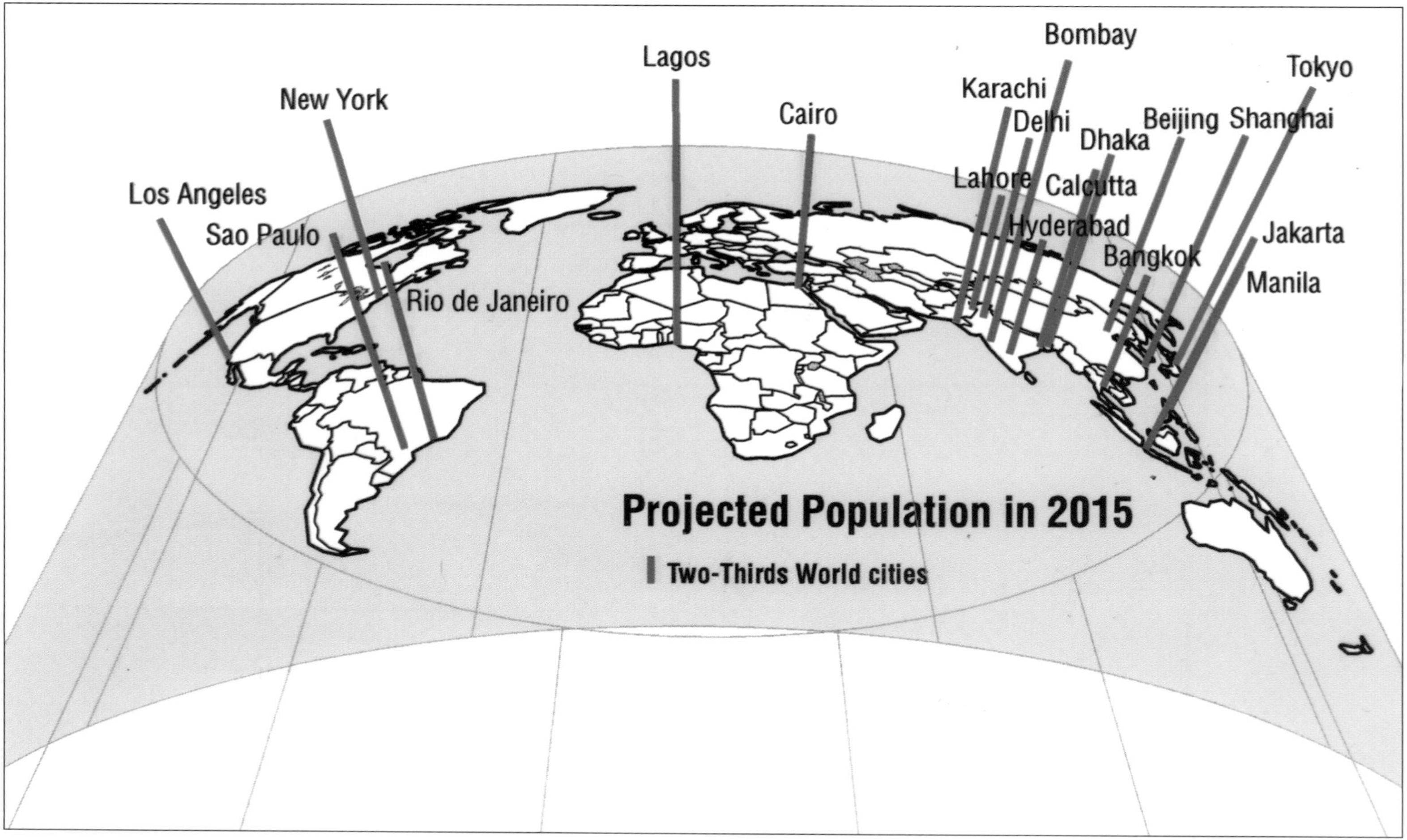

Plate 12.1. The growing cities in the south. (Source: MARC. Used by permission.)

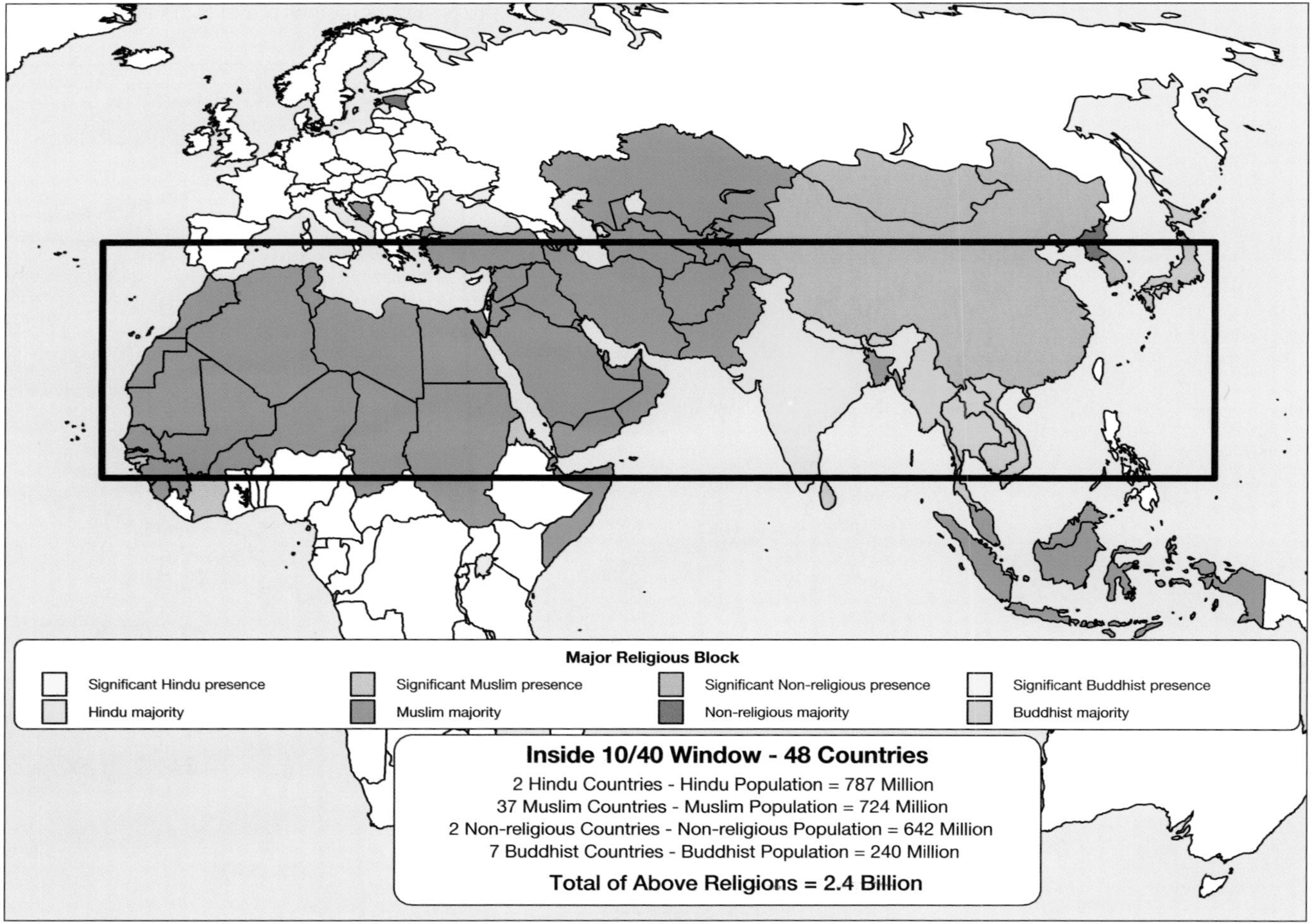

Plate 12.2. Four religious blocks and the 10/40 Window. (Source: Global Mapping International. Used by permission.)

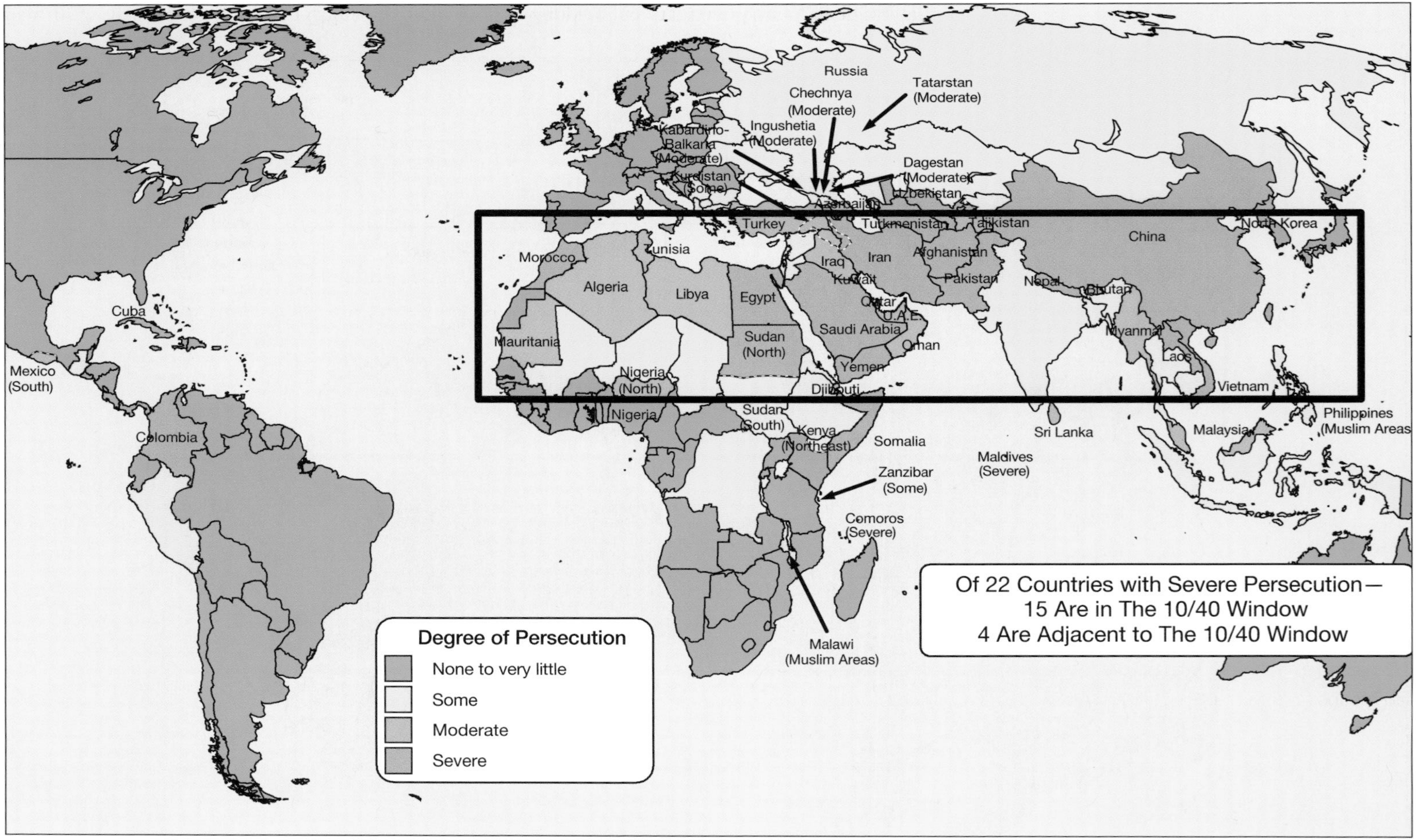

Plate 14.1. Christians under persecution and the 10/40 Window. (Source: Global Mapping International. Used by permission.)

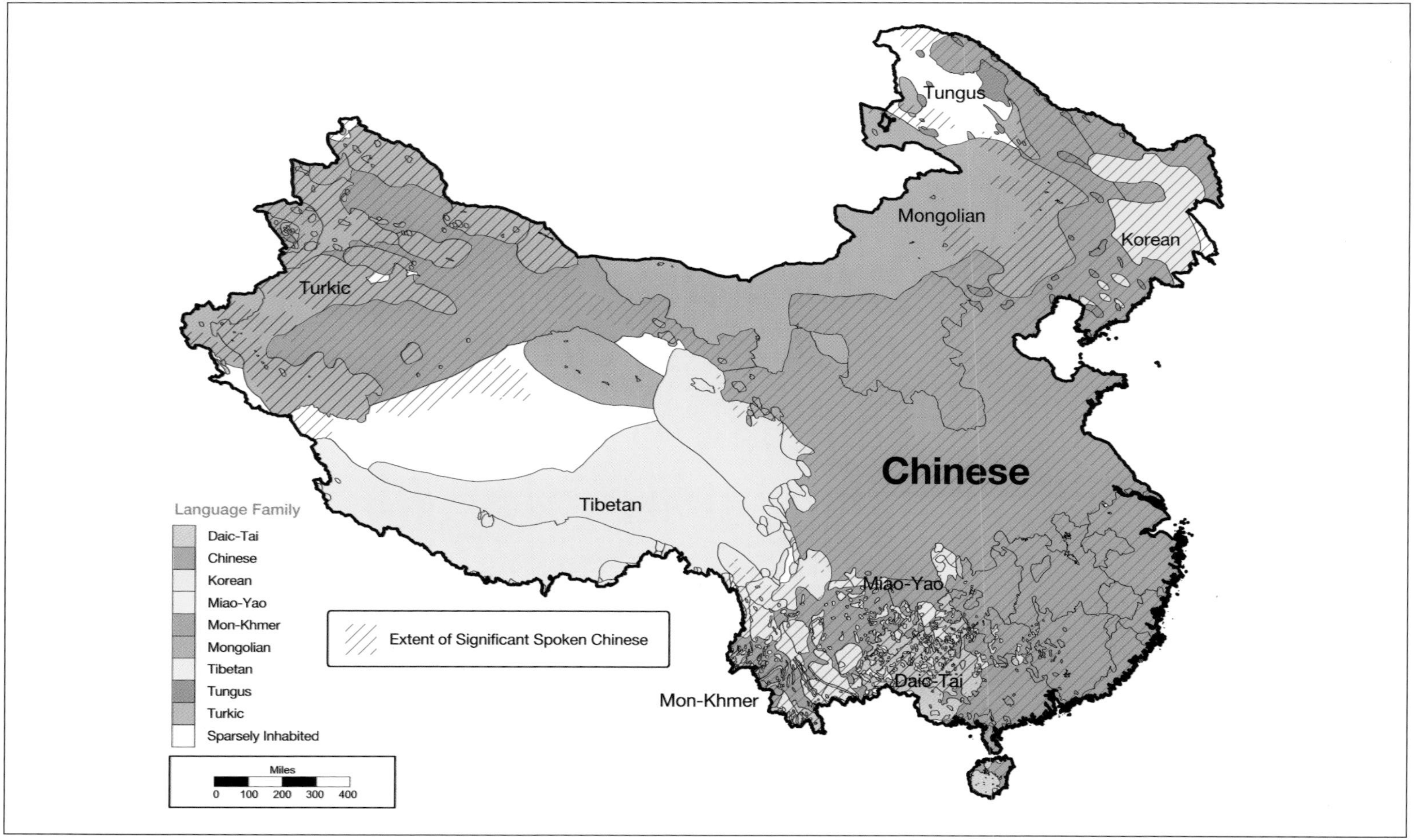

Plate 14.2. Language families in China. (Source: Global Mapping International. Used by permission.)

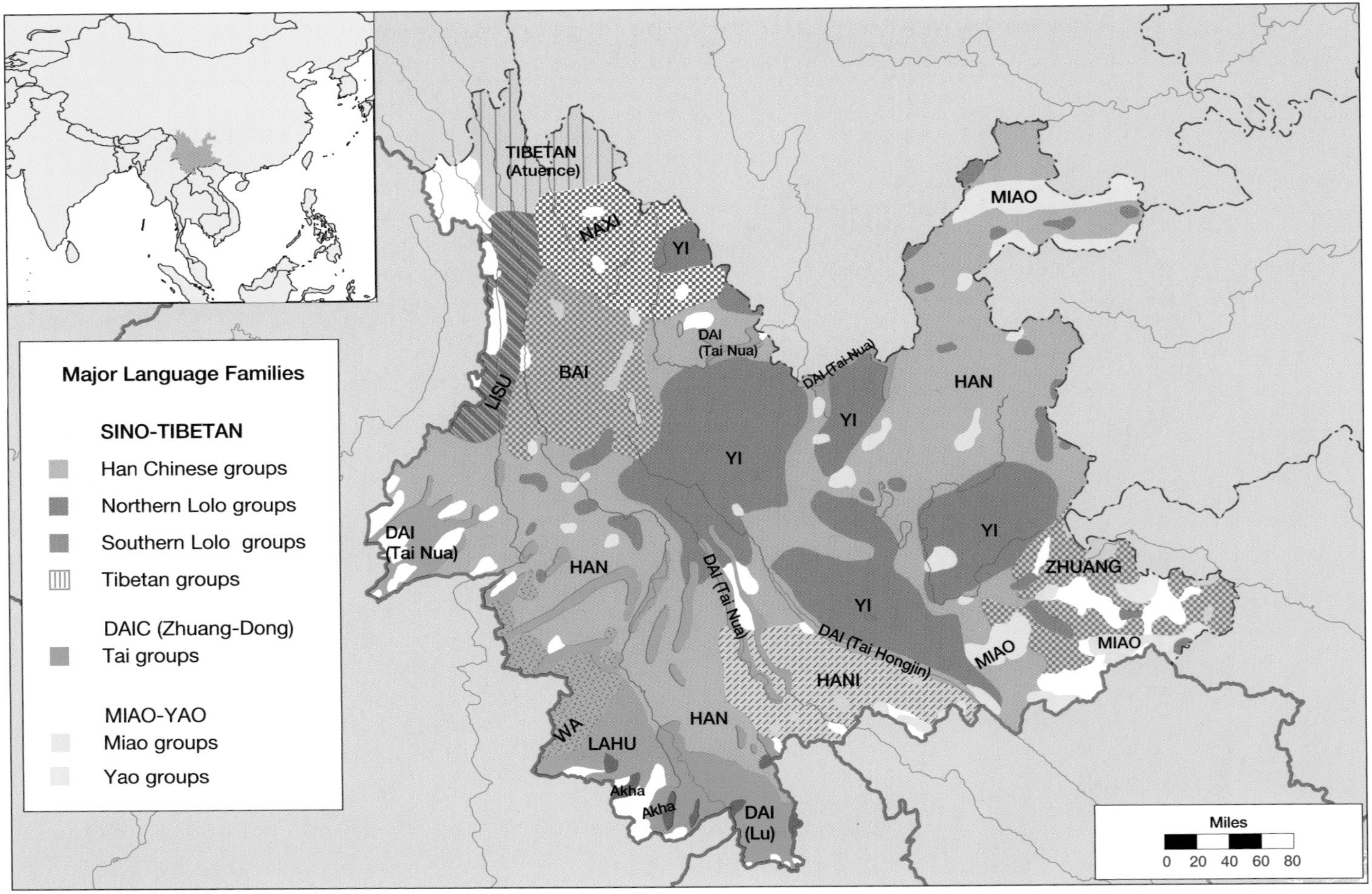

Plate 14.3. Major ethnic groups of Yunnan Province, China. (Source: Global Mapping International. Used by permission.)

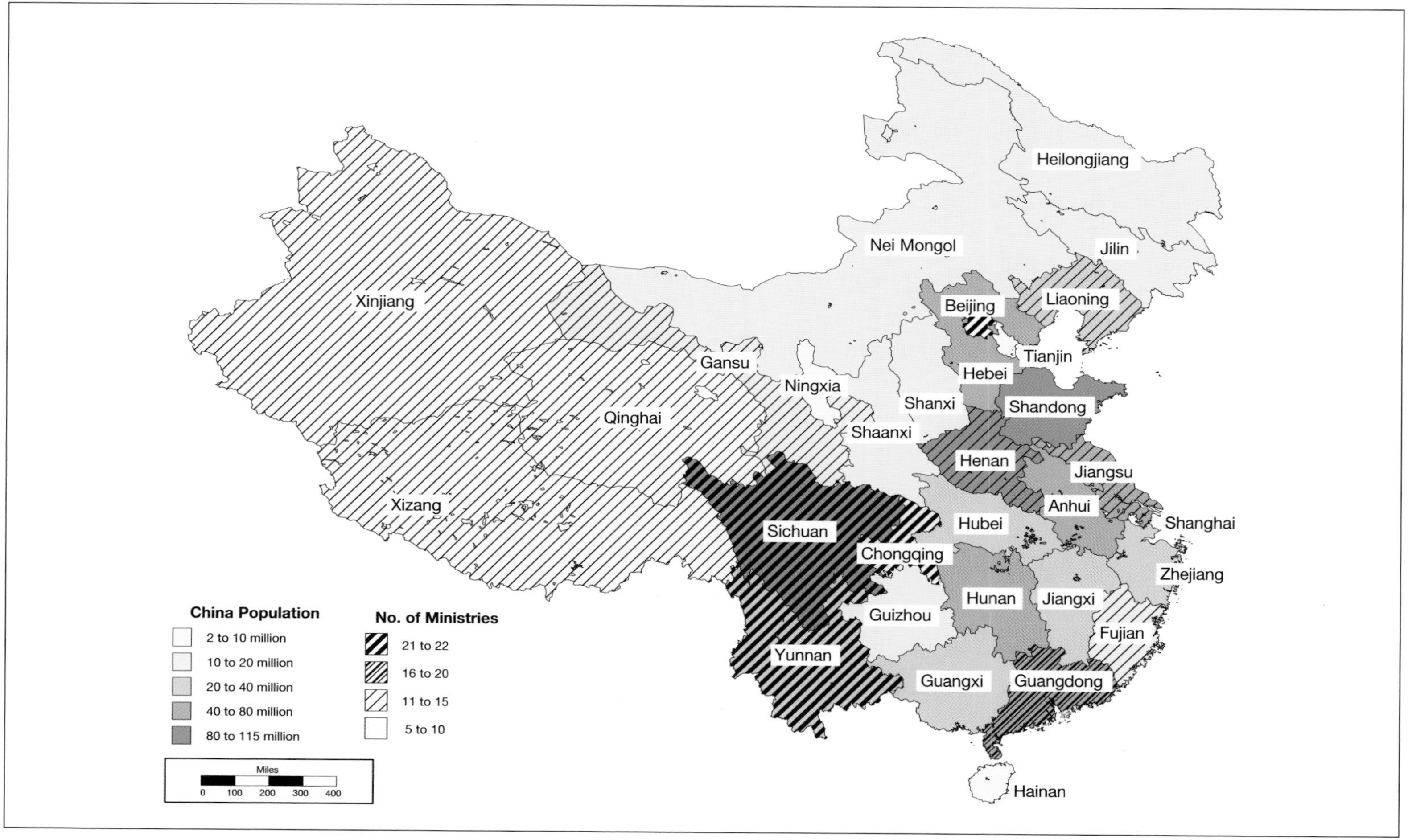

Plate 14.4. Ministry distribution and population in China. (Source: Global Mapping International. Used by permission.)

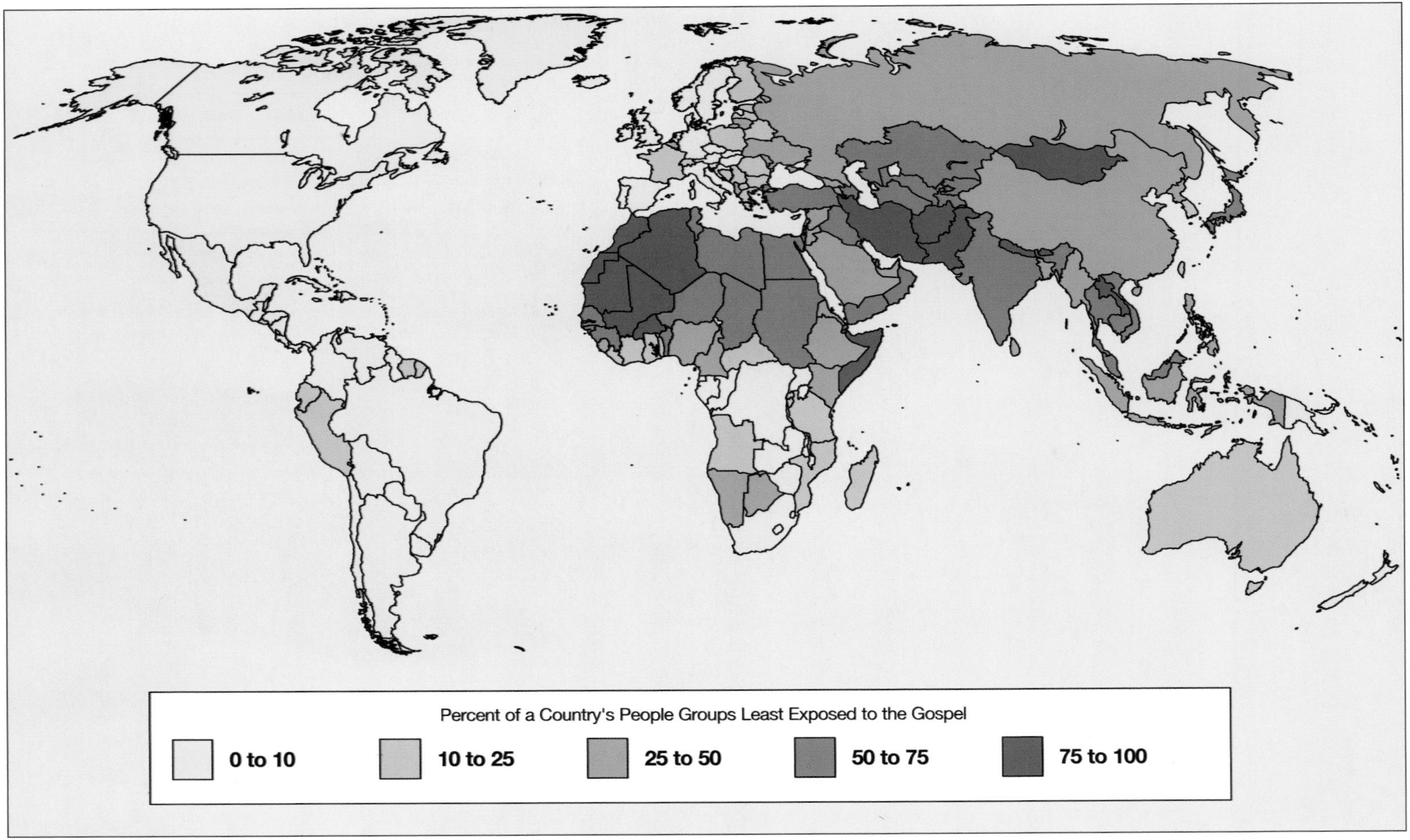

Plate 14.5. What percentage of people groups have not heard the gospel? (Source: Global Mapping International. Used by permission.)

side older career missionaries. One drawback is the volunteers' lack of life and career experience. Another is their frequent failures to comprehend how negative certain behaviors can be for the church in other world settings. As Craig Sheppard, missionary to Kosovo, has noted, "Short-termers hold the integrity of the gospel and the ministry of the church in their hands. I have seen and experienced volunteers compromise the integrity of the ministry."[13] The positive side is that young adults tend to be flexible (a good characteristic to have in cross-cultural mission) and willing to adapt to new situations. Even when they fall short of their high expectations of what can be accomplished in a year or two, their enthusiasm to change the world can be contagious. Their presence may push those with whom they minister to be more radical in sharing the gospel than they would otherwise.

Volunteer service for a year has more potential to produce lasting change in a person than will a 10-day trip. This is one reason why mission agencies need to offer significant midterm opportunities for young adults. Factors in the success and failure of young, midterm volunteers include how self-motivated they are, whether they feel they are part of something significant, and how thoroughly they understand what is expected of them. When young adults have mission experiences, the good and bad ripples from that can influence a church for years to come. As was previously noted, it is not uncommon to hear of full-time missionaries receiving their call while serving as midterm volunteers. Some midterm volunteers have even made seamless transitions into career missionary service.

Tentmakers

One group of hybrid longer-term mission volunteers is known as **tentmakers.** While other volunteers take time off from their jobs and use savings or raise funds from friends and family to go on short-term mission trips, tentmakers fund their mission experience by taking a secular job in another culture with the intention of doing evangelism, discipleship, and church planting in their free time. There are several options between the extremes of having a full-time tentmaking job and being totally supported by donors or churches in one's home country. William Carey did some tentmaking as he ran indigo processing plants and other business operations in India. Tentmaking has also been a way to do mission in creative access areas where visas and resident permits will not be issued to those doing missionary ministry in traditional ways. The downside to being a tentmaker missionary is that much of a person's day and energy is soaked up by a secular job.

One example of a tentmaker missionary was Kim Sun-il, a Korean kidnapped in Iraq in 2004. Kim was in Iraq working as a translator for a South Korean firm and doing evangelism during his free time. He was highly educated with college degrees in English, theology, and Arabic. His passion for mission work among unreached peoples led him to the dangerous task of working and trying to minister in a war zone. He had been in Iraq for a year when he was kidnapped by Jama'at al-Tawhid wa'l Jihad (in English, "Monotheism and Holy Struggle") terrorists. They threatened to kill him and released video footage of him pleading for his life. Sadly, after a month in the hands of his kidnappers, Kim's beheaded body was recovered outside of Baghdad. His killers posted an Internet message that read, "We have killed an infidel who tried to propagate Christianity in Iraq."[14]

Tentmaking should not be viewed as something less than the ideal, which is done mainly to get people into closed countries. Indeed, tentmakers' professional training and abilities can give them opportunities to minister in strategic settings in open as well as closed countries.

Pouring Out Their Lives

When the world sees millions of "retired" Christians pouring out the last drops of their lives with joy for the sake of the unreached peoples and with a view toward heaven, then the supremacy of God will shine. He does not shine as brightly in the posh, leisure-soaked luxury condos on the outer rings of our cities.[15] —John Piper

---

Evaluating Midtermers

Douglas Terry did his doctoral dissertation on the effectiveness of longer-term or midterm volunteers who have spent from six months to two years on a mission field. Terry tried to evaluate the midtermers' effectiveness by surveying them and the career missionaries and local Christians with whom they had served. According to Terry:

> Any mid-term missionary who contributed significantly to a mission ministry and its goals, witnessed effectively about Christ, was satisfied with his or her ministry, was deemed suitable for this ministry, was able to communicate adequately with those ministered to, had a good relationship with at least one on-site career missionary, had a good relationship with at least one on-site national Christian, and the recipients of whose ministry were satisfied with it, is by definition effective missionally.[16]

From this list of characteristics or variables Terry developed a **Missional Effectiveness Index,** or MEI. He then correlated volunteer's MEI scores with a number of other variables. The top three variables showing up in Terry's study all have to do with communication and relationship. The most important variable contributing to the missional effectiveness of midterm volunteers was language communication skills.[17] Cultural adaptation, which is inseparably tied to language learning, was the second most important variable in the high MEI scores. The third most important factor was the development and maintenance of good relationships. The fourth was spiritual readiness. Terry's study also showed age to be a significant variable. His research indicated that midtermers who had the best missional effectiveness scores were between 55 and 64 years of age.[18]

Most midtermers discover that one or two years of volunteer service go by very fast. They find themselves just starting to connect with people when it is time to go home. Thus, they need to be intentional about training others to do what they are doing or else their involvement and contributions will not continue after they leave. Because of the significant missionary ministry that midterm volunteers have given, some mission agencies have begun including them in the number of missionaries they report as being deployed.

A Win-Win Proposition

Volunteerism can benefit everyone involved. Fruitful short-term and midterm mission can assist not only the mission outreach of the church but also the spiritual maturation of individual participants themselves as they look beyond their own interests "to the interests of others" (Philippians 2:4, NIV).

In a *TIME* magazine editorial, Margaret Carlson noted the current popularity of volunteerism within American culture, "Volunteerism hasn't been cool since Camelot . . . [this is our] first chance to turn the Selfish Generation into something more like the Greatest Generation . . . to help our indulgent generation awaken to what [U.S. Senator] McCain describes as 'a cause larger than ourselves.'"[19]

By themselves, short-term mission programs cannot fulfill the Great Commission. However, there is a paradigm for using short-term volunteers that has win-win possibilities. Volunteer mission programs can have more than numerical success. Such programs can also be full of significance as they enable believers to contribute meaningfully to Kingdom purposes.

Questions for Reflection

1. Why would young people and retirees be the best sources of volunteers?
2. Why has there been such an explosion of growth of volunteerism within the Church?
3. Most missiologists believe that the primary beneficiaries of volunteer programs

are the people who go, not the people they go to. How may this ultimately benefit the Church?

4. What is a creative access area?
5. What are the seven Standards of Excellence?
6. What did Douglas Terry find to be important characteristics contributing to the missional effectiveness of midtermers?
7. Based on what is said in this chapter, how would you respond to the person who says, "Wouldn't it be better if we just sent the money overseas rather than spending it all on airline tickets and housing and food"?

10
DEVELOPING TOMORROW'S MISSIONARIES

Objectives

Your study of this chapter should help you to:

- Explain the difference between the general call to witness and the missionary call
- Recognize the essential steps for spiritual guidance
- Identify some secondary motivations for missionary service
- Understand the important role of the pastor in developing missionary candidates
- Identify the qualifications for missionary appointment
- Trace the steps leading to deployment as a missionary

Key Words to Understand

general call
Macedonian call
4-14 window
fruit of the Spirit
spiritual disciplines
mentor

In the 400s, Patrick felt God telling him to go to Ireland. In the 1800s, C. T. Studd sensed God wanted him to walk away from his family fortune and fame as a top British athlete and go overseas as a missionary. In the 1890s, Ida Scudder "met God face to face" and knew that He was calling her to India as a medical missionary.[1] In 1904, William Borden heard God's call to give up his inheritance in the family dairy business and go as a missionary to a Muslim people group in China. In the 1950s Wanda and Sydney Knox obeyed a call to go to Papua New Guinea.

Patrick, C. T. Studd, Ida Scudder, William Borden, and the Knoxes all did what they did because they decided that was God's will for them personally. They were all convinced that God had tapped them on the shoulder and asked them to become cross-cultural messengers of the gospel. For each of them, being called to be a missionary was different from the excitement that wells up inside people getting ready to do "something significant" during a short-term mission trip. The testimonies of these missionaries point to a personalized call in which God asks specific individuals to give a major portion of their lives to cross-cultural gospel proclamation.

> He is no fool who gives what he cannot keep to gain that which he cannot lose.[2] —Jim Elliot, missionary martyred in Ecuador

General Call

Scripture uses the words *call* and *called* in more than one way. In Romans 1:6-7, Paul speaks of being "called to belong to Jesus Christ" and being "called to be his holy people." In 1 Corinthians 1:2, 9 he uses very similar phrases: "called to be holy" (NIV) and "called . . . into fellowship with [God's] Son, Jesus Christ." These calls seem addressed to all believers as is the one in which God asks the Church as a whole to make disciples in every people group on earth.

Such calls, none of which are addressed to specific individuals, are examples of the **general call** of God. Because congregations must respond to the general call to world evangelism, pastors normally are ecstatic when a parishioner testifies to being specifically called by God to go across cultural boundaries as a missionary. It is in response to that general call to evangelize the world that believers become mobilizers of mission prayer and financial support in their own local church. Indeed, obedience to that general call demands that every Christian get involved somehow in reaching the unreached.

It was to a sense of general call that Francis Xavier tried to appeal in the

1540s when he pleaded for young people to join him as missionaries to Asia. From India while on his way to Japan, Xavier wrote back to his alma mater, the University of Paris, "Tell the students to give up their small ambitions and come eastward to preach the gospel of Christ."[3]

Some, like George Verwer of Operation Mobilisation, have sounded a similar note. Verwer, a proponent of radical discipleship, has said, "If you're not called to stay, then go!"[4] In the early 1980s, Keith Green had a song with the words, "Jesus commands us to go; it should be the exception if we stay." Verwer, Green, and others like them see the general call to be so urgent that they have said all believers should expect to enter missionary service unless they feel a specific call not to go.

The Missionary Call

Sentiments like George Verwer's "if you're not called to stay, go" underscore the pressing nature of the mission task. They reflect how heavily world evangelism weighs on the heart of God. However, using the general call to motivate individuals to become expatriate missionaries is not in line with the way God called individuals in Bible times. It does not fit either with the testimonies of missionaries throughout Church history. Paul, for example, wrote about the clear sense he had that God had asked him to go to the Gentiles. Paul did not go to the Gentiles simply because he saw the Abrahamic covenant saying that God wanted His people to reach out to all peoples. Rather, Paul went to the Gentiles because He became convinced that the Lord was telling him personally to go.

Because missionaries have testified to being called in different ways, what constitutes a missionary call can seem hard to define precisely. Indeed, God's call to special service may come in a variety of ways. God startled Moses with His unexpected call through a burning bush (Exodus 3:1—4:17). God's call may come during a dramatic vision, as it did to Isaiah (Isaiah 6:1-13). God's call may come as a voice in the night as it did to a little boy named Samuel (1 Samuel 3:1-11). The call may give rise to some uncertainties that need to be cleared away, as was the case with Gideon (Judges 6:36-40). The realization of a divine call may arrive like the gradual dawning of a new day, beginning in a dim way and then increasing in intensity and clarity. The call can be a simple "Come, follow me," as it was for several of the Twelve (Matthew 4:19; 9:9). In their situation, as it has been for many today, the Lord's clear leading was through a series of small steps with missionary service not being envisioned at first. When John left his father's fishing business on the Sea of Galilee, for example, he had no idea he would eventually become the leader of the church in the Gentile city of Ephesus.

Say "Yes" If He Calls

The answer was NO. I was 16 and I didn't want to be a missionary. I wanted my own will. That led to another no. It wasn't long before I found myself very far from God. I began to make choices that were to *my* liking. It was fun for a while, but it didn't last. My reputation was ruined, and I had lost many of my church friends. My heart was empty. I was lost, and I didn't even know how to admit that I needed Christ to save me.

It happened one Sunday morning when my closest friend stopped and said, "Claudia, I cannot agree with all you are doing, but I want you to know I still love you."

That touch of love was the turning point, for I had decided not to go to college. I soon found myself a student at what is now Point Loma Nazarene University, following a friend who hadn't given up on me.

It was at the close of the fall revival that I slipped into the dorm prayer room. I locked the door, and I knelt down and began to pray. I prayed most of the night. When I came out in the early morning, I was a "new creature" in Christ!

That was the beginning of real joy! The Holy Spirit sanctified me a few months later, and He so graciously gave me back the call He had given me 2 years before.

I look back now on 32 years of missionary service. They have been exciting and fulfilling. I continually find great inner peace in doing the Father's will. Would I choose to go back to a life of my own will and sinful living? No! Never!

I almost made a major wrong choice in my life. It would have taken me far from where I am today.

I count it a great privilege in serving Christ as a missionary. Say yes if He calls you. You will never be sorry![5]

—Claudia Stevenson, missionary to Nigeria

Paul's Macedonian Call

Sometimes people cite Paul's **Macedonian call** (Acts 16:9) as an example of a missionary call. The purpose of that particular vision, however, was not to recruit Paul for missionary service. When Paul had that vision, he had already been commissioned as a missionary by the Antioch church (chap. 13). When the Macedonian vision came, Paul was in Troas in the middle of his second missionary trip. The man from Macedonia in that vision was used to direct Paul and his team westward toward peoples on the European continent.

People testifying to a missionary call have sometimes felt that God was calling them to a specific place, somewhat like what happened in the Macedonian call. Indeed, for much of the Protestant era of mission, it has been expected that people testifying to a missionary call would also name the place to which God was calling them. Today, with the exception of people feeling called to the 10/40 Window area, that does not seem to happen as much. One reason may be that 21st-century missionaries are much more mobile than they were when travel was slower and more arduous. It is not uncommon now for missionaries to fulfill their call by serving in multiple countries on more than one continent.

Hearing the Call

Young people sometimes struggle as they try to understand whether or not they have a call from God. Maybe it would be less complicated if God used a cell phone, e-mail, or text messaging. Alas, He does not. There are, however, some instructions in Psalm 25 on how to get divine direction. David begins that psalm by imploring the Lord to "show me . . . teach me . . . guide me" (vv. 4-5). Then David holds up humility and submissiveness as keys to receiving divine guidance, "[The Lord] guides the humble in what is right and teaches them his way" (v. 9) and "The LORD confides in those who fear him" (v. 14).[6]

Veteran missionary Joe Mattox helps educate future missionaries at the HEART Institute, a simulated Third World village near Lake Worth, Florida. While visiting a class on the campus of Southern Nazarene University, Mattox talked about what people could do to understand if God was calling them to missionary service:

1. Immerse yourself in the Word—all of it, not just a few favorite phrases.
2. Listen to the Holy Spirit.
3. Look to God as sovereign. He may lead by opening and closing doors.
4. Seek the counsel of mature Christians, such as an older believer, a pastor, or a trusted mentor.

Sometimes, to make His call heard, the Lord speaks through Scripture passages. At other times He uses the stories of missionaries as the background for calling people to missionary service. Among the stories God has used is the one told on film in *Through Gates of Splendor* (1978) and *End of the Spear* (2006). That story is about five American missionaries who died in Ecuador on the banks of the Curaray River, killed by the very people to whom they were trying to take the gospel. Not long afterward, Elisabeth Elliot, widow of one of the slain missionaries, took her three-year-old daughter and went to live among those who had killed her husband, Jim. Many of the Waodani eventually became Christians, including those whose spears had killed the missionaries. Elliot's writings about her missionary experiences have been used by the Holy Spirit to spark mission interest among succeeding generations of young people.

In whatever way it comes, an authentic call from God invariably carries with it a firm conviction that cannot be shaken. God seems to find ways to let people know He is calling them even if, like Jonah, they choose to run the other way.

Timing of the Call

The missionary call has often come to people when they are quite young. Researchers like George Barna and Lionel Hunt have said that people worldwide generally come to faith in Christ between the ages of 4 and 14. Because that period of life seems propitious for Christian conversion worldwide, Dan Brewster has coined the phrase 4-14 window. While the 10/40 Window defines a geographic area, this 4-14 window designates a period of life. Research has also shown that this 4 to 14 age is the time when many missionaries first felt God calling them.

All the Peoples of the Earth

When I was a junior high school student, I tried to read the Bible through. Like most teenagers, I really had a struggle with the Old Testament. But an awesome thing happened while I was wading through 1 Kings. Verse 60 of chapter 8 was thrust into my consciousness, "That all the peoples of the earth may know that the LORD is God and that there is no other." In the stillness of my bedroom, the Lord said to me, "That is to be your life's work." God had ignited a call to mission in the life of a teen. —Charles Gailey

---

Motives

The Holy Spirit's call to missionary service can be accompanied by some secondary motives. For instance, some people like to travel. The romance of learning to live in other cultures intrigues and beckons some people. Others see missions as the highest form of Christian service, and they want to do everything they possibly can for God. One must not, however, mistake the allure of secondary motives for a missionary call itself. For example, when John Wesley went to the New World in 1735 as a missionary to the Indians, he was hoping for a breakthrough in his personal spiritual life. Because Wesley lacked a sense of a definite missionary call, the secondary motivation that took him across the Atlantic was not enough to keep him in Georgia when discouragement came a few months later.

Seeing Needs

One secondary motivation causing Christians to consider missionary service has been seeing the needs of the world. That was the background of William Carey's call. To be sure, 2 Corinthians 5:14 says that believers are compelled by the love of Christ to be concerned about human need. As Christians become painfully aware of some of the world's great needs, they want to cry out with Isaiah, "Here am I. Send me!" (Isaiah 6:8). Becoming aware of human needs may be an initial step to being called as a missionary. However, while such awareness opens the door to hearing God speak, an authentic missionary call is more than people realizing they have the ability to meet some world needs. Missionaries are not God-called simply because they have seen a need; they are called because God has tapped them on the shoulder.

The Moravians of the 1700s seemed to understand the importance of being sure the motivation for cross-cultural evangelism was God himself calling and not just a compassionate response to other humans in need. The Moravians living as religious refugees on Count Zinzendorf's estate were very touched by their encounter with Anthony, an ex-slave who had unevangelized family members still living as slaves on West Indies sugar plantations. However, though feeling a burden to reach Anthony's family and other slaves with the gospel, the Moravians then spent more than a year trying to be sure of God's will before sending their first missionaries to the Caribbean.

Deep Peace

For missionaries to survive the tensions and disillusionments that accompany cross-cultural ministry, they need the deep inner peace provided by having said yes when God called. A strong conviction that being a cross-cultural missionary is God's will can steady a person like a ship's ballast in the rough journey through culture shock, dark testing times, and other problems of cross-cultural missionary service. John Seaman, missionary to West Africa, wrote, "Without a genuine God-placed call it is too easy to bail out when the going gets tough. On more than one occasion—once very early in my career and another in my later missionary years—if it had not been for the certainty of the 'call,' I just would not have made it."[7] So, while there may be accompanying secondary motives, the determining motivation for people to enter missionary service should be an unmistakable sense that this is God's will.

Those truly called to be missionaries will never have peace or contentment until they do what God wants them to do. In a lecture titled "The Call to the Ministry," Charles H. Spurgeon, British Baptist minister in the 1800s, recalled the advice of an older minister, "Do not enter the ministry if you can help it."[8] That is good advice for anyone thinking about missionary service. If there is anything else that a person can do and feel content and at peace with the Lord, they should do it. H. F. Reynolds was the Nazarene missions leader in the early 1900s. He found himself talking to Roger Winans, a young man who testified to being called by God to South America. While Reynolds's denomination did not think it had the funds to send Roger Winans overseas, Reynolds was wise enough to say, "Brother Winans, we cannot send you to South America, but if God has called you, you will go or backslide."[9] Winans did go and successfully pioneered church planting among indigenous peoples in the mountains of Peru.

Qualifications for the Missionary

Those wondering if they have what it takes to be a missionary may have difficulty finding a typical missionary against whom they can measure themselves. Missionaries come in all personality types. There are outgoing missionaries who seem to never stop talking. There are quiet missionaries. There are missionaries who see the big picture but who never quite master the details. There are missionaries who are great with detail work. There are missionaries who are incredibly optimistic. There are others who see themselves as "more realistic."

Since sending agencies want missionaries who will exercise their calling in truly incarnational ways, they look for people bearing an abundance of the fruit of the Spirit mentioned in Galatians 5:22-23. The "sent ones" (apostles/missionaries) are commissioned to be conduits through which God's love will flow to the global mosaic of cultures. Mission boards, therefore, look for people with versatility, humility, adaptability, and a sense of humor. Mission agencies also know that people who practice spiritual disciplines like regular church participation (Hebrews 10:25), prayer and fasting (Acts 13:3), Bible study, and submission to others (Philippians 2:5-8) will be more likely to have productive cross-cultural ministries than those who do not.

The rigors and stresses of cross-cultural missionary ministry can exacerbate physical and emotional weaknesses. So, in addition to spiritual qualifications, mission boards want future missionaries to be physically and psychologically healthy. Even if physical health-care needs exceeding those of the average person can be met on a mission field (which is not always possible or advisable), some medical problems require resources beyond a missionary's financial capabilities. As to psychological health, in the 21st century, getting along with coworkers and serving under indigenous leadership may be the biggest challenges missionaries will face. A missionary with personality issues will flounder in interpersonal and intercultural relationships. The struggles of missionaries to get along with each other cause some to drop out and return home early. Indeed, denominational leaders and mission boards regularly cite personal incompatibility as the number one cause of shortened careers and failure of missionaries to achieve their potential. Emotional issues are not, of course, the only reason why missionaries do not get along. However, because it is a significant reason, many mission boards attempt to deal with psychological issues ahead of deployment by giving personality and psychological tests and then following up with individualized counseling.

It has often been said that a call to serve is a call to prepare. Most mission agencies want missionary candidates to have college or seminary training for cross-cultural service. Generally, missionaries will be more effective if they have grappled with major missiological questions before arriving on the field. Most mission boards want missionary candidates who fully understand core Christian beliefs and who know how to communicate Christian faith to unbelievers. A basic grasp of various world religions is considered helpful. Missionaries need to know how to enter another culture as well as how to constructively critique their own. Missionaries need to know how to absorb culture shock and most need to know how to learn another language. Missionaries need to be aware of how paternalism, ethnocentrism, and racism can be cancerous to the health of the Church.

In addition to classroom studies, future missionaries will find that mission boards like for them to have had some cross-cultural ministry experience before deployment. Of course, even when missionaries have received specialized mission training, they should view that as only the beginning of their missiological education. People heading to a missionary assignment should be encouraged to subscribe to journals like *Evangelical Missions Quarterly, Mission Frontiers,* and *International Bulletin of Missionary Research* as one avenue of continuing their education. To be sure, even the best missiological training is no guarantee that missionary life will be problem-free and that there will be no unsettling days. Good training can, however, cushion the impact of discouraging problems and enable the missionary to confront them effectively.

> If God calls you to be a missionary, don't stoop to be a king.[10]
>
> —Jordan Grooms

What Do Missionaries Do?

For a time, it was common to categorize all missionary work as being of three types: preaching, teaching, and medical work. Of course, to see how that was an oversimplification, one has only to look at the huge variety of things that missionaries like William Carey did.[11] Missionary assignments do not just come in the three categories of teaching, preaching, and medical work. What missionaries do is evangelize, supervise disaster relief, recruit and develop church leadership, facilitate economic development projects, and run broadcast and print media programming. Missionaries are anthropologists and linguists who translate the Bible and other books. They train village health-care workers. They coordinate incoming short-term mission teams. They start Bible colleges and Theological Education by Extension programs. They develop programs for youth and children. They pilot airplanes and boats and do computer systems support. They account for finances and wrestle with the red tape of government bureaucracies. And, along the way, missionaries will also teach, preach, and do medical work. One thing missionaries rarely do is pastor local churches unless they are in a pioneer setting mentoring a new believer who is about to take over.

Working Themselves Out of a Job

It used to be said that one primary task of missionaries was to "work themselves out of a job." Today, rather than using the working-ourselves-out-of-a-job phrase, missionaries today talk about themselves as **catalysts.** By that they mean they are filling a role such as that of the apostle Paul during his missionary journeys around the northern rim of the Mediterranean. The catalyst metaphor is taken from chemistry where a catalyst is a substance that starts or accelerates a chemical reaction without itself being consumed. At any point in the chemical reaction, the catalyst can be removed intact from the mixture. Using *catalyst* as a metaphor for missionaries is a recognition that these expatriates are aliens who are around for a while to get things going, but their presence will not be needed forever. To be sure, the catalyst metaphor has one major drawback. It can give the impression that missionaries remain unchanged by cross-cultural encounters. That is not true.

Representative or Incarnational?

As has been noted, God's plan has always been to wrap His message up in people and send them to communicate that message to others. This makes the words of Paul about believers being envoys or ambassadors (2 Corinthians 5:20) especially applicable to missionaries. As representatives of a government, ambassadors are entrusted with messages to deliver. When missionaries are seen primarily as ambassadors, delivering the Good News by direct evangelism becomes by far the most important thing to be done.

Another way of looking at missionaries is to view them as "little Christs" or Christ-bearers. It has sometimes been said that Christians are the only Jesus some people will see. In this sense, therefore, the missionary is an incarnation of the gospel for another culture. Mark Elmore, mission volunteer in Slovenia, said it well, "If you minister out of love, you will never be a failure."[12] Using the incarnational model with its emphasis on being the "aroma of Christ" (2 Corinthians 2:15) will foster a holistic approach to missionary work.

So, which view is the proper model for the missionary: the ambassadorial representative or the incarnational "little Christ"? It is some of both, with each being ways that the missionary is fulfilling the Abrahamic covenant principle that when God blesses people, He expects that they will pass on the blessing.

The Pastor and Missionary Candidates

Spirit-filled leadership in the first-century Antioch church played a key role in setting people apart for missionary service and sending them (Acts 13:1-4). Missionary sending still follows that model. While the actual missionary sending contract will be signed by a mission board, the sending needs to start with the candidate's home church. Clearly, therefore, local pastors play key roles in the deployment of missionaries.

Mentoring

In trying to highlight the importance of children and youth, people will sometimes call them "the church of tomorrow." That is both true and false. Today's young people and children are going to be the leaders of the church of tomorrow. However, they are also an important component of the church of today. God-called young people must do more than sit on the sidelines waiting to grow up and go off to a school somewhere so they can be trained for future ministry.

> If your Christianity doesn't work at home, it doesn't work. Don't export it.[13]
> —Howard Hendricks

Before being expected to take the gospel across cultural and language boundaries, potential missionaries of every age-group must discover and hone their ministry gifts and talents in their mother tongue and within their own culture. So, when people say that God is calling them to missionary service, their pastor should do more than offer a quick prayer and a pat on the back. The role of a pastor vis-à-vis a potential missionary is that of a **mentor** who encourages, instructs, and models. The pastor should take the lead in integrating people who feel a call into ministry roles. Training through hands-on experience is what Jesus and Paul did for their protégés. In the same way, missionary candidates need to become apprentices under those who have experience in ministry. While the goal of mission is not to clone the missionary's home church in another culture, one's home church is one of the best proving grounds (to borrow a phrase from industry) for developing missionaries.

A pastor who is mentoring other called people is fulfilling the training imperative of 2 Timothy 2:2, "The things you have heard me say in the presence of many witnesses entrust to reliable men who will also be qualified to teach others." Among the things future missionaries can learn from experienced mentors is that in ministry, adrenaline rushes do not come every hour on the hour. Future missionaries need to learn that one of the most important things about ministry is faithfulness in doing the small things.

Pastors and laypersons who mentor aspiring missionaries at the local church level can help them prepare in five areas:

1. Personal relationship to God
2. Churchmanship (living one's spiritual life as part of a community of believers)
3. Global awareness
4. Knowledge of the current status of missions efforts (this will likely include going on several short-term mission trips)
5. Development of God-given skills and talents

Processing the Call

When she was still a university student, Kimberly Jayne Rushing wrote that people generally pass through a succession of stages as they seek to clarify a call to ministry. Those stages are:

1. *A metaphysical encounter with God which establishes a sense of calling.*

   As has been noted, the encounter in which God calls someone may happen in a variety of contexts. It may happen in as dramatic a setting as Moses' burning bush experience in Exodus 3 or it may come through something like the gentle whisper which Elijah heard (1 Kings 19:12). However it happens, it will be a genuine encounter with God.
2. *A time of reflection or doubting of the calling.*

   While some people never have any doubt about their call, others go through times of wondering if they were mistaken. Even when people begin to doubt the authenticity of their call, this need not be seen as a spiritual problem. God patiently dealt with Moses when he was reticent and with Gideon who twice asked for a confirmation of his call (Judges 6:36-39).
3. *An affirmation of the call through the Body of Christ.*

   Good ecclesiology demands that an individual call be validated by the community of faith. Though Paul was sure God had called him to the Gentiles, he did not go to them until the Antioch church confirmed his call and sent him.
4. *A willingness to obey that puts no conditions on what God may ask or where one is willing to go.*[14]

No Place I Would Not Go

There's nothing I would not do; there's no place I would not go for the sake of Christ.[15]

—written by Esther Carson Winans, missionary to Peru,
on her application for missionary service

Pastors can play key roles in shepherding a person through those four phases, including guiding the person through the affirming of the call by the local church and eventually by a mission board. Prior to that, pastors can be interactive sounding boards, helping people talk about the times they believe God has spoken to them about missionary service. If a period of doubting arrives, pastors can assure people that this is often part of arriving at that strong conviction of being divinely called.

First Steps to Missionary Service

If people are called as children, 20 years could pass before they get to a mission field. On the other hand, for an adult it could take as little as a year or two from call to actual deployment. In either case, the process of getting to a mission field can be frustrating unless people see that going through the steps of that process is part of fulfilling the call. The steps to be taken from having become certain of a call to actually becoming an expatriate missionary can be summed up under three major headings:

1. Informal and Formal Training

The call to missionary service means a person should get serious about preparation. No missionary candidate should expect to show up at a mission board's offices, give a passionate testimony about a call and in return receive an airplane ticket for an overseas destination. Airline flights do not transform people into effective missionaries.

The person must find out a mission board's expectations regarding formal schooling. Most boards today want college graduates and some prefer those with master's degrees. Then, in addition to hands-on experience in their own local churches, it is now common for people to give a year or two of volunteer service before being appointed as career missionaries. An extended period of volunteer service gives the mission board an idea of how the potential missionary will perform in long-term cross-cultural situations.

2. Doing the Paperwork

Those who feel called to missionary service should register their call with the candidate offices of one or more mission organizations long before they are ready to be deployed. Even children and young people within the 4-14 window should inform a mission board's candidate office of their call and interest. Relationships with key people of mission organizations need to be developed on the phone, in person, and via e-mail. Those long-term relationships will be helpful for a mission board when it finally begins considering someone for deployment, a process that can take time as a match is sought between an individual and various openings around the world.

3. Creating a Network

Though they have been "set apart" in the words of Acts 13:2, future missionaries must not isolate themselves. People feeling a call should seek to develop relationships with veteran missionaries as well as with mission mobilizers and others who are passionate about world evangelism. Throughout their careers, missionaries need a circle of prayer supporters interceding for them. Missionaries need people they can turn to for advice and counsel. They need people who can provide financial resources. These networks take time to create; they cannot be put together the week before cross-cultural deployment.

How long it takes to walk through all the steps from hearing a call to deployment varies greatly from person to person and is, of course, somewhat dependent upon the age at which God's call comes. However, the faithful and even dogged walking through the various steps will demonstrate to a mission board how determined people are about fulfilling their missionary call. It will say something about the potential for effective service in a vocation that requires tremendous tenacity.

God does desire a relationship with every people group on earth. To that end, He calls people to be His agents of reconciliation, to bear the Good News to those of "every nation, tribe, language and people" (Revelation 14:6). The Church must pray the Lord of the harvest to send forth workers and then it must be ready to mentor, train, deploy, and support those workers.

Questions for Reflection

1. How is the general call to all Christians to witness both different from and similar to a missionary call?
2. What constitutes a call? What are some ways that a missionary call may be received?
3. What is the Psalm 25 pattern for receiving guidance?
4. Why not become a missionary because of the great need?
5. Why are there not enough missionaries to match the needs of world evangelization?
6. What is the significance of the 4-14 window?
7. In what ways can expatriate missionaries think of themselves in relation to the churches they are seeking to establish?
8. What can a pastor do to mentor a young person who has a missionary call? How can others in that person's life be mentors?
9. What qualifications are important for missionary candidates?

10. What are the major steps leading to missionary appointment?

11. What would you say to someone who tells you that he or she wants to be a missionary?

11
CONTRASTING PHILOSOPHIES AND STRATEGIES OF MISSION

Objectives

Your study of this chapter should help you to:

- Examine various philosophies of mission
- Explain why mission must be centered in the character and purposes of God
- Delineate key strategies for church growth
- Evaluate the merits of whether "reaching the unreached" or "going after the receptive" should have higher priority in a philosophy of mission
- Critically weigh the "three selfs" and understand their importance for indigenization

Key Words to Understand

philosophy of mission
holistic
truth encounters
power encounters
unreached people groups
receptivity
church planting
multiplication mentality
strategy
mass evangelism
personal evangelism
10/40 Window
JESUS film

Sometimes missionaries struggling to get along with each other do so because they have a different **philosophy of mission.** That can happen because people motivated by the very same things may have different philosophies about how to respond to those motivations. Motives are what energize people to take action while philosophies are collections of convictions about what is important. One's philosophy of mission is that set of principles that, consciously or unconsciously, guides decisions concerning strategy and methodology. Therefore, hashing out a philosophy of mission is a good way to get people in an organization on the same page. Philosophy is also different from strategy, with strategy being the specific ways in which a philosophy is put into action or implemented. Without a shared philosophy of mission, a mission team will find it difficult to effectively evaluate what is currently being done or to meaningfully plan for the future.

> Every movement is undergirded by a basic philosophy whether that philosophy is known and expressed or unknown and unarticulated.[1]
>
> —Harold Lindsell, *Christianity Today* editor emeritus

Most philosophies of mission can be broken down into a set of constituent attitudes. These component attitudes may include (1) how **holistic** one believes mission should be, (2) a conviction about whether the primary target should be unreached peoples or responsive populations, (3) feelings about whether the gospel should be presented primarily in **truth encounters** or in **power encounters,** and (4) how much of a work-in-progress concept one should feel comfortable in accepting. While it is tempting to think in either/or terms, the extremes on any of these issues are not the only viewpoints that exist. Most likely, the ingredients of one's philosophy of mission will be gradations of ideas or positions spread along a continuum.

Contrasting Philosophies

1. Holistic Versus Narrow Focus

One line or continuum of philosophical positions relates to how much focus should be placed on meeting spiritual needs and how much should be on meeting physical needs. In other words, should missionary work be only about getting people saved or should it also include responses to injustice, illiteracy, and poverty?

A recurring vision drawing people to missionary service is one of multitudes of lost people going out into eternity. Those who point to the need for a focus on direct evangelism plead for every penny to be poured into getting such lost people saved. Even William Booth, founder of the Salvation Army whose ministry is very holistic, once said:

> "Not called!" did you say? "Not heard the call," I think you should say. Put your ear down to the Bible, and hear Him bid you go and pull sinners out of the fire of sin. Put your ear down to the burdened, agonized heart of humanity, and listen to its pitiful wail for help. Go stand by the gates of hell, and hear the damned entreat you to go to their father's house and bid their brothers and sisters and servants and masters not to come there. Then look Christ in the face—whose mercy you have professed to obey—and tell Him whether you will join heart and soul and body and circumstances in the march to publish His mercy to the world.[2]

Finding God's Lost Children

God wants His lost children found.[3]

—Donald McGavran, missionary to India

Further down the continuum from those wanting a narrow focus on evangelism are those who say that global mission activities must reflect the compassionate character of God. Indeed, Christians have often been known for their compassionate acts. When unwanted Roman babies were thrown on garbage dumps to die, Christians gathered them up and nursed them back to health. The question on this position is: Are such acts of compassion to happen primarily as part of the individual Christian life or do they belong in the strategic plans of mission organizations?

An expansion of the options on this particular continuum came in the early 1900s when theological liberals began talking about the Church's primary mission as being the healing touch of Christ in the sense of a social gospel. There was nothing new about calling God's people to be involved in meeting human needs. In the late 1500s, Pedro Claver, Spanish missionary to Colombia, visited the holds of every slave ship arriving from Africa to give material aid and begin a relationship with the slaves, which he hoped would later allow him to preach the gospel to them. Even while doing direct evangelism, the Moravians and Hudson Taylor also met human physical needs. What was new in the 20th century was Walter Rauscenbush and others declaring that there was saving truth in all religions and that social ministry was all the Church should be doing. A watershed came in 1933 when the report of the Laymen's Foreign Missions Inquiry, *Rethinking Missions,* called on all missionaries to withdraw from direct evangelism. At that point, the opposite positions were no longer solely evangelism on the one hand and a mixture of evangelism and compassionate ministry on the other. A new position, social engagement with no evangelism, appeared further down the continuum.

Evangelicals reacted strongly against the call to reduce Christian mission to doing good things in Christ's name. In the backlash, some evangelicals began to classify compassionate ministry activities as distractions that detoured the Church from its urgent evangelistic task.

> Let my heart be broken with the things that break God's heart.[4]
>
> —Bob Pierce, World Vision founder

In 1968 the World Council of Churches meeting in Uppsala, Sweden, issued another call for missionaries to return to their home countries. That call drew as negative a reaction from evangelicals as the similar one had 30 years prior. At the same time, however, they began reminding each other that this was not necessarily an either/or subject and under the leadership of people like Ron Sider, social concerns were reembraced as legitimate Kingdom interests along with evangelism. Today, most evangelistic mission agencies stake out middle ground on this continuum, running social programs for the poor including child sponsorship and microfinance programs as well as doing direct evangelism. In recent years, social engagement has been evangelism's partner with compassionate ministries enabling believers to enter areas where immediate direct evangelism would have been counterproductive or perhaps even impossible.

2. Target: Unreached Frontiers Versus Responsive Peoples

A second philosophical issue with a continuum of positions relates to which groups of people should be the focus of mission efforts: those that are unreached or those that are responsive. Some point to the number of people groups still unreached while noting that the majority of missions resources are spent on groups already classified as reached. In making a plea for a focus on the unreached, Oswald J. Smith has said, "No one has the right to hear the gospel twice, while there remains someone who has not heard it once."[5]

An example of why the question of unreached versus responsive is raised can be seen by looking at Haiti and Saudi Arabia. In recent decades Haiti has been so responsive to the gospel that 30 percent or more of that country's population is now evangelical. Because the rest of the population, even though largely voodoo in everyday religious orientation and practice, is claimed by the Roman Catholic church, Haiti cannot be classified as unreached. On the other hand, while Saudi Arabia is unreached, it would probably not make anyone's list of responsive or receptive nations. So, mission organizations have to ask themselves: Should Haiti still get significant attention or should the resources going to it be diverted to a country like Saudi Arabia?

Reaching the Unreached

In the 2001 edition of *Operation World,* Patrick Johnstone described the Makhuwa of Mozambique as "the largest animistic unreached people group in Africa, possibly the world."[6] That designation may soon have to be changed.

When veteran missionaries David and Marquita Mosher transferred to Mozambique, they found that Jonas Mulate had already started 20 churches among the Makhuwa. It soon became clear that Mozambique, though devastated by a lengthy civil war, was seeing the birthing of a people movement as large numbers of Makhuwa turned to Christ. When leaders such as Jose Amisse reported to Mosher that some new churches had been started, Mosher would then visit the new congregations, writing follow-up reports like this:

> We baptized 118 adults and children and married three couples. We left and went to the next place where we baptized adults and children by the light of a kerosene lamp about 8:00 in the evening. The next morning at 6:30 we organized the church. At the next church we encountered 180 believers. We wrote certificates of baptism until we had no more certificates. In the late afternoon we baptized 151 children and adults. We arrived at the next place with no certificates left, but we walked to the river, which really was only a mud puddle about knee deep. We then knelt in that mud puddle and with the strength of the Lord baptized 235 men, women, and children. To the Lord be all the glory![7]

Of this one missionary leader commented, "What is happening among the Makhuwa is like reliving the Book of Acts!" Another e-mail report said:

> We were undecided about going to Cotocuane since we had people waiting for us at Moma Sede . . . but the Holy Spirit guided us to go. We arrived to find a little chapel already constructed in a heavily wooded area . . . I preached an evangelistic message from 1 John 1:5-10, clearly explaining the difference between the life of darkness and life in the light of God . . . There were 30 new believers at the altar confessing their sins and asking forgiveness from the faithful God. . . . We then traveled down the dusky road to Moma Sede and, facing a brisk wind, went to the beach on the Indian Ocean and baptized the first believers there. The waves were rolling, but each person entered, even a blind young woman, and all demonstrated to the people on the beach their salvation in Jesus Christ.[8]

One Easter weekend 446 new Makhuwa believers were baptized. In one area, all of the churches almost doubled in a single year. The people movement to Christ continues with 10,000 members now having been gathered into 175 churches. What formerly was an unreached people group is now being reached.

—Charles Gailey

At the initial Lausanne Congress on World Evangelization, Ralph Winter pleaded for a focus on what he then called the hidden or bypassed peoples. Winter noted that most global mission resources were going to areas where missionary activity had been going on for years. Samuel Zwemer, who became known in the early 1900s as the apostle to the Muslims, spoke of least-evangelized areas as "unoccupied fields." Those areas scarcely touched by evangelism efforts are where Winter wanted mission agencies to focus their energies and resources. The terminology used most often today is *unreached people groups,* though a few also use *unengaged people groups.* By *people group* is meant the largest group through which the gospel can flow without encountering significant barriers of understanding and acceptance. Even if there are Christians within a people group, it may still be defined as unreached if its indigenous Christians are too few to evangelize their own people without outside personnel and assistance.

The existence of unreached people groups has long been a prime motivator for global mission. Unreached peoples described by Captain Cook grabbed William Carey's attention and set him ablaze. Unreached peoples in the interior of China drew the attention of Hudson Taylor and led him to found the China Inland Mission. Unreached indigenous groups in Central America so caught William Cameron Townsend's attention that he started SIL/Wycliffe Bible Translators.

In responding to Winter's plea to focus attention on the unreached, David Barrett and other missionary strategists have divided the earth's population into three categories or worlds. World A is made up of people who have never heard the gospel and who have no access to it. In some cases those in world A are separated geographically from Christians. In other cases, world A people are in proximity to groups of Christians, but there is such cultural and linguistic separation that missionary methods will be needed to span the chasm. World B is made up of people who have access to the gospel but have not yet accepted it or else have rejected it. World C people are those who profess to be Christian.

Recent research indicates that there are about 4,000 unreached or least-reached sociolinguistic groups in world A. Because that figure was over 15,000 a few decades ago, progress has been made. Some would say that available mission resources should be spent in evangelizing the remaining unreached groups. Others would say that mission strategy is more complicated than checking off people groups as church planting movements are started. One complicating factor is the issue of **receptivity** or responsiveness. Several of the unreached or least-evangelized groups are also resistant. No matter how much is invested in evangelizing them, the harvest will likely be somewhat meager. The history of missionary endeavors in Eastern Europe after the fall of Communism shows the difficulty of knowing which groups will be resistant and which will be receptive. On occasion an unreached people group may be immediately receptive when the gospel arrives (see "Reaching the Unreached" sidebar) and rapid church growth occurs—the best of both worlds for missionary strategy!

3. Proclamation Versus Church Development

A third set of building blocks for a philosophy of mission relates to whether the primary goal should be proclamation of the Good News to large numbers of people as quickly as possible, or whether that primary goal should be developing self-sustaining and self-replicating church planting and discipleship ministries.

There are those who, seeing worldwide gospel proclamation as an eschatological sign (Matthew 24:14), say the Church's task as an ambassador is proclamation and that the results of that proclamation should be left to the Lord. This view sees widespread seed planting as the primary missionary task. Being inclined toward proclamation as a primary goal does not necessarily signify a disinterest in planting churches. Rather, it is a philosophy of harvest that views missionaries as the ones driving the combines in the harvest fields. Those with this philosophy do not see it as their responsibility to organize the transport of the harvested grain and or to build the grain mills.

> As we plant more churches, the result will be a dramatic increase in our overall growth rate.[9] —Paul R. Orjala

On the other end of this continuum are the missiologists who say that the most effective way to move forward with God's mission on earth is to plant lots of new churches. After retiring from missionary service in India, Donald McGavran was influential in getting missiologists and church leaders to embrace aggressive **church planting** as a primary strategy. McGavran argued that the missionary enterprise's supreme goal was that of spawning clusters of growing churches in every segment of the world cultural mosaic. Although criticized for his homogenous unit principle, McGavran is credited with having fathered the modern church growth movement. It needs to be noted that the Euro-American model of church planting has included the construction of buildings as a part of the strategy. The place that building construction has in one's philosophy will determine important things about the shape and size of church multiplication efforts.

4. Sturdy Construction Versus Work-in-Progress

Another constituent element of many philosophies of mission relates to when missionaries feel comfortable stepping away from leadership roles. The choices along this particular continuum involve the comfort level of leaders in terms of what they can tolerate in the way of loose ends. Some want to build quickly and get the scaffolding down; others move ahead more carefully, wanting to be sure they build in ways that will last. Strategies based on the extremes of this constituent component of a philosophy of mission produce very different results. One example is what two denominations have experienced in Haiti. Both groups have been there over 50 years and both are rooted in the same theological tradition. One group has three churches, all of which are being pastored by missionaries who say they are having difficulty recruiting and training reliable Haitian leaders. The second group has more than 500 congregations, all pastored by Haitians. While the results are rarely so far apart as happened in this case, the example does illustrate how one's philosophy can shape the end results.

Naturally, there are hazards to both extremes. When large numbers of people in a culture come to faith in Christ, questions will be raised about the movement's validity. Some will wonder if the movement is, as African theologian Tokunboh Adeyemo has lamented about African Christianity, "one mile long, but only one inch deep."[10] Another downside to accepting a work-in-progress can be illustrated by the experience of Karl F. A. Gutzlaff in China in the mid-1800s. Gutzlaff was a tentmaker missionary whose secular job did not leave a lot of time for pioneer evangelism work. He recruited large numbers of Chinese itinerant evangelists, even setting up a school to train them. At one point Gutzlaff had 300 of these evangelists who were supposedly distributing New Testaments he provided and reporting back the numbers of converts. For a while, Gutzlaff and his Chinese workers seemed to be doing well. The reports he sent home of conversions and Scriptures distributed made other missionaries to China look unproductive.

Unfortunately, Gutzlaff had not developed an effective accountability system for his workers, and it was eventually discovered that many of them were deceiving him. Quite a few were opium addicts who simply made up conversion statistics. To support their opium habit, they were selling Gutzlaff's New Testaments back to the printer who was then reselling them to Gutzlaff. The flaw was not in Gutzlaff's strategy; the flaw was in a faulty system of accountability.

Self-Government, Self-Support, and Self-Propagation

In 1854 Henry Venn began talking about getting churches on mission fields away from their dependency on the mission organizations that planted them. By 1861, Venn and Rufus Anderson were expounding on the three-self principles: self-government, self-support, and self-propagation. In 1890 Presbyterian missionary John Nevius used very similar concepts in helping birth the Church in Korea. Nevius felt strongly that foreign funds should never be used to pay local pastors.

Although the three-selfs of Venn and Anderson fueled a thrust forward in indigenization, it has become clear that a Three-Self church is not automatically indigenous or contextualized. A church, for example, that is governing itself and caring for its own financial needs and reaching out to new people could still be thought of as a foreign transplant by non-members. So, while the **three-self formula** has been helpful, it is incomplete in describing the eventual goal of missionary work. Because the three-selfs are largely external things, Paul Hiebert suggested adding a **fourth self,** self-theologizing, as a criteria for authentic contextualization.[11]

Where the pace is slower, there will be great temptation to use mission funds to pay church workers. This almost always creates an unhealthy economic dependency, developing what Brett Elder has called an "ecclesiastical welfare system." Elder points out that rather than birthing strong churches, economic dependence generally breeds status-quo stagnation characterized by feelings of powerlessness, helplessness, and futurelessness.[12]

In contrast with what tends to be a one-by-one addition in the sturdy construction philosophy is the **multiplication mentality** of those who believe things can move more quickly. Multiplication refers to replicating the expansion of the Church described in the New Testament. A multiplication mentality emphasizes the idea that the Church must be aggressively expanding. The focus in multiplication is not on laboriously building up individuals or working to consolidate existing churches but on multiplying believers and ministries.

5. Truth Encounters Versus Power Encounters

Another continuum of attitudes that often go into a philosophy of mission relates to how the gospel message should be delivered. People on one end of this attitude continuum are sold on apologetics. For them the gospel needs to be presented through truth encounters in which reasoned arguments are made for the truth of the gospel. Those holding positions on the other end of the continuum like to point to power encounters in which the Creator of the Universe defeats evil in dramatic ways, demolishing obstacles to His kingdom.

David Brainerd's brief missionary career tends toward highlighting power encounters. His journal entries speak of hours in prayer and then of God dramatically breaking in on church services. Brainerd's first journey to the forks of the Delaware included an incident that caused a tribe of Indians to revere him as a prophet. It happened one evening while Brainerd was camped near an Indian settlement where he planned to preach the next day. Unbeknownst to Brainerd, he was being spied on by warriors waiting to kill him. Australian pastor F. W. Boreham described what happened:

> When the braves drew closer to Brainerd's tent, they saw the paleface on his knees. And as he prayed, suddenly a rattlesnake slipped to his side, lifted up its ugly head to strike, flicked its forked tongue almost in his face, and then without any apparent reason, glided swiftly away into the brushwood. "The Great Spirit is with the paleface!" the Indians said; and thus they accorded him a prophet's welcome.[13]

In the early 700s a missionary serving in what is now Germany decided that drastic measures were needed to communicate the gospel to the people he was trying to reach. So, in front of amazed onlookers, missionary Boniface chopped down an oak tree dedicated to the thunder-god Thor. It was an in-your-face power encounter act showing there was no supernatural power in either the tree or the god it represented. Boniface's chopping down of the sacred Oak of Donar triggered such a turning to Christ that Philip Schaff has called the action "a master stroke of missionary policy."[14]

Another example of a power encounter came in 1946 during a severe drought on Fogo island in Cape Verde. Believers began praying for water and one night in something reminiscent of what happened with the Israelites at Horeb (Exodus 17), water began flowing from a rock.[15] Cape Verdian believers often point to that flowing spring as the sign of Yahweh's power and presence.

While those on the truth encounter end of the continuum would argue the importance of showing rationally why Christianity is true, those on the power encounter end insist that Yahweh always shows himself worthy of worship and adoration in dramatic ways. Paul Hattaway's *The Heavenly Man* is a good example of the reports of divine intervention characterizing the house church movement in China. On the apologetics end of the continuum, one could point to how encountering the truth of the gospel transformed well-known authors such as Lew Wallace, C. S. Lewis, Charles Colson, and Lee Strobel. An evangelistic tool like the *Four Spiritual Laws* pamphlet would be an example of a printed truth encounter way to present the gospel.

Strategies

Strategy refers to the approaches and plans used to reach one's goals. Strategy grows out of the various philosophical positions one holds even if those have not been clearly articulated. Mission strategy has to do with envisioning and developing structures and systems for extending the church into new areas and communicating the gospel in all parts of the global mosaic of cultures. Strategizing forces believers to focus on God's purposes for the world and to come up with ways they can assist in accomplishing those purposes. While what works in one place will not necessarily work everywhere, some characteristics that will enhance every mission strategy are:

- Shedding unnecessary foreignness
- Looking for relevant methods of communication
- Establishing viable roles in the community
- Working relationally
- Looking for things in the culture and language that could be redemptive analogies
- Having missionaries live among the people rather than clumping together where a missionary subculture develops
- Getting missionaries to commit time to assimilating the culture of the people (mother tongue language, history, social structures, institutions, leadership style, aesthetic values, literature, religious beliefs, and core identity issues)
- Establishing multigenerational church planting and discipleship movements that express biblical faith

> Let us bear in mind that the best methods cannot do away with the difficulties of our work which come from the world, the flesh and the devil, but bad methods may multiply and intensify them.[16]
>
> —John Nevius, missionary to China and Korea

One strategy issue has to do with the way to do evangelism. The ways evangelism takes place can be divided into two categories: **mass evangelism,** where the gospel is communicated to people in large groups, and **personal evangelism,** where the gospel is presented one-on-one to an individual. John Wesley, Dwight L. Moody, Charles G. Finney, Luis Palau, and Billy Graham are examples of those who have had success doing evangelism with large crowds of people. While Jesus regularly used mass evangelism, He also talked to people one-on-one as happened in the episodes in John 3 and 4 with Nicodemus and the Samaritan woman at the well. Paul Orjala used to say that a major reason for church growth in Haiti was that Haitian believers "gossiped the gospel" throughout their country's network of open-air markets.

Depending on God?

> Making plans while praying and searching for God's will is not a denial of divine sovereignty but an acceptance of the fact that God works through faithful servants . . . Many movements stagnate because Christian leaders have not developed the creative capacities for strategic planning.[17]
>
> —Gailyn Van Rheenen, former missionary among the Kipsigis

Occasionally someone will rebel against the idea of doing strategic planning. They say church leaders and missionaries should just depend on God. Actually, good strategies or plans entail having diligently sought the mind and will of God. Paul had a strategy that was conceived in prayer. Other missionaries have followed his model by being outstanding persons of prayer who also devised and followed strategies and plans. David Livingstone, for example, was found kneeling by his bedside at 4 A.M., having died in prayer. Livingstone was also a man of strategy who sought to map the interior of Africa for future missionary work. There was no contradiction in Livingstone's life between his dedication to prayer and his trying to work strategically.

Modern missionaries use a variety of strategies. Harmon Schmelzenbach III has combined a new strategy with an old one as he captains a boat around the islands of the South Pacific in the style of missionaries in the 1800s. However, in his 21st-century island-hopping ministry, Schmelzenbach uses modern technology to show the *JESUS* film and raise up groups of new believers that are formed into churches.

Missionary George Patterson, who planted more than a hundred churches in Honduras, emphasized the development of reproducing chains of churches that he called daughter, granddaughter, and great-granddaughter congregations. In the model exemplified by Patterson's work, evangelism and discipleship are done mainly along family and kinship networks. Missionaries stay in the background. Rather than utilizing a lengthy training program people must complete before being handed responsibilities, leadership is quickly raised up with new churches being linked to experienced pastors who mentor new leaders who then are expected to begin mentoring other new ones. Formal ministerial education is done on the job following the Theological Education by Extension model.

Highlighting the Need: The 10/40 Window

In 1989 Luis Bush got missions strategists talking about the 10/40 Window (see plate 11.1). That was what he started calling the oblong area of the globe that lies between 10 degrees and 40 degrees north of the equator and stretches from North Africa to China and Japan. Drawing attention to the missionary task yet to be done, the visually dramatic 10/40 Window concept has inspired many to offer themselves for missionary service. Two-thirds of all people on earth live within the 10/40 Window. While not all unreached people live there, almost all of the 55 least-evangelized countries are located there. Even though Bush coined the term *10/40 Window*, he has also used Patrick Johnstone's *resistant belt* phrase to refer to the same area. Christians living in this part of the world often suffer physical persecution. In several resistant belt nations, conversion to Christianity is punishable by death. In addition to being relatively unreached with the gospel, that area of the globe is home to 8 out of 10 of the poorest of the poor. The 10/40 Window concept has fostered the development of specialized forms of missionary service for creative access areas, including such things as running restaurants to provide places where people can meet inconspicuously.

Case Study of a Tool: The *JESUS* Film Project

The *JESUS* Film in Mevali, Tanzania

The whole village came to watch the film. As it reached the point where Christ began to suffer, we heard weeping in the crowd. When the whip fell across Christ's back, women began to cry out with each cruel blow. The sight of our Lord being dragged through the streets of Jerusalem on His way to Calvary brought more sobbing from the crowd. The crowd watched as the Roman soldiers put Jesus on a cross and drove nails through His hands and feet. The crying turned to wailing, and we felt God's convicting Holy Spirit on the audience.

Pastor Righton Kyomba grabbed my arm. "Now is the time for the invitation!" he exclaimed. "The Spirit of God is here!"

I stopped the film and turned on the lights. Pastor Righton invited the people to come forward. Within moments people were throwing themselves to the ground beneath the screen. They wept bitterly, calling out in the night to ask God's forgiveness of their sins. I saw children praying in loud voices with such conviction in their hearts. Young people knelt in obedience in the Spirit and poured out their struggles at the foot of the Cross where Christ still hung suspended on the screen. More than 125 people came, seeking forgiveness . . .

The Spirit of God swept through the crowd for almost 20 minutes before we gathered the people in the church for counseling.[18]

—Tim Eby

In the 1970s, Bill Bright, founder of Campus Crusade for Christ, dreamed of producing a film of Christ's life that would be an evangelistic tool. The result was the ***JESUS* film** in which all of Jesus' words come directly from the Gospel of Luke. Since its first showing in 1979, the *JESUS* film has been dubbed into more than 900 languages and has been shown so widely that it is by far the most-watched full-length feature film ever. Campus Crusade's goal is to dub the *JESUS* film into the 1,154 languages that have at least 75,000 native speakers each. Reaching that goal will make the film understandable by 99 percent of the people on earth.

After almost two decades of using the *JESUS* film, Campus Crusade leaders realized that, in order to better conserve the fruits of the film showings and draw resulting new believers into a local church, they needed to partner with mission boards and agencies focused on discipleship and church planting. The resulting partnerships have been very fruitful. Thousands of new churches have been established by follow-up programs now accompanying film showings.

The *JESUS* film has also been contextualized in some ways. For example, the version shown in Islamic areas starts with Creation. There is a children's version with specific scenes added for children. A women's version is also in production. In cultures where group decision making is prevalent, the film is often shown four or five times before any response is expected, allowing the group decision-making process to take place.

In contrast, the *JESUS* film has had virtually no effect in the U.S. and Europe. Why? Is it because there are many films of Jesus' life available on video and being shown on television? Is it in part because the technology itself does not have an attraction for Westerners? Whatever the reasons, this experience reminds missions strategists that there is no tool that will be uniformly effective everywhere.

Philosophy Determines Strategy

Many convictions go into a philosophy of mission. This chapter has focused on a few. One's philosophy of mission is always the starting point for developing world evangelism strategy. That philosophy of mission will also shape various tactical elements of that strategy as they are implemented and tweaked.

Questions for Reflection

1. What are the differences between motives, philosophy, and strategy? How do the three relate to each other?

2. What do you think the constituent parts of Christ's philosophy of mission would be if He were on earth today?

3. How should one respond to those who argue that we should just rely on God rather than doing long-term planning and strategizing?

4. Why is it said that church planting may be the most effective method of fulfilling the Great Commission?
5. What are both the positive and negative aspects of Venn's three-self formula?
6. On what basis should groups be identified as unreached or unevangelized?
7. What are the respective strengths of making either the unreached or the receptive a priority?

12
NEW CONTEXTS FOR MISSION

Objectives

Your study of this chapter should help you to:

- Comprehend the new context that mission faces today
- Delineate the key forces leading to global urbanization
- Evaluate various approaches to people of other faiths
- Assess the universal quest for the supernatural
- Relate the universality of the supernatural quest to the Wesleyan concept of prevenient grace
- Develop a personal framework for witnessing across cultural and religious boundaries

Key Words to Understand

contexts
urbanization
nominalism
postmodernity
cultural diversity
gateway cities
Consultation on Mission Language and Metaphors
Rethinking Forum
inclusivism
prevenient grace
animism
religious approach
magical approach
exegeting the culture

As the Church seeks to fulfill its global mission, it finds itself confronting changing contexts. Today's contextual challenges include: a rapidly growing world population, **urbanization** on a scale never before seen, other world religions including the resurgence of animistic practices, **nominalism** in Christianity, the AIDS epidemic, and **postmodernity.**

Burgeoning Population

On or about October 12, 1999, the earth achieved an epic milestone. On that day earth's population reached 6 billion people. Even more mind-boggling than the actual number is the speed with which it went from 2 billion to 4 billion. It took from the beginning of the human race until 1804 for the world's population to attain a total of 1 billion people. When global population hit that first billion, William Carey had just arrived in India. The second billion was added after 123 more years, coming in 1927 not too long before William Cameron Townsend began Wycliffe Bible Translators. Reaching the next milestone, 3 billion, took only 33 more years, coming in 1960 when Loren Cunningham founded Youth with a Mission. World population topped 4 billion after only 14 more years, reaching that mark about the time of the 1974 Lausanne Congress on World Evangelization. The 5 billion mark came 13 years later in 1987, just a year before Wycliffe Bible Translators completed their 300th New Testament translation. The jump to 6 billion came in only 12 more years. Now, 7 billion is just over the horizon. Those numbers pose challenges for the Church as it tries to fulfill its covenant responsibilities.[1]

Urbanization

The world today is more urban than ever. One hundred years ago, the world had 300 cities with 100,000 or more inhabitants. Today there are more than 4,000 cities of over 100,000. A century ago there were only 20 cities of over 1 million in population. Now, with half the world's population living in cities, earth has more than 400 cities of 1 million or more.[2] Megacities of 10 million or more inhabitants are appearing with projections saying there will be 26 of them by 2015. Each of those cities will, by themselves, have more inhabitants than entire European countries like Greece, Portugal, or Belgium, and they will have twice as many people in them as live in smaller countries like Nicaragua, Finland, and Jordan.

If the Great Commission is true, our plans are not too big; they are too small.[3] —Pat Morley, businessman and author of *Man in the Mirror*

The non-Western world is being urbanized at an even faster rate than the West. While it took England 79 years and the United States 66 years to go from under 10 percent to more than 30 percent urban, it took Japan only 36 years to make that same jump from 10 percent urban to more than 30 percent. Although Africa and Asia were relatively late arrivals on the industrial scene, urbanization is going on there at an extremely rapid pace.

The movement of the world to the cities has brought both uneasiness and excitement for the Church. Christian urbanologist Ray Bakke has argued that massive migrations of people into cities provide great opportunities for the Church. Looking at the changes brought on by rapid urbanization, Bakke said, "The Lord is shaking up the world."[4] The result is an urban context full of challenges for evangelism, church planting, and discipleship.

In more affluent nations, the pull of urban jobs combined with an idealization of rural life has produced suburbia where people live away from the city core but remain connected to it by umbilical cords of rapid transit systems and freeways. In his book *The Exurbanites,* sociologist A. C. Spectorsky described business executives in the U.S., Canada, and Australia moving out beyond the suburbs to what he dubbed the exurbs. Those exurbanites also remain tied to the central city.

Why Is This Happening?

The biggest reason people move to the cities is to improve their standard of living. The promise of a better life, even though frequently illusory, has turned cities into powerful magnets for rural populations. Urbanization has also been fostered by the mechanization of farming, which enables fewer farmers to feed more people. In the United States, for example, the percentage of the population employed in farming has dropped from 35 percent in 1900 to less than 2 percent today. Even so, mechanization has allowed the U.S. to remain a net exporter of foodstuffs. Another reason for the move to the cities is to allow children educational opportunities not available in rural areas.

> One poignant memory of a recent visit to Africa was seeing a woman trying to carry a refrigerator carton down a path in a rainstorm, with the wind constantly blowing her off the path. She persevered, reminding me of millions of others throughout Africa. The miles and miles of shantytowns surrounding every metropolis are mute testimonies to the precarious existence of many. In addition, there are the homeless who do not even have a shelter of their own, and who live under bridges or in culverts.
>
> —Charles Gailey

In developing nations, shantytowns have sprung up as the rural poor arrive in large cities with dreams of earning more income or of helping their children better themselves. Many of those families wind up living in makeshift shelters made from cardboard, pieces of plastic, or discarded roofing tiles. Hoped-for jobs do not materialize. Life is precarious and criminal activity is rampant. Sadly, the growth of cities has facilitated the rise of organized crime empires whose power rivals or even surpasses that of some national governments. In many cities the sex-slave traffic has swept up young people and, tragically, even children.

Collections of high-rise apartment buildings have turned many cities into very densely populated areas. In China, for example, Shanghai has one district with 126,000 people per square kilometer. By way of contrast, Paris, the most densely populated city in the West, averages 25,000 people per square kilometer while low density Los Angeles only has 2,730 people in that same space. The growth of cities has been especially rapid in the Southern Hemisphere. In less than 30 years, for example, the Brazilian city of São Paulo doubled in population to about 20 million. Doing effective evangelism, discipleship, and church planting in densely populated, rapidly growing urban areas will require creative ministries, unceasing prayer, and dogged commitment.

Urbanization and Cultural Diversity

The increasing cultural diversity of the cities, and thus the potential diversity of churches, will present new challenges to the 21st-century global mission enterprise. Cities are so culturally disparate and multilingual that unprecedented cross-cultural contact occurs daily as people jostle each other in city markets. This urban cultural diversity will mean large city churches will likely become multiethnic while rural churches remain mostly homogenous.

Gateway Cities

Because cities are doorways into national cultures, they can be good places for disseminating the gospel in much the same way as cities were in the first century. Cities in creative access and least-evangelized areas are especially pivotal in this regard. Calling them **gateway cities,** missiologists have identified 100 population centers that could serve as portals to unreached and least-evangelized peoples of the world. Those gateway cities include Cairo, Dakar, Casablanca, Tripoli, Baghdad, Damascus, Karachi, Delhi, Kabul, Tehran, Shanghai, Chengdu, and Jakarta (see plate 12.1).

World Religions
(see plate 12.2)

Some have used THUMB as an acronym to talk about unreached peoples in terms of religious orientation. The letters of THUMB stand for tribal, Hindu, uncommitted (such as the Confucian Chinese), Muslim, and Buddhist. The question is: How do Christians approach those unreached peoples of other religious backgrounds? One Judeo-Christian theological doctrine essential to historic Christian mission is the affirmation that there is only one God. Authentic cross-cultural evangelism can only be built on a monotheistic foundation. By discounting the existence of territorial and tribal gods, monotheism makes possible a genuinely global faith. Having said that, can there be a search for some kind of common ground or must Christians always proceed as though they are in enemy territory? In proclaiming the *shema* of Deuteronomy 6:4, "The LORD our God, the LORD is one," do Christians use confrontational methods like the Spanish writer and martyr Eulogius did in the 800s? Opposed to any feeling of affinity with Muslim culture, Eulogius advocated using a missiology of martyrdom to confront Islam. In 859 he himself was killed while sheltering a young woman who had converted to Christianity from Islam.

For many years Christians regarded Islamic cultures as impenetrable, in part because of the frequent union of religion and state. That pessimism about evangelizing Muslim areas is being questioned today with some researchers saying it is harvesttime in the Muslim world. One of those is Robert Blincoe, U.S. head of Frontiers, who has written, "More fellowships and churches of Muslim background believers have begun in the last 40 years than in the previous 1400 years."[5] In a similar vein, Iranian-born evangelist Lazarus Yeghnazar wrote about his homeland: "More Iranians have to come to Christ in the last 20 years than in the last 14 centuries."[6] Many conversions have also taken place in Southeast Asia, which has a larger Muslim population than does the Middle East. In one South Asian country, a pastor recently baptized 80 former Muslims in one service. The flattened world of global connectivity holds possibilities for facilitating the discipling of believers in those areas in ways that were not possible until recently.

As Christians relate to people of other religious groups, they must be very sensitive to language issues. While recognizing that the gospel itself "is an offense and a stumbling block to those who reject it," a recent Consultation on Mission Language and Metaphors suggested that certain words used in the missionary enterprise are needlessly abrasive.[7] The consultation warned in particular against military-sounding language, including words like *target, army, crusade, mobilize, beachhead, advance, enemy,* and *battle.* While evangelical Christians use those terms in a purely spiritual sense, the images they conjure up in the minds of others are often different from what Christians are thinking.

For example, after a long and brutal civil war in one African country, the leader of the victorious side read parts of an expatriate missionary's prayer letter on national radio. With rising intensity in his voice, the new president read what the missionary had written: "Pray for us here on the front lines as we battle the Enemy." Pausing, the African leader then said, "This proves that the missionaries were collaborating with [our opponents]!"

What the African leader did not understand is that when Christians talk about a battle they do not mean against "flesh and blood, but against . . . the spiritual forces of evil" (Ephesians 6:12). However, because a paragraph in a missionary newsletter was misunderstood, two American missionaries were imprisoned in that country for a year and many churches were shut down. With the passage of time, that nation has repudiated the ideology of its former president, allowed closed churches to reopen, and invited Christian missionaries to return. Though that unfortunate episode is fading from people's memories, the lesson that words can be misunderstood with tragic results needs to be remembered.

To be sure, Islam has its own militant-sounding vocabulary, but the point is not to win a debate over whose terminology is more militaristic. Christians seeking to gain a sympathetic hearing for the gospel must understand how certain terms may be misunderstood. In most cultural contexts, using the biblical themes of love, blessing, reconciliation, submission, suffering, and forgiveness will be far more profitable than confrontational-sounding words and phrases.

In Jesus' encounter with the Samaritan woman at the well recorded in John 4, the Lord masterfully demonstrated how to deal with confrontational speech and move past it. The Jews and Samaritans despised each other. The Jews called the Samaritans "dogs" and some even believed that the Samaritans were possessed by the devil (John 8:48). The rift between the two cultural groups was so deep that most first-century Jews would walk miles out of their way to avoid traveling through Samaria.

With that cultural context as a background, John wrote that Jesus "had" to go through Samaria (4:4). As Jesus and His disciples approached a town on their journey northward they stopped at a well where Jesus spoke to a Samaritan woman, asking her for a drink of water. In spite of the shocked woman's attempt to reestablish the wall of hostility—"Jews do not associate with Samaritans" (v. 9)—Jesus leads her to a point of receptivity and she winds up saying, "Sir, give me this water" (v. 15). Ultimately, because of the woman's testimony, many from that Samaritan town accepted Jesus as the Messiah.

This story is more than a revelation of Jesus' modus operandi. It can be a model for the Church's mission outreach. Between the time the woman went to town and came back, Jesus said something to which mission mobilizers have pointed as a biblical mandate for mission, "Open your eyes and look at the fields! They are ripe for harvest" (v. 35). Some biblical commentators have suggested that as Jesus spoke those words, He was gesturing toward Samaritans arriving from town, thus pointing out to His disciples that their ministry needed to include people that were not Jewish. The disarming methods Jesus used on that occasion and others are relevant to building a strategy for Christians to become agents of reconciliation among the earth's diverse population groups.

Christian Worship Adaptations for the Muslim World

1. Facility for washing prior to service is provided
2. Worshipers remove shoes and sit on the floor
3. Bibles are placed on folding stands like those used for the Qur'an
4. Prayer is offered with uplifted hands and eyes closed
5. Chanting of attributes of God, the Lord's Prayer, and personal testimonies is encouraged
6. Worshipers embrace in Muslim fashion
7. No particular emphasis is placed on Sunday
8. "Followers of Isa" is used instead of "Christians"
9. Churches are organized along the lines of the loose-knit structure of the mosque[8]

—Phil Parshall

Missionaries have experimented with a variety of ways of evangelizing and discipling in the Muslim world. Recidivism, or falling away, is a huge problem in trying to evangelize people in Islamic societies. Islam is a very all-encompassing religion. Thus when a Muslim comes to faith in Christ, he faces the question of how much of his culture he will walk away from. For example, can a Muslim convert continue such things as praying five times a day and keeping month-long fasts? Is it possible to talk of Christian mosques in the same way that Jewish believers talk of messianic synagogues? Some would point to 2 Kings 5 where Elisha simply responds "Go in peace" when the new convert, Naaman, speaks of continuing to go to the temple of Rimmon.

To help in discussing strategies for the Muslim world, missionaries have come up with a C1 to C6 scale to differentiate six models of Christ-centered communities used in Islamic areas. These range from the C1 traditional churches using outsider language to C4 contextualized communities that follow many Islamic practices (avoiding pork, keeping fasts, following local forms of Islamic dress) and on to C6 communities of believers who feel they need to be extremely secretive about their worship of Christ.

Religious Fundamentalism

In this third millennium after Christ, Christians are looking for ways to communicate the love and compassion of the triune God to those of other religious backgrounds. An example of this is the Rethinking Forum, which focuses on contextual witness among Hindus and endeavors to promote "the birthing of Christ-centered movements within Hindu cultures and communities."[9]

Sadly, sectors of some religions are extremely fundamentalist in the sense of rigidly emphasizing what are considered their defining or founding principles. Such religious fundamentalists see themselves as aliens in the midst of depraved cultures. Their resulting combativeness produces considerable social instability. The appeal of religious fundamentalism, says Phill Butler, "fuels Islamic, Hindu, and right-wing nationalists in such diverse places as France, Italy, Russia, Afghanistan, Algeria, North India, and Indonesia."[10] Finding ways to evangelize these ardent fundamentalists poses a tremendous challenge.

Lostness of "Heathen"

One question that often comes up is: What happens to those who die without ever having heard of Jesus? Sometimes that question does not get serious consideration. For example, recently one Internet blog site seemed to scorn the question with these words, "Are the heathen lost? This is the question of the college campuses, the skeptic and the agnostic. This is the question of those who wish to deflect making a personal commitment to Christ. This is the question of those who like to play mental gymnastics with God."

If the author of that paragraph was saying one should not even reflect on the fate of the unevangelized, he was wrong. The question of people's eternal fate deserves a thoughtful answer. Since what one believes about people's eternal destiny will shape a philosophy and strategy of mission, it does matter which of the following positions Christians take on the salvation of people of other religious ideologies:

1. Restrictivism (also called particularism or ecclesiocentrism)

Restrictivism says that all the unevangelized are tragically damned because they are part of the sinful human race (1 John 5:11-12; John 14:6; Acts 4:12; Romans 1:20-21; 1 Corinthians 3:11; Zechariah 10:2; and Psalm 16:4). This position resonates with the biblical worldview that sees one ramification of the solidarity of the human race as being that all humans are sinners because of the sin of Adam and Eve.

2. Universalism

Many liberal Christians are universalists who believe that everyone, including the unevangelized, will be saved. They do not see how God, who is ultimate goodness, could allow anyone to be eternally separated from Him (Luke 3:6; Isaiah 40:5; John 12:32; Romans 5:18; 1 Corinthians 15:22-28; Philippians 2:9-11).

3. Religious Instrumentalism

Religious instrumentalism holds that non-Christian religions can have a saving potential paralleling that of Old Testament Judaism (Matthew 5:17). This viewpoint says that sincere believers of other religions can be saved without ever hearing the story of Jesus of Nazareth because their religious faith has validity as a valid form of worship of the true God. Hindus and Buddhists would applaud the all-encompassing nature of this position.

4. Universal Evangelization

Some hold the belief that God will ensure that the gospel will somehow get to all those who are truly searching for Him (John 4:23; Acts 8:26-40). One criticism of this position is that it seems to imply that human beings have already begun searching before God takes His first step.

5. The "If" Theory

The "if" position says that God will save those who would have accepted Christ if they had heard about Him (Matthew 11:21-23). This viewpoint has a tint of Calvinism about it in that it has God deciding people's fates somewhat apart from their actual choices.

6. Postmortem Evangelization

The postmortem position says that people will have the possibility to hear about Christ and accept Him at the time of death or some point thereafter (Matthew 12:40; Mark 16:15-16; John 15:22; 2 Thessalonians 1:8; 2 Timothy 1:16-18; 1 Peter 3:19-20). This is the position with which Mormons, who baptize on behalf of the dead, would agree.

7. Wider Hope (called inclusivism by some writers)

This position says that salvation is possible apart from the actual hearing of the Good News from the Bible. Those who hold this position say that the unevangelized will be saved or lost on the basis of how they follow what light of the triune God they have seen through His prevenient grace (John 1:9; 3:16-17; 12:32; 1 Timothy 1:15; 4:10). One variation of this position, accessibilism, says that God enables everyone to respond to His self-revelation on at least one occasion in his or her life in a way that leaves him or her accountable for his or her response.

Of these seven positions, the two most often embraced by evangelical Protestants are (1) the one labeled restrictivism or particularism, and (2) some variance of wider hope or inclusivism, which sees the possibility of what have been labeled "implicit" Christians.

Animism and Spiritual Warfare

As they approach people of other religious faiths, Christians must be careful not to think that their central strategy should be that of coming up with counterarguments for textbook listings of the doctrines of those religions. What people actually believe and the ways they practice their faith will differ from what textbooks say about their religion. For example, it is often said that the majority of those categorized as Muslims and Hindus and perhaps 20 percent of those who are nominally Christian are actually animistic. Many Buddhists are animistic as well, as is evidenced by the little spirit houses outside homes and businesses throughout Southeast Asia.

The traditional short definition of **animism** is "the belief in spirits." However, to get a proper understanding of that term, one must go back a hundred years to anthropologist James George Fraser. In his monumental 13-volume *The Golden Bough,* Fraser noted that people in every culture are involved in a quest for the supernatural. Through the years anthropologists have continued to affirm what Fraser said about the universality of religion, putting it on their lists of cultural universals. Even where leaders have claimed their followers were atheistic, this has never been true for the whole of a culture. Witness the survival of religion in Albania during the Communist years even though the attempts to erase all vestiges of religion included sandblasting crosses off of tombstones.

That all groups of people seek the supernatural should not be surprising in the light of the prevenient aspect of God's grace in which divine grace is understood to precede or go before the arrival of the missionary. Though Don Richardson does not use the term *prevenient grace,* that was the foundation for his words in *Eternity in Their Hearts* when he wrote, "God has indeed prepared the Gentile world to receive the Gospel."[11] John Ellenberger, professor of missions at Alliance Theological Seminary, has also pointed to several examples of the Holy Spirit's preparatory activity in cultures prior to any contact with the gospel message.[12]

As Fraser examined cultures throughout the world, he saw two ways that people approached the supernatural, ways he called the religious and the magical (see fig. 12.1). Either approach can be used by believers of all religions. They are not mutually exclusive and are often mixed in practice.

The **religious approach** to the supernatural, anthropologists say, is characterized by submission. One example of that is the prayer of Jesus in the garden of Gethsemane just prior to His arrest. His submissiveness in that prayer is exemplified by the words, "Not my will, but yours be done" (Luke 22:42). Submission is also a key attitude in the religion of Islam; indeed, the word *Islam* means "submission" in Arabic. For many, Buddhism is also a religion of submission to the point of being fatalistic.

The **magical approach** to the supernatural is characterized by manipulation. People using this approach want supernatural forces to do something for them. The supernatural quest by animists often uses such a magical approach.

Through a séance, a visit to a shaman, or some other means the supplicant seeks to control or influence supernatural powers. If the attempt involves an enemy, the shaman may be asked to work a spell, mix up a potion, or create a representative doll to try to bring harm to someone. The shaman, medium, or practitioner usually receives a fee for his or her efforts and there is often a fear that one's enemy may go to a shaman who can more effectively manipulate the supernatural than the person to whom he or she has just paid a fee. Such fear is dysfunctional, both for the person and the culture.

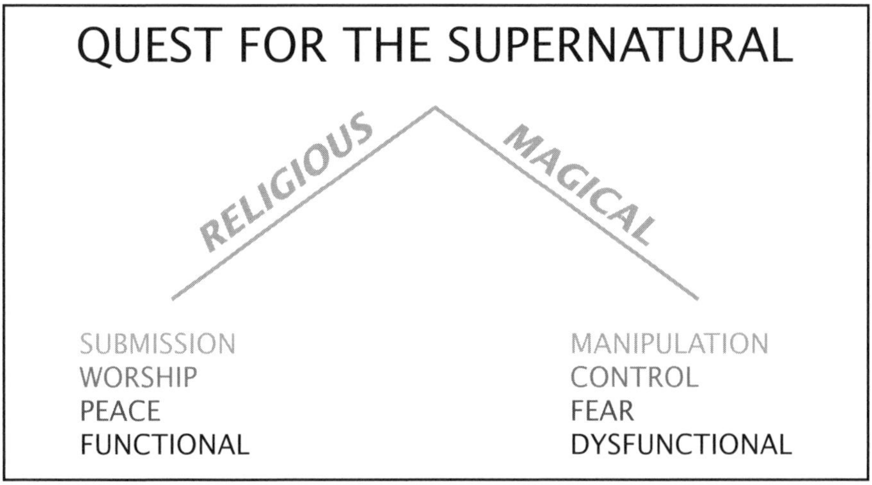

Fig. 12.1. Quest for the supernatural

What Would You Do If . . . ?

Several different approaches have been used by Christians in efforts to understand those of other religious faiths. Bringing up classically stated doctrines of another world religion or even those of Christianity may do little more than spark long and even heated discussions. A far better technique is to pose a simple question, "If you had a great need—perhaps your child was dying—what would you do?" The answer will be very revealing about a person's core religious beliefs. Many self-professed Muslims or Hindus will say, "Oh, I would go down the street to that lady who reads the tea leaves or who will work a spell." Finding someone to work a spell is not, of course, true Islam or Hinduism. It is animism.

For such people, Christians can offer a better way, a way of submission and worship. Sadly, Christians may not always be prepared to do that. Some time ago Paul Hiebert wrote an article about the "flaw of the excluded middle" in which he said Western missionaries were often unprepared to minister in cultures in which there was widespread animism.[13] Hiebert noted that believers in the West had well-developed theological understandings about God and about the natural world but their formal studies often ignored what he called the "middle area" of spiritual forces like angels and demons.

As C. S. Lewis noted in the introduction to his delightful *Screwtape Letters,* Westerners generally approach the idea of unseen spiritual forces in two ways. On the one hand, as Paul Hiebert noted, the worldview of many Westerners has no place for the unseen realm of spiritual beings and their power. Such Westerners have written off those spiritual forces as unimportant or else have not acknowledged them as real. The extreme rationalism of this approach ultimately strips Christianity of supernatural content, oxymoronically turning the faith into a secularizing force. The other extreme that Lewis mentioned is represented by books such as *Engaging the Enemy,* which urge Christians to learn about "territorial spirits" so that they can pray "against them."[14] In some people's minds, that way of talking about spiritual forces reduces Christianity to the level of magic and animism.

AIDS/HIV Crisis

Another contextual challenge facing Christianity today is the AIDS epidemic. Though the pandemic is worldwide, it has hit parts of sub-Saharan Africa hard with HIV prevalence rates of over 20 percent in Botswana, Lesotho, Swaziland, and Zimbabwe and more than 15 percent in South Africa and Zambia. The results of such high infection rates pose tremendous challenges to the Church in Africa. As children have lost both parents to AIDS complications, millions of orphans have been created across Africa. This high profile problem is attracting money as churches and agencies scramble to help those in the hardest hit areas. Sadly, unless the outside funding for alleviating AIDS-related problems in Africa is used with great wisdom, it could spawn a fresh set of dependency issues. The challenge is thus not only to respond to the AIDS crisis but also how to do so without creating other long-term problems.

Nominalism

Another characteristic of today's global mission context is the huge number of people who are Christian in name only. In *Biblical Perspectives on Evangelism,* Walter Brueggemann talked about the back-to-the-Torah movement under Ezra and Nehemiah in which "forgetters" in Israel were transformed into "rememberers." Europe (eastern as well as western) and North and South America are populated by millions of nominal Christians who could be termed *forgetters.* That the Church faces a serious challenge in evangelizing these nominal Christians was pointed out when three major reports from the Consultation on World Evangelization held in Thailand focused on nominal adherents among Roman Catholics, Orthodox, and Protestants. Many of the people labeled as nominal Christians in both Protestant and Roman Catholic areas of Europe think of themselves as post-Christian. They have not rejected Christianity; they see it as part of their heritage but they feel they have moved on beyond it. The Church is struggling to find ways to reevangelize countries like Denmark where more than 85 percent of the population claims to be Christian but church attendance sputters along between 1 percent and 4 percent.

Postmodernity

The coloring that postmodernity gives to the thinking of people around the world is another aspect of the context in which mission is done today. In postmodernity there is skepticism about concepts such as progress, objectivity, reason, certainty, personal identity, and grand narrative. Postmodernity is characterized by the feeling that all communication is shaped by cultural bias, myth, metaphor, and political content. Postmodernity, typified by parody, satire, and self-reference, sees society as dominated by a mass-media that has no originality. In much of postmodernity, meaning and experience can only be created by the individual and cannot be made objective by an author or narrator. Postmodernity and globalization have combined to produce a culturally pluralistic yet profoundly interconnected global society that lacks a dominant center of political power, communication, or intellectual production.

The context produced by postmodernity will affect how evangelism and discipleship are done. Postmodernity will also shape how support for world mission must be generated. Some see in the postmodern fascination with story an opportunity for the Christian story to get a good hearing. Narrative theology, which grapples with the theological messages of the narratives of Scripture rather than attempting to do systematic theology, is a way of doing theology that should appeal to postmoderns.

Exegeting the Culture

Global population growth, urbanization, changes in other religions, the resurgence of animism and postmodernism are features of the context in which today's Christian global mission is being done. The church growth movement fathered by Donald McGavran urges church leaders to study thoroughly the context in which they are ministering. Scholars sometimes discount the insights of church growth studies, saying that those are simply crass attempts to market the church. What they do not see is that church leaders must be **exegeting the culture** with the same dogged determination they use to exegete or understand Holy Scripture. It is a mistake to summarily dismiss the usefulness of the social sciences in understanding the context in which the Church must minister today. Mission leaders must be reading cultures and seeking to understand the context of today and to anticipate trends of tomorrow. If Christians are going to effectively do what God has called them to do, they must exegete their world.

Questions for Reflection

1. What factors have led to global urbanization?
2. Why do you think a quest for the supernatural is present in every culture?
3. In what way should the idea that the supernatural quest is universal be an encouragement to missionaries?
4. How does the universality of the supernatural quest relate to the concept of prevenient grace?
5. What are the two approaches to the supernatural that Fraser delineated? In what way are they functional/dysfunctional?
6. If a Muslim or Hindu family moved into your neighborhood, how would you seek to communicate your faith to them?
7. What does it mean for church leaders to exegete a culture?

13
MOBILIZING THE LOCAL CHURCH

Objectives

Your study of this chapter should help you to:

- Evaluate the importance of mission vision in keeping a local church healthy
- Delineate four objectives of a global mission program in the local church and how they may be accomplished
- Recognize how important a mission-minded pastor is to the development of a mission ethos in a church
- Diagnose a local church's mission education and promotion program
- Develop a personal mission vision

Key Words to Understand

action-to-information ratio
mission fatigue syndrome
mission education
mission-minded pastor

Not infrequently, the mere mention of a global mission offering will cause some church member to frown and say, "Well, I just don't see why we have to send so much money overseas when we have so many needs right here!"

Fatigue Syndromes

One reason people like that seem unfazed by the world's heart-rending physical and spiritual needs is the compassion fatigue caused by media overload. People have heard it all and seen it all. Their televisions carry nonstop stories about abuse, neglect, malnutrition, and suffering brought on by disasters. When that stream of bad news merges with the pleading ads of relief agencies in magazines and on television and billboards, the result can be mind-numbing compassion fatigue. From that point on, challenges to ease world hunger or give to disaster relief move people about as much as do toothpaste commercials.

Another fatigue syndrome, mission fatigue, can hinder efforts to mobilize believers for fulfilling the Great Commission. Visiting missionaries' messages about God's heart and the needs of the world, no matter how clearly illustrated, may not be enough to overcome the deadening effects of mission fatigue. That paralyzing fatigue is usually brought on by one or more of the following four things:

1. Inadequate Understanding of Ecclesiology

When the missionary enterprise is seen as peripheral or optional, mission promotion produces more fatigue than it does action. People who feel they are already committed to enough things around a church will tune out appeals to become burdened for world evangelism. Congregations full of this kind of people will likely not be zealous for world evangelism until believers shed the notion that the church is a salad bar of activities and emphases in which involvement in global mission outreach is just one more option like singing in the Christmas musical or helping with a weekly children's ministry.

> Sympathy is no substitute for action.[1]
>
> —David Livingstone, missionary to Africa

2. Lack of Knowledge

People tend to have low **action-to-information ratios.** As a result, what can seem like disinterest or sinful apathy may be simply the result of people not having enough information to cause them to act. People do not know what to pray for, so they do not pray at all. They do not know there are places where missionaries are discouraged and about to burn out. They do not know large cultural groups are still untouched by the gospel. They do not know where the Holy Spirit is moving. They do not know there are ways they can get personally involved. They do not know that most organizations have accountability systems in place to ensure that mission funds are properly used. They do not know there are very receptive groups where an even larger harvest could be gathered if more resources were available. They do not know their mission organization is very involved in meeting physical as well as spiritual needs.

3. Erroneous Theology

Wrong beliefs can make people susceptible to mission fatigue. Even evangelical believers can get infected with the religious relativism associated with postmodernity. Since what people believe drives their behavior, religious relativism can blunt the urgency of appeals to get the gospel to underevangelized and unreached peoples. Believers can also be affected by a universalism that says that surely everything is going to come out OK in the end for almost everybody.

Wicked Selfishness

I feel now that Arabia could be evangelized within the next thirty years if it were not for the wicked selfishness of Christians.[2]

—Samuel Zwemer, writing in the early 1900s

4. Selfishness

Carnal selfishness also fosters **mission fatigue syndrome.** Too many Christians in materialistic cultures find themselves working to pay for consumer goods they do not really need and that are often used up before they are paid for. Sometimes those who have quite livable incomes find themselves saying, "We're just barely making ends meet; we can't really afford to give anything right now for overseas missions work." Outright selfishness has kept them from internalizing Jesus' words in Luke 14:33, "Those of you who do not give up everything you have cannot be my disciples."

Raising Up a Mission-Minded Church

Because mission is best done when there is a sending, then having a missionary sending base filled with passion, fervor, and commitment is of paramount importance. Oswald J. Smith, founder of Peoples' Church in Toronto, Canada, felt so strongly about the priority churches should place on world evangelism that he reportedly said, "Any church that is not seriously involved in helping fulfill the Great Commission has forfeited its biblical right to exist."

Thus, the inertia that too often makes believers lethargic when it comes to world evangelism has to be overcome. Leaders must get people to comprehend the seriousness of what Smith said, pushing their churches into prayer support, financial backing, and the development of an atmosphere in which children and youth can clearly hear God's call to global mission.

> The Church must send or the church will end.[3]
>
> —Mendell Taylor, church historian

Although some things in support of global mission can happen spontaneously, global mission rarely becomes a priority in a local church unless leadership intentionally makes an effort to push it to the forefront and keep it there. When a tsunami comes ashore or an earthquake strikes, local churches and groups of believers around the world will respond quite spontaneously. However, assuring support year after year for career missionaries and various global ministries as well as creating an atmosphere conducive to people feeling a call to missionary service necessitates having some kind of missions committee charged with doing publicity, promoting intercessory prayer, educating the congregation, setting up events, and carrying on other needed activities. Such a group, in whatever ways it is organized, should aim at promoting world evangelism in four ways:

- By educating people about what is happening in missions, about God's heart for all peoples, and about the task yet to be done
- By mobilizing prayer support for world evangelization
- By challenging children, youth, and adults to learn about and embrace the global mission of the church to the point of offering themselves for missionary service
- By raising funds for the world mission enterprise

Some denominations have a model structure that congregations copy to create the needed mission committee or council. In other situations, a mission promotion structure must be organized from scratch by each local church.

Mission Education

Ralph Winter has said, "God cannot lead you on the basis of facts that you do not know."[4] One key task, therefore, for local mission mobilizers is gleaning relevant mission information from various places and passing it along. Such mission education is aimed at intentionally opening people's eyes and calling for action. Good mission education must show believers that the cause of world evangelism merits giving up leisure time to pray for, to mobilize for, and to participate in. Mission education must lead believers to see that global mission is worth the investment of more than pocket change and perfunctory prayers.

Some mission boards help local churches with mission education by providing curriculum materials. In terms of information content, some churches give their members a well-rounded look at global evangelism by cycling through a different mission emphasis every month of the year, often with a call to pray for, give to, or get personally involved in that particular aspect of world mission. Such monthly emphases include volunteerism, compassionate ministries, gospel broadcasting, training for indigenous leadership, and missionary care and nurture.

While the Internet can provide lots of useful information, caution must be exercised. Sadly, global information networks have made it easier for charlatans and inept leaders to find gullible local churches and individuals and milk them for money for fake or badly conceived mission projects. Thus, individual local churches that are not working through a denominational or reputable mission board must be extremely careful, lest all they do is "make a hole in water."

Given the normal low action-to-information ratios, local mission leaders must use every avenue available to get mission information to believers: material in church bulletins and newsletters, printed flyers passed out before a service, informational material on bulletin boards, displays in church hallways or foyers, "mission moments" in worship gatherings, brief video and PowerPoint presentations, promotional skits, e-mail newsletters, church Web sites, and even entire church services devoted to the cause of world evangelism.

The part music plays in mission inspiration and education is too often overlooked. Kenneth Osbeck, music director for the Radio Bible Class and professor at what is now Cornerstone University, has written that Christians "are really the people of two books, the Bible and the hymnal."[5] While many churches do not use printed hymnals, Osbeck's point is that what people sing can influence them almost as much as does Scripture. Mission education leaders must be continually encouraging music leaders in local churches to make use of missions songs or at least songs that allude in some way to world evangelism.

Missionaries can be a valuable source of information and inspiration. Fortunately, the flattened world described by Friedman has made it easier than ever for local churches to develop relationships with missionaries on the field. Most missionaries have periods of home assignment where they are encouraged and even expected to spend a considerable amount of time speaking in churches. Short-term opportunities in which local members go to a mission field are also ways of helping them and the people they talk to on their return to learn about missions. Effective local mission promotion and mobilization will therefore include facilitating involvement in short-term mission opportunities.

One key responsibility of local mission leaders is that of developing and cultivating other mobilizers, particularly younger ones, within the congregation. Avenues of mission education for preparing these local leaders include training events like the 14-week "Perspectives" courses now taught in several countries. There are also national and international missions mobilization conferences aimed at young people (such as the triennial Urbana meetings in the U.S.A.). Many denominational mission organizations also hold annual conventions that can train and inspire local mission mobilizers.

Prayer

It may be impossible to overemphasize the importance of prayer in the global mission enterprise. Across the years prayer has been the lifeblood of mission with every great missionary advance having been sparked and then fueled by the intercessory prayer of ordinary church members. Churches should be full of intercessors who give high priority to praying for the establishment of clusters of reproducing churches in unreached people groups. When prayer for world evangelism is not being mobilized by local church leaders, individual believers need to find ways to create their own little cells of fervent mission prayer support.

> The whole history of missions is a record of the achieving power of believing prayer.[6] —William Remfry Hunt, missionary to China

In *The Power of Prayer,* R. A. Torrey, successor to Dwight L. Moody, wrote, "The man or woman at home who prays often has as much to do with the effectiveness of the missionary on the field, and consequently with the results of his or her labors, as the missionary."[7] Unfortunately for the cause of world evangelism, most prayer requests in church services have to do with people's illnesses and injuries. Thus, prayer time in many local churches sounds like roll call time in a sick bay. Those involved in mission promotion and mobilization must seek to change that, helping believers become just as burdened about an unreached people coming to Jesus as they are about their relatives' health issues.

Prayer support can be marshaled in many ways. Local churches have sometimes organized monthly prayer meetings for global mission needs. Coinciding with the Islamic Ramadan fast each year is the 30 Days of Prayer for the Muslim World. Several organizations sponsor a World Day of Prayer and others promote a World Week of Prayer that focuses on world evangelism. *Operation World* contains a year-long daily prayer calendar. Many missionaries print photo prayer reminder bookmarks or cards that can be kept in a Bible or put up on a refrigerator or bedroom mirror. E-mails from missionaries keep local churches up-to-date on answers to the needs for which they have been interceding as well as passing along new requests.

Sometimes local churches will set up prayer chains in which requests can be passed quickly from family to family or person to person. Such prayer chains, while continuing to mobilize people to pray for the sick people of that congregation, can marshal intercessory prayer for unexpected opportunities that mission leaders encounter and for political crises and natural disasters that affect world mission efforts.

Some missionaries establish a special time when they want supporters to pray for them. For example, when Fred Huff was a missionary in Africa, he went around asking people to join his 714 Club. That club was a network of prayer supporters who prayed for Huff and his work each day at 7:14 in the morning and again at 7:14 in the evening. Huff took the "714" number from 2 Chronicles 7:14, which says, "If my people, who are called by my name, will humble themselves and pray and seek my face and turn from their wicked ways, then I will hear from heaven, and I will forgive their sin and will heal their land." Huff used that challenge to create a prayer support network for evangelism and discipleship ministries across sub-Saharan Africa.

Children and Youth

Sending Its Best

No local church can afford to go without the encouragement and nourishment that will come to it by sending away its best people.[8]

—David Penman, missionary to Pakistan and Lebanon

Exposure of children and youth to world evangelism must be an intentional part of local church programming. Because many missionaries report receiving their missions call prior to the age of 18, promoting missions in ministries for children and youth is of critical importance. Local churches need to look for ways to get their youth involved in hands-on mission trips. Children and youth need to become involved in praying and giving as well as being encouraged to think about their own future involvement. They need to have direct contact with missionaries who visit their church.

Raising Funds

Evangelizing the world takes financial resources. Churches must encourage their members to so embrace the cause of world evangelism that they rein in personal spending in order to free up more money for global mission. Believers need to encourage each other to live with great intentionality in employing all their resources—time, money, gifts, and abilities—for the task of world evangelism. In His Sermon on the Mount, Jesus said the use of money revealed the focus of people's passions, "For where your treasure is, there your heart will be also" (Matthew 6:21). Implied in that passage is the principle that the need for believers to give far exceeds the mission enterprise's need to receive such giving.

Many Christians will say they wish they could give more money to missions. Tragically, missions offerings too often get reduced to bothersome intrusions in busy church activity calendars. At the mention of a special missions offering, church members scramble to see how much can be spared from their bank account or from whatever amount of cash they are carrying at the moment. Sadly, what they wind up giving is often less than they would like for it to be.

One way of enabling people to give to global mission in the way they would like has been a program called Faith Promise. That system of giving originated with Canadian pastor Oswald J. Smith who called on believers to make yearly commitments of what they believed the Lord was asking them to give to world evangelism. In the faith promise concept, missions giving—like the tithe—comes off the top of a person's income rather than being scraped together from leftover money at the end of the month. The faith promise system has been successful because people find they give more to missions when they do it on a weekly or monthly basis rather than through one or two big offerings in a year.

Churches that raise money for world evangelism through faith promise plan an annual missions weekend. During that special event, a special speaker (usually a missionary) will challenge people to commit to what they feel God wants them to give to world evangelism during the following year. These commitments are usually paid out on a weekly or monthly basis. People are urged to step out on faith, to go beyond what seems humanly possible and to make a *faith* promise. Often, in a moment of praise, the total of these promises will be announced at the conclusion of the commitment service. Occasionally faith promise has been promoted with the idea that God is going to provide extra money to be given, the implication being that if God does not provide the extra money, nothing needs to be given to global mission. That is a distortion of the concept.

While faith promise time serves to gather financial commitments, it is also an opportunity for a local church to host a missionary or a missionary family as special speakers. It is also a chance to educate those who are being asked to fund a mission program as to where the missions money raised in that church will be going. It is even a good time to teach a new global mission song or two to a congregation.

Church leaders need to guard against falling prey to the temptation to add things to their faith promise budget, such as raising local building funds or paying other obligations. Trying to piggyback on the inspirational tide of a missions weekend to raise money for other purposes is a mistake that can backfire. The church leadership's integrity may be questioned if the emotional pull of outreach to unreached peoples is used to solicit money for local construction projects.

Faith promise is not, of course, the only way global mission money is raised by congregations. Many churches take special missions offerings during holiday seasons. For instance, the Women's Missionary Union of the Southern Baptist Church promotes the Annie Armstrong offering at Easter and the Lottie Moon offering at Christmas. Others take offerings for gospel broadcasting, missionary medical care, compassionate ministries, and global construction needs at special times throughout the year. Such offerings are not just a chance to collect money; they serve a mission education purpose.

Raising Up a Mission-Minded Pastor

In addition to an active missions committee or council, a **mission-minded pastor** is almost indispensable for a local church that wants to assume its global responsibilities. Missions committees, therefore, need to see that one of their primary jobs is developing mission-minded pastors. Once in awhile, people zealous for the cause of world evangelism will criticize a pastor's level of enthusiasm for global concerns. Those critics need to understand that what they are doing is counterproductive. Pastors do not suddenly become mission-minded because mission committee members snipe at them.

Lay mission leaders can take advantage of the voracious reading habits of most pastors by regularly giving them a book on global mission or sometimes a book on the place where people from the church will be going on a mission trip. Pastors who like to collect out-of-print classics may appreciate a copy of something like John R. Mott's *The Pastor and Modern Missions: A Plea for Leadership in World Evangelization* or Andrew Murray's *The Key to the Missionary Problem.* Though published a hundred years ago, books like these can still be found in second-hand bookstores and on Internet bookseller sites. Visiting missionaries can be asked to suggest book titles for future gifts to a pastor. In addition to the goodwill generated by the gift-giving, a mission committee may be able to transform a pastor's thinking, praying, and preaching in regard to world evangelism. Sometimes that change will be the radical result of reading one book. More often, the transformation of a pastor into a truly mission-minded leader will come through a series of small but incremental steps.

Missions Books for Pastors

From Jerusalem to Irian Jaya by Ruth Tucker
Let the Nations Be Glad by John Piper
Loving the Church, Blessing the Nations by George Miley
Mission on the Way by Charles Van Engen
Missions in the Third Millennium by Stan Guthrie
Missions in the 21st Century by Tom Telford
The New Global Mission by Samuel Escobar
The Open Secret by Lesslie Newbigin
Operation World by Patrick Johnstone
Unveiled at Last! by Bob Sjogren

Pastors who become truly mission-minded will model, guide, and lead in at least three ways related to world evangelism.

1. Guiding Congregations into Seeing the Bible as a Missionary Book

It is a mistake to allow believers to continue to think that the Great Commission in Matthew 28 and Mark 16 is the only scriptural foundation for mission. As pastors see how replete the Bible is with references to God's heart for world evangelism, they should begin passionately preaching and teaching until people in their congregations see it as well. While a missions committee or council can do a lot of educating about the status of world mission work, it is the pastor who carries the most weight in pointing out the biblical and theological foundations for global mission.

> A church that neglects mission will—sooner or later—die out.[9]
> —Jan A. B. Jongeneel, professor of missions, Utrecht University

The richness of material on Christian missions in books like those listed in the "Missions Books for Pastors" sidebar can aid pastors as they search for sermon ideas and illustrations. Mission committees can help both their pastors and their cause by watching for sermon material that relates to global evangelism and passing along that material to their pastor.

2. Helping Congregations See That a Church Is Most Healthy When It Is Passionate About Reaching Lost People Everywhere

Unselfish global outreach and a healthy, growing local program often go hand in hand. Occasionally a pastor, not realizing how those two things complement each other, will become fearful that a focus on anything other than local ministries weakens a congregation. That was not the case with Harold John Ockenga when he became pastor of Boston's Park Street Church. At one of his first board meetings, Ockenga asked that church to allow him to challenge church members to give sacrificially in a special offering for world evangelism. At that time, Park Street Church was giving only a tiny fraction of its income to others while struggling to keep its building painted. Although it seemed like the Conservative Congregational Christian Conference church needed every bit of its income just to survive, Ockenga pleaded for it to get out of a survival mind-set. The church board accepted their new pastor's challenge to make global mission a priority and that decision fueled a transformation of Park Street Church. On the crest of an expanding missionary program that sprouted from Ockenga's call for a sacrificial missions offering, Park Street Church became a strong and influential church. Today that congregation has a full-time global outreach coordinator and gives twice as much to missions as what it keeps to run its local programs—an amount that, incidentally, has been more than sufficient to keep the church's building painted!

> The real problem of foreign missions, then, is the home churches, and without the pastor it cannot be solved. . . . The multitudes of the distant nations cannot come to speak for themselves, even were they conscious of their need. Nor can the missionary do so. The missionary visitor may arouse temporary interest. But it is the missionary pastor who makes a church a missionary power the year through.[10]
>
> —John R. Mott

3. Modeling Mission Passion

People respond to what pastors say; they respond even more enthusiastically to what pastors do. Global missions concerns need to be a part of worship service prayer times. During their public pastoral prayers, pastors should pray often for missionaries by name and enthusiastically model for their congregations what it means to passionately support global mission.

In the early days of Paul Cunningham's pastorate of a tiny, struggling church in Olathe, Kansas, he had a vision of his congregation stretching itself to give a record missionary offering. Cunningham, fresh out of seminary, decided he needed to lead the way for his flock. To that end, he got a personal loan from a local bank so that he could put a significant amount into that offering. That same church, which now has over 3,000 members, recently committed more than $1 million in its annual faith promise event. The groundwork for what that church is doing today was laid when a young pastor took the audacious step of taking out a loan so he could be a pacesetter in a missionary offering.

Such stories should not give the impression that pastors need to embrace mission in order to produce gains in other areas of ministry. The stories of Ockenga and Cunningham are told to illustrate how congregations can be profoundly influenced by mission-minded pastors.

> The mark of a great church is not its seating capacity, but its sending capacity.[11]
>
> —Mike Stachura, past president
> Advancing Churches in Missions Commitment

Raising Up a Mission-Minded You

As a small girl riding around a Quebec lumber camp with her father in the late 1800s, Susan Norris saw a fight among some Indian workers. When she got home, Susan asked her mother why the men had been so mean to each other.

When her mother explained that liquor made people behave like that, Susan asked, "If it makes them mean, why do they drink it?"

"I guess they don't know Jesus," her mother replied.

"Someone should tell them about Him!" said young Susan.

That incident sparked in Susan Norris a lifelong passion to reach people who did not know about Jesus. In her early years she took that ever-present burden as a sign that she would someday go overseas as a missionary. Then, tragedy struck. At 14 years of age, Susan became very ill and was confined to her bed for almost two years. One day she had a dream about Christ's second coming. In the dream she was happy until she saw that not all people were going to heaven. She woke up wondering why she had had such a sad dream, but then she seemed to hear a voice quoting Mark 16:15, "Go into all the world and preach the gospel to all creation."[12]

Because Susan thought that meant God was calling her to be a missionary, she was excited! However, when she eventually applied to be a missionary, she was turned down over health issues. In the midst of her discouragement over being rejected, she was reading the Bible when Ezekiel 3:5 caught her attention, "You are not being sent to a people of obscure speech and strange language." That day, Susan felt the Lord was saying to her that she was not to be a missionary. However, because she did feel she was supposed to be in some kind of ministry, she went off to a Bible college. Marrying another young preacher, she became Susan Norris Fitkin. Not long after their marriage, her husband left the active ministry for a business career and Susan became the master pulpiteer of the family. Wherever Susan N. Fitkin spoke in churches as an evangelist and world mission promoter, she encouraged people to take care of their missionaries and to provide financial resources for world evangelism outreach. Elected founding president of a denominational mission society, she became the most visible missions promotion leader in her church, holding that position for almost three decades.

S. N. Fitkin, the name by which she often went in print, was a woman of prayer as well as a great organizer. Using those two gifts, she enabled global outreach efforts to survive the Great Depression. Before e-mail was even dreamed of, Susan Fitkin carried on an extensive correspondence with missionaries and fed information to local churches from those exchanges. Long before short-term mission trips came into vogue, Susan Fitkin went overseas several times at her own expense and infused excitement and information from those mission field visits into her messages to missionary conventions across the U.S.A. She encouraged local churches to organize missions mobilization committees and inspired families in the U.S. to give to missions even in the midst of economic struggles. One of Susan Fitkin's oft-repeated sayings was, "We never test the resources of God until we attempt the impossible for Him."[13]

Ways to Assist Missionaries

Communication support
Financial support
Logistics support
Moral support
Prayer support
Reentry support

Individuals can be involved in supporting missions in many different ways. The Church needs some very visible people like Susan Fitkin. Others are needed who will work behind the scenes. This can be in seemingly little things like sending cards for birthdays and other special occasions. Notes of support and encouragement from a local church can lessen the danger of missionary burnout in which high levels of stress cause deterioration in both ministry and personal spiritual life. Missionaries sometimes need help with housing during deputation travels or with finding a car to use on home assignment or in locating special supplies or equipment for their ministry. Individual believers can help with all kinds of logistics problems, such as collecting and getting materials to missionaries, driving a vehicle to a shipping point, or pulling together a meeting of potential supporters for a meal when a missionary is in town.

A well-functioning local missions committee is a plus, but even when there is not one, individual believers can provide global mission flavoring for a congregation by what they do with music, in children's ministry, with the youth program, or by material put up on bulletin boards. Individuals can pass on copies of missionary e-mail letters to Sunday School classes or Bible study groups, helping a missionary communicate with entire congregations. Members of churches where the rest of the congregation is not giving much to missions can still get very involved in funding global outreach. To be sure, they must guard against feeling superspiritual when other believers do not share their passion or do the same things they are doing. **World Christians** must understand their need to be cheerfully giving in sacrificial ways regardless of what others do. People also can get very involved in praying for specific missionaries even if there is not a lot of prayer support for global mission in the rest of their church.

Helping missionaries may mean supporting them as they go through reentry upon coming home. Missionaries often need someone to talk to, whether they are simply coming back in for a time of home assignment or are returning permanently from the field. Sometimes missionaries need someone they can open up to without fear that what is said will be repeated. Believers will do well to sense when something is amiss for a missionary and be willing to listen without telling the whole world things for which a missionary just needed a listening ear.

> As I traveled around and saw whole nations of people where there were only 50 or 100 believers in the whole country, what I saw was it's either God's will for it to be this way (and we know that's not true) or it's somebody else's fault.[14]
>
> —Keith Green

Goals for Local Churches

Some local churches set very audacious global mission goals for themselves. An example is the West Covina (California) Christian Church, whose leadership came up with the following goal statement:

"Because our blessings have brought equal responsibilities, we therefore set the following goals:

- World evangelization permeates church life throughout the year.
- Every member expects to have some role in the global harvest.
- God's heart for the nations is heard in almost every service.
- Church leadership continually challenges couples and singles to consider going overseas.
- Going on short-term mission trips is the expected norm.
- The average lay member of this congregation, knowing God's heart for all nations is a major theme of the Bible, can name several scripture passages about world evangelism.
- Global mission needs will be met even before the local church electric bill is paid.
- Most members will know the church's adopted missionaries, where they serve, and what their needs are.
- Mission information and prayer times are mainstream.
- The church aims to give no less than 25% of its income to world missions.
- World evangelization is seen as half the reason that local church exists."

Because the essence of the gospel—the Good News—is such that it must be shared with all people everywhere, mission cannot be left to a few missionary-minded people. Because global mission is on the heart of the triune God, it must be on the heart of the local church.

Questions for Reflection

1. How can a local church move beyond just having only a sprinkling of missionary-minded people involved in world mission?
2. What are some ways a church can educate its members about mission?
3. What additional thing—such as more knowledge, more love, more dynamic, greater conviction—do you think would cause believers you know to respond to world need?
4. What are ways a pastor can assist his or her congregation in developing a new vision for mission?
5. What are ways a healthy church can maintain a clear mission vision?
6. Suppose your local church hired you as a consultant to help them improve or develop a mission program, what would you say to them?

14
FUTURE CHURCH

Objectives

Your study of this chapter should help you to:

- Understand the changes affecting mission today
- Evaluate the need for strategic partnerships
- Identify the vital importance of prayer in the Christian world mission
- Be aware of the amount of persecution of Christians
- Develop a theology of suffering
- Reflect on the relationship between suffering and receptivity
- Develop a personal response to God's call to mission

Key Words to Understand

panta ta ethnē
futurology
world Christian
International Day of Prayer for the Persecuted Church
persecution
suffering

As Christianity's third millennium gets underway, God's people are facing a rising tide of global changes that has the potential to lift them to a new level or else render them irrelevant. This is a critical time for global outreach because the world is moving through a significant hinge point, a hinge that is opening doors to entirely new worlds. Christian futurist Leonard Sweet put it this way:

> Events that have happened in the aftermath of the postmodern earthquake have generated tidal waves that have created a whole new world out there. In your lifetime and mine, a tidal wave has hit . . . The Dick and Jane world of my '50s childhood is over, washed away by a tsunami of change.[1]

It is difficult to forecast in detail all that this tsunami of change will mean for the Church. However, what does happen and how the Church responds is extremely critical in terms of whether God's yearning to see the globe blanketed with gospel proclamation will be honored. The Greek phrase in Matthew 28:19-20 rendered as "all nations" is ***panta ta ethnē,*** a phrase with the same nuances as the Hebrew word *mishpahoth* or "all peoples" used in the Abrahamic covenant in Genesis 12:3. How all those peoples living in today's changing environment will be reached is the challenge the Church faces.

Looking Forward

Trying to predict what the future holds is risky business, as can be seen in how far off the mark IBM founder Thomas Watson was in 1943 when he said, "I think there is a world market for maybe five computers."[2] Those in the past who tried predicting where the mission enterprise would be today rarely did much better than Watson in their forecasting. In terms of missionary work, no one predicted the Theological Education by Extension movement that revolutionized the delivery of leadership training. No one foresaw the huge short-term mission movement that now involves more than 1.5 million people each year. Who could have foreseen the phenomenal evangelistic and church planting results of the *JESUS* film? In Hudson Taylor's day, who could have predicted missionary communication tools like e-mail, Web pages, and Internet voice communication? For that matter, no one envisioned in the 1700s that William Carey would come along to mobilize Protestantism for global mission. In the beginning days of the Pietist movement, no one thought that historian Gustav Warneck would one day evaluate its missionary impact with the words, "In spite of [Pietism's] 'fleeing from the world,' it became a world-conquering power."[3] A hundred and fifty years ago, who would have predicted the mobility that today's global air traffic system could give to those involved in world mission? On the other hand, just because **futurology** is risk-prone does not mean that one should shy away from it. While Christians cannot change the past, they can help shape the future and the more those involved with global mission have thought about that future and reflected on possible scenarios, the better prepared they will be to face what actually does come.

> If you had really believed in what you tell us is the Christian message, you would have been here long ago.[4]
>
> —response of a man in China

It is quite clear that paradigms developed in the Industrial Age and the Enlightenment period are being superseded and discarded. Much of the human race now lives in a postmodern period that has been called the third wave or the information economy. Even that information age has begun to wane with Stan Davis and Christopher Meyer, authors of *Future Wealth,* predicting that a bioeconomy period is now getting underway that will hit full stride by the 2020s. In a *TIME* magazine article, Davis and Meyer talked about what they expected in the near future:

> Generation Xers born after 1964 . . . will experience two major economic shifts: first, from the crunching to the connecting halves of this information economy and, second, from a microwave-based connected universe to the cell-based world of biologic and bionomics. Those of you in Gen Y may have to go through three![5]

Radically **new paradigms** of church and mission may or may not now be germinating in the soil of these global changes. To be sure, the Church is centuries old and while it has experienced some enormous changes through the centuries, some things that people thought would change have remained the same. About three-quarters of the way through the 20th century, some predicted that preaching was about to radically change and maybe even disappear. For most pastors, even very successful ones, it has not. Without a doubt, some new ways of doing old things will come along and be embraced. The fact that people change jobs and even careers several times during their lifetime is affecting how people view missionary service. Missionary candidates used to think in terms of spending the rest of their lives on a mission field. Now, people applying for missionary service are willing to commit for 10 to 15 years and then reevaluate where God may be leading them. Some other changes will be in the area of how financial support is given. Already people in some countries give to mission organizations by credit card or automatic bank withdrawal. Some changes will be in communications with missions organizations likely doing more and more communicating with supporters through electronic rather than printed means. In the early 1970s some people predicted the demise of large churches and the disappearance of denominations by the year 2000. Neither of those things happened. In fact, there are now more megachurches than ever and little in the way of denominational merging has gone on in the last 30 or 40 years. Thus, dealing with what seem to be new trends requires discernment so that in the rush to be on the cutting edge leaders do not blindly embrace scintillating fads that turn out to be ephemeral. For example, not long after the Internet arrived, believers began gushing about how it would revolutionize evangelism. However, no effective models of that being done have emerged. While the Internet is a great communication and information-disseminating tool, it has not become an evangelistic powerhouse.

Future = New

Trends coming into focus for the immediate future include even more cooperation among churches and mission agencies, a renewed emphasis on prayer, new inspiration from key pastors, new questions begging to be answered, and new expansion.

New Cooperation

There is a growing sense among churches and mission agencies that networking, cooperation, and partnering will be hallmarks of future Great Commission efforts. Phill Butler has reported, "Denominational groups like the Southern Baptist and interdenominational ministries like Campus Crusade . . . with reputations for 'going it alone,' have taken dramatic steps to reach out and link with other ministries."[6] One example of such cooperation is the development of *JESUS* film partnerships between Campus Crusade for Christ and various groups.

Such collaborative efforts can integrate the strengths and ministry strategies of differing groups into goal-reaching coalitions. In local churches the gifts and abilities of individual believers complement each other to create healthy body life and effective outreach and discipleship ministry. In similar fashion at the level of organizations, the gifts and strengths of various groups can complement each other in the cause of world evangelization. New cooperation will also be expressed through short-term mission teams from multiple countries working together on projects.

Renewed Emphasis on Prayer

Facilitated by new forms of communication, worldwide prayer networks are springing up. The Window International Network, formerly the Christian Information Network, has reported huge numbers of people committing to pray specifically for unreached people groups. It has been estimated that more than 50 million Christians regularly pray for the unreached peoples of the world. Leaders like David Bryant have been instrumental in encouraging concerts of world mission prayer in a variety of global venues.

Throughout history, great missionary outreach, like great revival, has begun after people have prayed. David Bryant noted the relationship that exists between local spiritual revival and world evangelism:

> In any prayer movement, dynamic tension must always be maintained between church renewal and world evangelization. Each thrives on the other and drives us to the other, if kept in proper balance. Renewal prevents "burn-out" on the task of missions and missions challenges "cop-out" on the fruits of renewal. If we maintain this tension, the ministry of intercession will be our most effective step in pioneering faith for Christ's global cause.[7]

New Inspiration from Pastors

Through the ages, God has raised up leaders to provide vision and inspiration for lifting the world mission enterprise to new levels. Those key inspirational leaders have often been pastors. Britisher Charles Spurgeon was a promoter of world missions in the last half of the 1800s. Following on his heels was New York pastor A. B. Simpson, who promoted global missions even more heavily than Spurgeon. Simpson went so far as to say that a Christian "is not obedient unless he is doing all in his power to send the Gospel to the heathen world."[8] Not long afterward, Oswald J. Smith boosted mission support in Canadian and U.S. churches through the faith promise system of giving. Singer Keith Green, who had his life cut short in a plane crash, was a mission motivator for a generation of Americans. Baptist pastor and prolific author John Piper wrote *Let the Nations Be Glad,* a best seller expounding the biblical foundations of world evangelism. More recently, California pastor and author Rick Warren has emerged as a very visible promoter of world evangelism.

The World Around the Corner

You all will forgive me, I trust. I have been primarily concerned with our little corner of the world when I should have been concerned with the world around the corner.[9] —Jerry Gass, pastor

Warren's *The Purpose-Driven Life* has been very influential among Christians in the first years of the 21st century. Originally written in English, that book has sold more than 25 million copies worldwide, influencing believers in both hemispheres. Recently, people arriving for services in a 6,500-member church in Campinas, Brazil, were greeted with a huge Forty Days of Purpose banner in Portuguese. *The Purpose-Driven Life,* which was on the *New York Times* best-seller list for months, stressed that global mission passion is a necessary component of the Christian life. "The Great Commission is your Commission," Warren wrote. He urged believers to "shift from local thinking to global thinking." That is powerful stuff from a pastor most known for taking a church of 3 members and building it into a megachurch of 20,000 people. In *The Purpose-Driven Life,* Warren called on Christians to "read and watch the news with Great Commission eyes," and concluded that, "if you want to be like Jesus, you must have a heart for the whole world."[10]

Some indication of the fascination people have with the concept of global mission can be found in the level of participation in short-term mission. Such participation in and support for world missions in local churches reflects how well pastors have been developing members of their congregations into world Christians, a phrase that means almost the same thing as missionary-minded. Though world Christian has been widely used only recently, it was coined by Daniel Fleming in his 1919 book *Marks of a World Christian.* World Christians, said Fleming, are disciples whose life directions have been inspired and transformed by a divine vision of the world. For world Christians, God's global cause is the integrating, overriding priority of their life.

New Questions

Throughout this book several strategic questions have been raised. There are others that need answering. How does the Church get the Bible into all of those languages that do not yet have it? How does the rest of the global Church interface with the huge house church movement in China? Will leaders in the West be able to cleanse themselves of vestiges of paternalism? In a changing world, can the missionary enterprise be proactive as opposed to reactive? Will the Church hear Rick Warren's cry for believers to become passionate about global evangelism, or will that cry get submerged in a cafeteria approach in which global mission is just one of many good things the Church does? Will what looks like fruitful evangelism in the Islamic world continue and can we do things to help it accelerate? Can tomorrow's missionaries be the strategists, catalysts, and facilitators that the mission enterprise needs? As the Church grows rapidly in some world areas, will it find ways to quickly develop the needed mature, reflective leaders?

New Expansion

The last decades have seen an acceleration of global evangelization initiatives. There are more missionaries than ever before deployed around the world, with the total expatriate missionary force from all branches of Christendom (Protestant, Roman Catholic, and Orthodox) now numbering about 443,000.[11] Mission budgets have grown to new records, including a nearly 22 percent increase in one recent three-year period. According to the editors of the *Mission Handbook,* that jump represents "the greatest [percentage] increase ever seen from one edition . . . to the next."[12]

Intensified Persecution

At the same time mission organizations are seeing new cooperation, finding new inspiration, and experiencing new expansion, believers also are experiencing an increase in persecution, especially in that area of the world called the 10/40 Window (see plate 14.1). Sadly, the 20th century saw more Christians killed for their faith than had been martyred in all the first 19 centuries of Christian history combined. That pace does not seem to be slackening. A research report in the *International Bulletin of Missionary Research* said that 169,000 Christian believers lost their lives in one recent 12-month period.[13] In one instance guerrillas surrounded the home of Nazarene Pastor Peter Nyabusa. They tied up his wife and forced the pastor to sit on her. They then slit his throat. Blood flowed all over the wife as she and the guerrillas watched Pastor Nyabusa die.

In recent years Christians have encountered severe persecution in China, India, Indonesia, North Korea, Pakistan, and Saudi Arabia. Conscious of the dangers they face, Pakistani Christians often sing with one hand on their neck to signify that they are ready to die for Jesus. In another nation, news cameras took photos of a large banner being waved by some young people. On the banner was written: "TOLERANCE IS NONSENSE; SLAUGHTER CHRISTIANS." "'Burn churches!' shouted others in the restless crowd, estimated at upwards of 200,000. Although it sounds like something from Nero's persecution of Christians in the first century, this particular scene took place not long ago."[14]

It is difficult for most Western Christians to imagine living under the constant threat of being punished or killed even though every day many Christians throughout the world live with that threat. There are parts of the world where just trying to share one's faith with a nonbeliever is punishable by death. An example of what believers face in parts of the world can be seen in the following report:

> This week the Lord once again allowed me to meet men and women that are committed to God even through tremendous persecution. This nation has gone through extreme political unrest over the last several months . . . The streets around our churches became hot-beds of riots, killings, burnings and destruction.
>
> Our pastors told stories of [religious extremists] surrounding their church during services and demanding them to stop the services or face the burning of their church. They have been forced to meet in homes to hide from danger. One pastor . . . was lured to his church because of a plea for help—only to find that the [religious extremists] had set up an ambush. They executed him on the spot. They knew that his son [who was also a pastor] would come to the funeral and tried many times to take his life, too.[15]

Suffering and Growth

One of the realties of our world today is that in areas where material resources are abundant, the church is growing little if at all while in areas where resources are few, where there is conflict and persecution, and where trained pastors are in short supply, the church is growing rapidly. Is there a relationship between affluence and spiritual vitality? Robert Coleman wonders, "Can it be that in our preoccupation with the good life, we have missed the church-growth principle of suffering woven all through the New Testament?"[16]

—Terry Read

In spite of situations like this, the Christian church in that particular country is growing rapidly—so rapidly that the government of that country has stopped publishing religious affiliation statistics! Though persecution of God's people has intensified in the last century, it is not something new. Elisabeth Elliot has reminded believers, "Christians who think they should never suffer forget that God allowed John the Baptist to be beheaded, Stephen to be stoned, and his son to be hung on a cross as a love gift to the world."[17] Elijah, Zechariah, Jeremiah, Daniel, James, Peter, Paul, and John all suffered persecution. Hebrews 11 talks about the persecution of God's people in both Old and New Testament times. All this suffering does, however, bear fruit for the Kingdom. Terry Read, missionary to Haiti and Rwanda, has joined others in noting that suffering has often accompanied the expansion of Christianity (see sidebar "Suffering and Growth"). Indeed, Tertullian, an Early Church leader, said that "the blood of the martyrs is the seed of the church."[18]

The rise in the physical persecution of Christians has affected many churches and mission organizations. One horrific example is what happened to Australian missionary Graham Staines and his two young sons, ages six and nine, who were killed while on an evangelistic mission in India. Staines, director of the Leprosy Mission in the state of Orissa, had served in India for more than 30 years. Fluent in several languages, he had been influential in getting the New Testament into the Ho dialect. Just after midnight on January 23, 1999, Staines and his sons were sleeping in their jeep when Hindu extremists arrived with the intention of burning them alive.

> The windows were broken out of Staines' jeep; gasoline was poured on and ignited; the jeep was then enveloped in flames. The screams that were emitted did not incite sufficient help to prevent the horror from continuing. But they may have awakened the nation. There are at least two obvious things

> that India has been made keenly aware of: the horrors of the Hindu and fundamentalist movement's most radical fringe and an authentic faith with a depth of Christian spirituality hitherto unrecognized by many in India.[19]

Within days of the killing, Graham's wife made a public statement forgiving the perpetrators of the crime. At the funeral, she and her only surviving child, Esther, sang a Bill and Gloria Gaither song, "Because He lives, I can face tomorrow, / because He lives, all fear is gone."

21st-Century Persecution Hot Spots

Chechnya: Radical Muslims in Chechnya kidnap and martyr Christian believers.

China: Chinese house church leaders face arrest.

India: The Hindu Nationalist movement in India has a violent, anti-Christian side to it.

Indonesia: Over 500 Christians have been killed on the island of Ambon, although most of Indonesia's population is not extremist.

North Korea: North Korea has been called the last Stalinist state. There are only three Christian churches for visiting Westerners. Korean Christians do exist, but they are deep underground.

Pakistan: Blasphemy laws were amended not long ago in Pakistan to permit courts to issue death sentences.

Saudi Arabia: Expatriate Christians have been arrested and imprisoned on charges in Saudi Arabia that they engaged in Christian worship.

The forgiveness offered in the Staines' case has impressed people in India. Russell Shubin of Salem Communications reported that one Hindu exclaimed, "This is true spirituality."[20] The unconditional forgiveness displayed by Graham Staines' wife fueled increased receptivity to Christianity in Orissa as hearts and minds became more open to Christ than ever before. This incident should help Christians know how to pray as well as see how important it is to forgive those who are their persecutors.

About 300,000 churches worldwide now observe a mid-November **International Day of Prayer for the Persecuted Church.** When Christians learn about the suffering of the persecuted church they must use that awareness to step up to new levels of commitment and stewardship. When Elisabeth Elliot was asked what advice she would give to newly appointed missionaries, she replied, "I would say to them, 'Take up your cross daily, and follow Him.'"[21] Western Christians who see their freedom from persecution as a sign of divine blessing need to hear again the words of Matthew 5:10, "Blessed are those who are persecuted because of righteousness, for theirs is the kingdom of heaven." Read adds, "Several contemporary theologians write about 'a theology of the cross.' Incarnational ministry implies that the messengers of the Cross share in the sufferings of those they serve."[22] As they face a world in which there is new and intensified persecution of Christians, tomorrow's missionaries will need to embrace a theology of risk and suffering.

We call him Joseph. He lives in a country we cannot name. When word got out that Joseph was translating the Scriptures, local officials asked him on three different occasions to renounce his faith. Each time he refused. The first time he lost his job, the next time his son was kicked out of school, and finally he and his family were chased out of town.

Joseph asked for prayer, but his request was not for the obvious—that he would get his home or his job back. Instead, he said, "Pray with me that I will be able to carry my cross all the way to Calvary and not set it down in the middle of the road."[23]

Third Millennium Church

Example from China

With more than 20 percent of the world's population, China is a huge country. A rapidly urbanizing nation with consequent cultural clashes, China has a dynamic, growing church that bathes its ministries in fervent prayer. What is happening with the church in that country may portend mission trends of the 21st century: a persecuted church with visionary leaders in a key nation of the 10/40 Window that is a single country encompassing several cultures (see plates 14.2 and 14.3).

In the 1940s the work of the Church of the Nazarene in China was centered in Daming in Hebei province. A church building still stands in this area with a typical early 20th-century sign over the pulpit reading "Holiness unto the Lord." At the time missionaries were forced out in 1941, there were 5,500 church members in and around Daming. Recently, a government official reported that same area now has 500,000 people claiming to be Christian. Where there were 54 churches in 1947, the number of congregations today exceeds 1,000! A Communist government official recently said to a visiting denominational representative, "I have been watching you as you have interacted with the people. There is something about you that is different—and very, very special."

Hungry for the Gospel

China is hungry for the gospel. We discovered that immediately upon our arrival in Beijing. On Easter Sunday morning we told our guide, "We must go to church. It's Easter Sunday. We are Christians, and we must go to church." However, we had a difficult time finding a church. The taxi driver in that atheistic country was not really familiar with taking people to church services. But finally, going down an alley and through a gate in a thick wall, we arrived at a church.

And what a church it was! It was standing room only with over 2,000 people crowded into that building for an Easter Sunday morning service. With people standing in the back, in the vestibule, and everywhere else imaginable, we sang a joyous song about the Resurrection. The atmosphere was electrifying. Then, in that Communist land where they had just enacted a law threatening immediate imprisonment for Christian witnessing, a soloist sang about Christian hope in this life. We felt bathed in the glory of God from that great group of Chinese believers who had been turned "from darkness to light, and from the power of Satan to God" (Acts 26:18). Fifty people were baptized that Easter morning.

While all this was going on, our guide became hungrier and hungrier for the Good News. She began to ask me questions, and before the day was over, she prayed to receive Jesus Christ as her Savior.

We had a week of Bible studies with her before we left. Because of the new law, I was not allowed to officially witness to her. But we found a way. The next day, we went to the Temple of Heaven (I thought that would be a good place to talk about religion), and we found a secluded place on the grounds where there was a bench. Doris, my wife, was the lookout, and we had our first Bible study.

Another day, the three of us rented a paddleboat and went out into the middle of the lake at Beihai Park for prayer and Bible study. After a week, we got on a plane to Russia. We were happy because we were leaving behind a brand-new Christian in China.

On the plane, God placed a Chinese gentleman, Professor Wu (not his real name), next to me. We talked about his field of study for a while, and then our discussion turned to spiritual things. He had not realized that God wanted to be our Friend and that we could talk to Him. I sensed a deep spiritual hunger in Professor Wu. After we talked awhile he said, "I would like to pray."

"Would you like to pray right now?" I responded.

"Yes!" he said.

I then led him in a prayer of repentance and salvation. Right there in midair, over frozen Siberia, the Chinese gentleman gave his life to the Lord and was born again. His burden rolled away! The professor grabbed my hand in gratefulness, squeezed it, and said, "Thank you, thank you, thank you!" He squeezed my hand so hard it seemed ready to break.[24]

—Charles Gailey

The stories in the sidebar "Hungry for the Gospel" are typical of the receptivity to the gospel in China (see plate 14.4). While such openness to God has not come without a price, leaders of the church in China know that God is "not wanting anyone to perish" (2 Peter 3:9). Energized by seeing humanity as God sees it, these Chinese believers are determined to do something about the world's lostness and brokenness. Even though they know it may be dangerous, they are looking to expend themselves to reach others with the gospel. Consider the vision of "Joe," a young leader of the church in China. Recently, Joe told a Western Christian, "We will evangelize every person in China. Then, we will line up on the western border of China and, in the power of the Holy Spirit, we will march to, through, and beyond Jerusalem planting the Church!" Is it any wonder the church in China is growing so rapidly? Because of the vision and zeal of Christians like Joe, millions in China are finding God. What a great example the Chinese church is for churches everywhere else in the world. Churches elsewhere in the world need to look to the church in China as a model because of how clearly it understands that to be Christian is to be missionary.

Mission-Centered Church

Like holiness, global mission is birthed in the very nature and character of God himself who both seeks and sends. Since Yahweh is a missionary God, the church that truly submits to His sovereign Lordship must be infused with a passion for global mission. When believers start becoming like Him whose name they profess, they, too, will become senders and seekers. Missionary Doug Perkins summed up the challenge facing the Church:

> The greatest threat to the Church in the third millennium is not the post-modern age of moral relativism, nor is it a generational problem. It's not a music problem nor is it a problem of baby boomers and their values. The greatest threat to the Church is that we are not drawing near to Christ and not going out in His name to make a difference in our world.[25]

What Perkins said echoed the sentiments of South African Andrew Murray who wrote a hundred years ago in *The Key to the Missionary Problem* that lack of love for Jesus Christ was why the Church was failing to fulfill the Great Commission.

The Church of Jesus Christ must respond to the challenges before it. Missiologists dream about the Church being able to send a team of missionaries to each unreached people group within a decade (see plate 14.5). That is not an impossible dream. The Church could likely do that if three things were to happen:

- 100,000 additional missionaries could be mobilized
- a great avalanche of prayer could be initiated
- current global missions giving could be doubled

The Church of Jesus Christ is standing on what could be the brink of a new era of mission. However, every day that the Church fails to mobilize adequate resources for world evangelism, 55,000 unreached people die without ever hearing the gospel. Every day the Church fails to mobilize itself, opportunities are lost. The Church can and must go so that "those who were not told about him will see, and those who have not heard will understand" (Romans 15:21, quoting Isaiah 52:15).

Questions for Reflection

1. What reasons do we have to be optimistic or pessimistic about the future of the Christian world mission?
2. What factors highlight the need for strategic partnerships in the third millennium?
3. What should be the Christian response to increased persecution?
4. What are some elements of a theology of suffering? What is your theology of suffering?
5. What explanation would you give for the rapid growth of the Church in several non-Western areas?
6. What are the characteristics and purposes of God that should lead us into global mission?
7. How will you personally respond to the call of God to global mission?

APPENDIX
CASE STUDY: MISSION IN THE CHURCH OF THE NAZARENE

The Church of the Nazarene was born at the end of the great century of Protestant missions. That timing may have something to do with the missionary ethos that characterizes Nazarenes. It certainly seems more than a coincidence that a denomination born in an era of intense Protestant missionary activity is today a major missionary-sending denomination.

As several groups were coalescing into what would become the Church of the Nazarene, two global visionaries emerged to nurture and shape the missionary vision and strategy of the new denomination. Both of those people, H. F. Reynolds and Susan Fitkin, were part of the Association of Pentecostal Churches of America in the northeastern U.S., one of the three groups that merged in 1908 to form the Church of the Nazarene.

When those three Holiness groups united at Pilot Point, Texas, leaders did not need to figure out how they were going to start a global outreach program. They already had one going. Prior to the merger, all three of those groups had overseas missionary work with the Pentecostal Churches of America in the East and the Holiness Church of Christ in the South being the most active.

At the time of that 1908 union, the man who would become one of the most famous names in Nazarene missionary history was already on the field. The previous year, 1907, Harmon Schmelzenbach had left what would become Southern Nazarene University to go to Africa where he remained as a missionary without furlough until traveling back to the U.S. for the 1928 Nazarene General Assembly. After that assembly, though he was in frail health, Schmelzenbach insisted on returning to Africa where he died the following year.

After the 1908 merger, H. F. Reynolds became the denomination's mission administrator, taking on the task of integrating the separate missionary endeavors of the three groups into a unified enterprise. Reynolds was also elected as one of the three Nazarene general superintendents. The passion for world evangelism that Reynolds brought to the general superintendency may have been what assured that world mission would frequently occupy center stage in the Church of the Nazarene.

In 1913-14 H. F. Reynolds made an around-the-world trip. He spent an entire year away from the U.S., visiting every Nazarene mission field. That trip, which was financed by a denomination-wide offering, set a precedent. Today Nazarene church members would think it strange if general superintendents were not going on trips to visit mission fields and giving some direct supervision to world missionary work.

Susan Fitkin came from that same group in the northeastern U.S. Early in life she felt a burden for the unreached and assumed the Lord wanted her overseas. However, when she applied to a mission board, they turned her down for health reasons. Rather than becoming bitter, she turned her energy to missions promotion and mobilization. In 1899 Susan Fitkin organized the Women's Foreign Missionary Auxiliary for her association of Holiness churches in the northeast. Ten years later the denomination that her own group helped form came into being without setting up a mission auxiliary. For the next seven years Susan Fitkin worked behind the scenes lobbying for official authorization of a world mission auxiliary. When the 1915 Nazarene General Assembly got around to setting up an auxiliary to promote awareness of its global mission outreach and raise financial and prayer support for it, church leaders turned to Susan Fitkin. For the next three decades she was that organization's president. That particular position was not a paid one, but she threw herself into it as though it were, using personal money to travel overseas as well as in the U.S. speaking in district missionary conventions and local churches.

In 1923 the denomination moved to a centralized budget system that for decades was called General Budget and now is known as the World Evangelism Fund. Using one cooperative fund curbed some administrative chaos and cut down on the number of fund-raising appeals being made to local churches by several "general boards." That move would also keep the denomination stabilized through the economic duress of the Great Depression of the 1930s. Through those years, the world mission administrative leader (as distinct from the promotion and publicity role of what is now the NMI) was J. G. Morrison. During lean financial times, he helped Susan Fitkin's auxiliary with fund-raising by repeatedly begging Nazarenes, "Can't you do just a little bit more?"

Early on, Nazarenes fell in love with great slogans and challenging goals. During the war-torn 1940s, world mission administrator C. Warren Jones promoted the reach toward "a million for missions," the giving of $1 million for missions in one year.

The 1944 General Assembly was what Franklin Cook has called "one of the most forward looking" ones for Nazarenes.[1] That is because, even with a World War still going on, Nazarenes took three key actions at that quadrennial gathering: (1) startup of a Spanish department that led to global publishing in scores of languages, (2) startup of the Radio League, which led to the global communication program of the denomination, and (3) startup of a graduate seminary that would eventually have a School of World Mission as one of its key components. The end of World War II brought more firsts for Nazarene missions. One was having the first non-Anglophone speaker at a General Assembly. The year was 1948, the city was St. Louis, and the speaker was Alfredo Del Rosso, itinerant Holiness evangelist from Italy who was merging his four independent congregations into the Church of the Nazarene. Del Rosso's presence at the General Assembly podium signaled a giant step forward in the process in which Nazarene leaders in other countries would be recognized as equal partners with those from the U.S., Great Britain, and Canada. Another key visitor at the 1948 General Assembly was Samuel Bhujabal from India, who was the denomination's first non-Anglo district superintendent. During a six-month tour of churches in the U.S., Bhujabal made quite a spectacular impression wearing his red turban.

During World War II some Nazarene missionaries were imprisoned by the Japanese in China. One of those prisoners, Mary Scott, came home after the war to become director of the promotional and fund-raising organization founded by Susan Fitkin (which would soon change its name to Nazarene World Missionary Society). At that point the organization was a somewhat independent though loyal auxiliary. Its focus was on mobilizing districts and local churches for the cause of global mission. It raised money, solicited prayer support, did mission education, and tried to make sure children and youth were involved in the local missions organization.

That movement of the Church of the Nazarene into new world areas accelerated through the 1960s, 1970s, and 1980s, and it exploded in the 1990s. By 2006, the denomination was working in more than 150 world areas. One key element of this expansion was the widespread use of volunteers. The door to that was opened in the early 1960s when youth groups began going to mission fields on short-term mission trips. That began calling into question the idea that global mission was something that used only professionals. By the 1970s, the internationalization of Nazarene church government began taking on clear outlines. That process had its beginning, however, more than a half a century earlier. Back in the 1920s the decision was made that general superintendents would preside at all district assemblies. The people who made that decision may not have realized what the outcome would eventually look like, but with that decision they put all districts worldwide on the same footing, a somewhat unusual decision in a time when people still divided the nations of the world into civilized and backward categories.

In 1972 a first-ever meeting of national superintendents was held without the presence of missionaries. While that meeting made some older missionaries uneasy, it emphatically showed that full responsibility was being put into the hands of world leaders.

Under Jerald Johnson's leadership in the 1970s, the denomination adopted a four-step process by which districts could become *regular* and thus be considered on a par with districts in the U.S., Great Britain, and Canada. The first missions area district to achieve this regular label was in Guatemala. Japan probably should have been the first. They had applied to become a regular district in the 1930s, but the denomination's General Board was caught off guard by their request and turned it down. At that point, American General Board members seemed not to know what to do with a mission field that wanted the right to send delegates to General Assemblies.

Now the process of becoming a regular district is well-defined, and regular districts have emerged all around the world. The strategy has been successful in places such as the island of La Gonave in Haiti. That island seemingly has few resources, but the church there is strong. A few years ago the Nazarene district of about 35 churches on that island went totally self-supporting. Since that time they have grown to more than 50 churches.

In 1974 the process of dividing the world into administrative regions began with the establishment of intercontinental zones. As regional leadership emerged, decision-making began to be shifted away from denominational headquarters in Kansas City. Such decentralization has enabled the Church of the Nazarene to administratively deal with the rapid pace of entering new areas (and probably has even fostered that). Then, the mission promotion organization that became NMI was moved from its auxiliary status on the general level to an integrated component of the World Mission office. On the district and local levels, Nazarene Missions International structures remained much the same.

It is difficult to predict what the Church of the Nazarene will look like a few decades from now. As General Assembly delegates increasingly reflect the diversity of the worldwide church, will the denomination's General Assembly remain the giant family gathering it has been? In trying to become a truly international church, Nazarenes have taken on an audacious undertaking. Only one or two other denominations have the goal of being an international church. Everyone else has opted for some variation of a loose federation of national churches rather than a unified global structure.

Denominational leadership has worked to move away from doing things that create financial dependency, and that has not been easy. Generally, funding from the World Evangelism Fund is now directed toward starting up things and one-time projects. In the last 30 years the denomination has moved completely away from subsidizing pastors' salaries on mission fields. Through Alabaster offerings and Work and Witness teams, the denomination sometimes helps with land purchases and building construction. In countries where there has been a pastoral pension program established, the denomination has sought to provide matching startup funds. Pastoral training programs are available at extremely low cost in impoverished areas of the world. Sometimes the denomination helps district and local leaders with travel costs to conferences of various kinds and responds to a few dire medical emergencies. Regional leadership facilitates evangelistic campaigns with the use of the *JESUS* film, one of the most fruitful partnerships of which the Church of the Nazarene has been a part. During less than a decade the *JESUS* film partnership teams showed the film to more than 40 million people, starting more than 10,000 new churches as a result.

All local Nazarene churches worldwide are now expected to contribute to the global World Evangelism Fund and other world mission offerings including Alabaster. A global mission giving goal for churches worldwide is set at about 10 percent of total local income. One purpose of having this goal in even the poorest countries of the world is to get local leaders' eyes off of survival and on to the global harvest field to which God is calling everyone.

Churches around the world joyfully embracing being participants in mission giving reflects what has happened since Nazarene mission leaders moved away from subsidizing local churches. As those subsidies have been phased out, the denomination has seen more aggressive evangelism and much greater spiritual maturity. In some areas, the church has seen a speeding up of growth after external pastoral subsidies were ended.

Nazarene general and regional leaders have tried to find ways to give people an incentive to fund programs locally. One of those is by treating leaders everywhere as equal partners with a voice and opportunities for service in the governmental structure. As was noted, the denomination uses a four-stage process through which districts (geographical groupings of churches) pass as they move toward full self-support. At each new level the district receives increased authority and voice in the international structure.

Money is not all, of course. There is that fourth self—self-theologizing. That has been slower to emerge and even more difficult to assess than the other three selfs, but it is now coming. To encourage this fourth self, the denomination established the graduate-level Asia-Pacific Nazarene Theological Seminary in the Philippines and through Nazarene Theological Seminary in Kansas City runs a doctoral degree program in Latin America. World Mission Literature also seeks to get into print material written by Nazarene writers around the world.

The Church of the Nazarene has also developed a multinational missionary force. Another thing that has contributed to the denomination's internationalization has been the decentralizing of the organization. Almost all funding, missionary deployment, and other similar decisions are now made in regional offices located in Singapore, Guatemala, Ecuador, the Caribbean, Switzerland, and South Africa rather than in the U.S. Each of those regional offices has people responsible for various ministry arms like NMI, NYI, Sunday School, *JESUS* film teams, and evangelism. In earlier years each country had a missionary as mission director. Now, with missionaries having been shifted out of several countries where work has matured, the regions have been divided into fields that usually encompass several countries and in which the work is directed or facilitated by a field strategy coordinator.

In the 21st century the Church of the Nazarene faces the same challenges that other mission organizations are encountering. There is, however, great optimism that Spirit-filled creativity and dogged determination will enable the church to successfully meet those challenges.

NOTES

Preface

1. Kenneth L. Woodward, et al., "The Changing Face of the New Church," *Newsweek* (April 16, 2001), 46-52.

Chapter 1

1. *Inn of the Sixth Happiness* was a 1958 movie on the life of Gladys Aylward. The 1986 film *The Mission* was loosely based on the life of a Jesuit priest in South America, and the 2006 *End of the Spear* film was about Nate Saint and other missionaries who died in Ecuador in 1956. The 1981 *Chariots of Fire* focused on Eric Liddell's participation in the 1924 Olympics rather than his later missionary service in China.

2. Phyllis Thompson, *A Transparent Woman: The Compelling Story of Gladys Aylward* (Grand Rapids: Zondervan, 1971), 183.

3. Paul Kollman, "The Roots and Consequences of the Term *Missio:* A Study in Religious Discursive Change," unpublished paper, University of Chicago (January 30, 1996), 2.

4. Johannes Verkuyl, *Contemporary Missiology* (Grand Rapids: Eerdmans, 1978), 3.

5. This is the Spanish spelling of the name often Anglicized as Raymond Lull.

6. Paul Orjala, "Retooling Our Missions Concepts," *Seminary Tower* (Summer 1965), 14-18.

7. Joon-Sik Park, "'As You Go': John Howard Yoder as a Mission Theologian," *Mennonite Quarterly Review* (July 2004), 370-71.

8. Richard Hutcheson, "Crisis in Overseas Mission: Shall We Leave It to the Independents?" *Christian Century* (March 18, 1981), 291.

9. John R. Stott, "Our God Is a Missionary God," sermon at Saddleback Church, Lake Forest, California (October 30, 2005).

10. Emil Brunner, *The Word and the World* (New York: Scribner's, 1931), 108.

11. Brooke Brown, interview and video presentation, Bethany, Oklahoma, First Church of the Nazarene (October 8, 2006).

12. Stephen Neill, *Creative Tension: The Duff Lectures* (London: Edinburgh House Press, 1959), 81.

13. Charles Van Engen, *Mission on the Way* (Grand Rapids: Baker, 1996), 152.

14. Ibid., 153.

15. John and Sylvia Ronsvalle, *Behind the Stained Glass Windows: Money Dynamics in the Church* (Grand Rapids: Baker, 1996).

16. John Piper, "Let the Nations Be Glad!" *Perspectives on the World Christian Movement,* 3rd ed., ed. Ralph Winter and Steven Hawthorne (Pasadena, Calif.: William Carey Library, 1999), 49-50.

17. Quoted by his colleague, Terry Barker. Southwest Oklahoma Nazarene Mission International annual convention (Bethany, Okla., June 6, 2006).

18. Quoted in *World Shapers,* ed. Vinita Hampton and Carol Plueddemann (Wheaton, Ill.: Harold Shaw, 1991), 3.

19. Dean Nelson, "Paul Orjala: Living the Language of God," *Holiness Today,* vol. 2, no. 10 (October 2000), 10.

20. Ray Tallman, *Introduction to World Mission* (Dubuque, Iowa: Kendall/Hunt Publishing, 1989), 17.

21. Paul E. Little, *How to Give Away Your Faith* (Downers Grove, Ill.: Inter-Varsity Christian Fellowship, 1966), 25.

22. Thomas L. Austin, "The Missionary Call," *Evangelical Dictionary of World Missions* (Grand Rapids: Baker, 2000), 645.

23. Kenichi Ohmae, *The End of the Nation State: How Regional Economies Will Soon Reshape the World* (New York: Simon and Schuster, 1995), 5.

24. Saskia Sassen, *Globalization and Its Discontents* (New York: New Press, 1998), xxv.

25. Brian Howell, "Globalization, Ethnicity, and Cultural Authenticity: Implications for Theological Education," *Christian Scholars Review,* vol. xxxv, no. 3 (Spring 2006), 25.

26. Philip Jenkins, *The Next Christendom: The Coming of Global Christianity* (New York: Oxford University Press, 2002), 81.

27. David Bosch, *Transforming Mission* (New York: Orbis, 1993), 4.

Chapter 2

1. Ralph Winter, "Missions" seminar, One in Love Conference (Montrose, Pa., January 5-8, 2005).

2. Gordon Wenham, *Word Biblical Commentary,* vol. 1, ed. John Watts (Waco, Tex.: Word Books, 1987), 32; c.f. W. H. Bennett, "Adam," *A Dictionary of the Bible,* vol. 1, ed. James Hastings (New York: Charles Scribner's Sons, 1898), 36.

3. Johannes Verkuyl, *Contemporary Missiology* (Grand Rapids: Eerdmans, 1978), 92.

4. Rick Wood, "Destination 2000 AD: Teaching the Missions Basis of the Bible," *Mission Frontiers* (May-June, 1994), 19 ff.

5. Martin McNamara, trans., *The Aramaic Bible: The Targums* (Collegeville, Minn.: Liturgical Press, 1994), 69.

6. Nina Gunter, keynote address, Quadrennial South Central Region Nazarene Missions International Workshop (September 26, 2003).

7. D. W. Van Winkle, "The Relationship of the Nations to Yahweh and to Israel in Isaiah XL-LV," *Vetus Testamentum,* vol. 35, fasc. 4 (October 1985), 449-50.

8. Dan Davidson, Dave Davidson, and George Verwer, *God's Great Ambition: A Mega Motivating Crash Course on God's Heart* (Waynesboro, Ga.: STL/Authentic, 2001), 6.

9. Thomas Carlisle, *You! Jonah!* (Grand Rapids: Eerdmans, 1968), 63-64.

10. J. Howard Edington, "The Field Is the World," address to Presbyterian Missions Conference (Atlanta: Peachtree Presbyterian Church, September 1998).

11. Alex Deasley, lecture, "The Church in Global Mission" (Nazarene Theological Seminary, February 16, 2000).

12. Quoted in Davidson, Davidson, and Verwer, *God's Great Ambition,* 45.

13. Eugene A. Nida, *God's Word in Man's Language* (New York: Harper and Brothers, 1952), 67.

14. Paul R. Orjala, *God's Mission Is My Mission* (Kansas City: Nazarene Publishing House, 1985), 20.

15. Brunner, *Word and the World,* 108.

Chapter 3

1. Michael Jaffarian, "What the WCE 2 Numbers Show" (excerpted from "The Statistical State of the Missionary Enterprise," *Missiology*), *International Bulletin of Missionary Research,* vol. 26, issue 3 (July 2002), 130.

2. Adrian Hastings, ed., *A World History of Christianity* (Grand Rapids: Eerdmans, 1999), 25.

3. George G. Hunter III, *The Celtic Way of Evangelism* (Nashville: Abingdon Press, 2000), 19-20.

4. Craig Sheppard, e-mail to Howard Culbertson from Kosovo (September 13, 2006).

5. Quoted in R. G. Tiedemann, "China and Its Neighbours," in Hastings, ed., *World History of Christianity,* 370.

6. Kenneth Scott Latourette, *A History of Christianity,* vol. 1 (Peabody, Mass.: Prince Press, 1997), 274.

7. Quoted in John Dear, *You Will Be My Witnesses* (Maryknoll, N.Y.: Orbis Books, 2006), 42.

8. Delno C. West, "Medieval Ideas of Apocalyptic Mission and the Early Franciscans in Mexico," *The Americas,* vol. XLV, no. 3 (January 1989), 293-313.

9. J. Herbert Kane, *A Concise History of the Christian World Mission* (Grand Rapids: Baker, 1982), 77.

10. Frederick Klees, *The Pennsylvania Dutch* (New York: MacMillan Company, 1950), 98.

11. Mark A. Noll, *Turning Points: Decisive Moments in the History of Christianity* (Grand Rapids: Baker, 2000), 240.

12. Quoted in Bob Kelly, *Worth Repeating* (Grand Rapids: Kregel Publications, 2003), 303.

13. Ralph Winter, "Four Men, Three Eras, Two Transitions," *Perspectives on the World Christian Movement,* 3rd ed., ed. Ralph Winter and Steven Hawthorne (Pasadena, Calif.: William Carey Library, 1999), 254.

14. J. E. Hutton, *A History of the Moravian Church* (Kila, Mont.: Kessinger Publishing, 2004 reprint of 1909 ed.), 174.

15. Kenneth Mulholland, "Planks in the Platform of Modern Missions," Missions and Evangelism Lectureship at Dallas Theological Seminary (November 2-5, 1997).

16. Quoted in Daniel J. Fleming, *Marks of a World Christian* (New York: Association Press, 1919), 84.

17. Lewis Drummond, *Women of Awakenings* (Grand Rapids: Kregel Publications, 1997), 247.

18. Ralph Winter, "The Diminishing Task," *Mission Frontiers* (November-December 1990), 4.

19. Noll, *Turning Points,* 269.

Chapter 4

1. Arthur Judson Brown, *The Foreign Missionary* (New York: Fleming H. Revell, 1932), 234.

2. For an excellent evaluation of Winter's sodality/modality concept, see Orlando Costas, *The Church and Its Mission: A Shattering Critique from the Third World* (Wheaton, Ill.: Tyndale House Publishers, 1974), 165-74.

3. Quoted in Randy C. Alcorn, *Money, Possessions, and Eternity* (Carol Stream, Ill.: Tyndale House Publishers, 2003), 243.

4. W. Harold Fuller, *Mission-Church Dynamics* (Pasadena, Calif.: William Carey Library, 1980), Appendix G.

Chapter 5

1. Patrick Johnstone and Jason Mandryk, *Operation World: When We Pray God Works, 21st Century Edition* (Waynesboro, Ga.: Paternoster USA, 2001), 21.

2. Wesley D. Tracy, "The Lamb Wins," *Herald of Holiness* (May 1993), 4.

3. Stephen B. Bevans and Roger P. Schroeder, *Constants in Context: A Theology of Mission for Today* (Maryknoll, N.Y.: Orbis, 2004), 279.

4. "The Fight for God," *The Economist,* vol. 365, issue 8304 (December 19, 2002), 32-33.

5. Patrick Johnstone, *The Church Is Bigger than You Think* (Pasadena, Calif.: William Carey Library, 1998), 114.

6. Ibid.

7. Simon Elegant, "The War for China's Soul, *TIME* (August 28, 2006), 43.

8. Timothy C. Morgan and David Neff, "The Church Vulnerable," *Christianity Today,* vol. 28, issue 4 (April 2004), 87-89.

9. Jaime A. Florcruz, et al., "Inside China's Search for Its Soul," *TIME* (October 4, 1999), 73.

10. Jenkins, *Next Christendom: The Coming of Global Christianity,* 2.

11. Andrew Walls, "The Expansion of Christianity: An Interview with Andrew Walls," *The Christian Century* (August 2-9, 2000), 792-99.

12. Woodward, et al., "The Changing Face of the Church," 46-53.

13. Paul Hiebert, "Cultural Differences and the Communication of the Gospel," in Winter and Hawthorne, ed., *Perspectives on the World Christian Movement,* 381.

14. Sherwood Lingenfelter, *Transforming Culture,* 2nd ed. (Grand Rapids: Baker, 1998), 12-13.

15. Lesslie Newbigin, *The Gospel in a Pluralist Society* (Grand Rapids: Eerdmans, 1989), 152.

16. Bong Bin Rho, "Four Reasons for Educating Asian Theologians in Asia," *Pulse* (November 21, 1984), 4-6.

17. Joon-Sik Park, "'As You Go': John Howard Yoder as a Mission Theologian," *Mennonite Quarterly Review* (July 2004), 369.

18. Tom Lochner, "Preacher Reflects on Waning Christian Values," *Contra Costa Times* (October 24, 2005).

19. Harvey Cox, quoted on the back cover of Jenkins, *Next Christendom.*

20. Jenkins, *Next Christendom,* 203.

21. Paul Orjala, "Retooling Our Missions Concepts," *Seminary Tower* (Summer 1965), 14-18.

22. Paul McKaughan, Dellana O'Brien, and William O'Brien, *Choosing a Future for U.S. Missions* (Monrovia, Calif.: MARC, 1998), 85.

23. This story was originally published in Chuck Gailey, *Mission in the Third Millennium* (Kansas City: Nazarene Publishing House, 2001), 27-28.

24. Terry Barker, personal interview with Howard Culbertson (Bethany, Okla., June 4, 2006).

25. Edward R. Dayton and David A. Fraser, *Planning Strategies for World Evangelization* (Grand Rapids: Eerdmans, 1990), 41.

26. Glenn Schwartz, "Dependency," in Winter and Hawthorne, ed., *Perspectives on the World Christian Movement,* 592.

27. Klees, *Pennsylvania Dutch,* 110.

28. William Reyburn, "Identification in the Missionary Task," in *Readings in Missionary Anthropology, II,* ed. William Smalley (Pasadena, Calif.: William Carey Library, 1978), 454.

Chapter 6

1. J. D. Douglas, ed., *Let the Earth Hear His Voice: International Congress on World Evangelization* (Minneapolis: World Wide Publications, 1975), 6.

2. Honorato T. Reza, *Our Task for Today* (Kansas City: Nazarene Publishing House, 1963), 20.

3. Rob Moll, "The Gospel for All People: It's Not Your Father's Mission Movement," *Christianity Today,* online version (November 10, 2005).

4. Rob Moll, "Missions Incredible," *Christianity Today* (March 2006), 30.

5. Johnstone, *The Church Is Bigger than You Think,* 115; see also Johnstone and Mandryk, *Operation World,* 747-51.

6. Ibid., 6.

7. Phill Butler, *The Power of Partnership* (Seattle: InterDev, 1998), 21.

8. Phill Butler, *The State of the Church and World Evangelism at the End of the '90s* (Seattle: InterDev, 1999), 17.

9. Donald McGavran, *Understanding Church Growth* (Grand Rapids: Eerdmans, 1970), 82.

10. Russell G. Shubin, "An Early Homecoming—A Tribute to Marilyn Lewis," *Mission Frontiers* (April 2000).

11. John L. Allen Jr., "Recovering Mission History—Through Third World Eyes," *National Catholic Reporter* (October 18, 2002).

12. David Hesselgrave, "The Role of Culture in Communication," in *Perspectives on the World Christian Movement,* ed. Winter and Hawthorne, 393.

13. Timothy Olonade, "Nigerian Church Takes the Gospel Back to Jerusalem with Vision 50:15," *Lausanne World* (June 2006).

14. Orjala, "Retooling Our Missions Concepts," 14-18.

Chapter 7

1. William Dunkerley wrote "In Christ There Is No East or West" for the *Pageant of Darkness and Light* at the London Missionary Society's exhibition "The Orient in London," which ran from 1908 to 1914. Many hymnals credit the words to John Oxenham, Dunkerley's pseudonym.

2. Bob Sjogren, *Unveiled at Last* (Seattle: YWAM Publishing, 1992), 29.

3. Edward B. Tylor, *Primitive Culture: Researches into the Development of Mythology, Philosophy, Religion, Language, Art, and Custom,* 2 vols., 7th ed. (New York: Brentano's, 1924 [original 1871]), 1.

4. Conrad Phillip Kottak, *Mirror for Humanity: A Concise Introduction to Cultural Anthropology,* 5th ed. (New York: McGraw-Hill, 2006), 63.

5. Ashley Montagu, *Man's Most Dangerous Myth: The Fallacy of Race* (London: Oxford, 1974), 444.

6. Rod Spidahl, "Making the Most of Short Term Muslim/Christian Relationships," Seminar at Fellowship of Short Term Mission Leaders annual conference (Atlanta, October 13, 2006). Quote was credited to reflections on material from Andrew Walls and Lesslie Newbigin.

7. This story was originally published in Gailey, *Mission in the Third Millennium,* 41-42.

8. Lula Schmelzenbach, *Missionary Prospector: A Life Story of Harmon Schmelzenbach* (Kansas City: Beacon Hill Press, 1937), 13.

9. Julie Woolery, e-mail to Howard Culbertson from Manila, Philippines (August 14, 2006).

10. Donald Larson, "The Viable Missionary: Learner Trader, Story Teller," in *Perspectives on the World Christian Movement,* ed. Winter and Hawthorne, 438-43.

11. Miriam Adeney, "Esther Across Cultures: Indigenous Leadership Roles for Women," *Missiology* (July 1987), 324.

12. E. Thomas and Elizabeth S. Brewster, *Bonding and the Missionary Task: Establishing a Sense of Belonging* (Pasadena, Calif.: Lingua House, 1987).

13. Richard Zanner, "Ten Imperatives Which Apply to All Christian Leaders," *Trans-African* (March/April 1995), 13-15.

14. Samuel Zwemer, *The Unoccupied Fields of Africa and Asia* (New York: Student Volunteer Movement for Foreign Missions, 1911), 222.

Chapter 8

1. This story was originally recounted in Charles R. Gailey, "Language as a Means of Conflict Resolution in the International Church," paper presented to the Association of Nazarenes in Social Research (February 9, 1990), 2.

2. "Praying Is Best in the Mother Tongue," *EKD Bulletin* 3 (2003).

3. J. Herbert Kane, *Life and Work on the Mission Field* (Grand Rapids: Baker, 1980), 130.

4. Quoted in Winter, "Four Men, Three Eras, Two Transitions," 260.

5. James and Marti Hefley, *Uncle Cam: The Story of William Cameron Townsend* (Waco, Tex.: Word, 1974), 182.

6. *Willowbank Report: Report of a Consultation on Gospel and Culture,* Lausanne Occasional Papers, no. 2 (Lausanne Committee for World Evangelization, 1978).

7. Johnstone and Mandryk, *Operation World,* 698.

8. E. Thomas Brewster, "Building Cross-Cultural Relations/Ministering Cross-Culturally," videotaped lecture (Pasadena, Calif.: United States Center for World Mission, n.d.).

9. Albert Mehrabian, *Silent Messages* (Belmont, Calif.: Wadsworth Publishing Company, 1971), 42-44.

10. This is the first phrase of Psalm 41:13 in English, Spanish, French, Romanian, Maori, and Haitian Creole.

11. Quoted in James Smith and Richard J. Foster, *Spiritual Formation Workbook, a Revised Edition* (New York: HarperCollins, 1999), 65.

Chapter 9

1. Seth Barnes, "Ten Emerging Trends in Student Missions," *Network* (June 2000), 19.

2. Roger Peterson, opening presentation at annual conference, Fellowship of Short-Term Mission Leaders, Atlanta (October 11, 2006).

3. David Armstrong, e-mail to Howard Culbertson (January 3, 2007).

4. Kurt Ver Beek, "Assessing the Impact of Short-Term Missions," paper presented at the North Central Region meeting of the Evangelical Missiological Society (Deerfield, Ill., April 9, 2005).

5. John Nyquist and Paul G. Hiebert, "Short-term Missions?" *Trinity World Forum,* vol. 20, no. 3 (1995), 3.

6. Julietta K. Arthur, *Retire to Action: A Guide to Voluntary Service* (Nashville: Abingdon, 1969), 38.

7. James Engel and Jerry Jones, *Baby Boomers and the Future of World Missions* (Orange, Calif.: Management Development Associates, 1989), 23.

8. Quoted in Croft Pentz, *The Complete Book of Zingers* (Wheaton, Ill.: Tyndale House Publishers, 1990), 201.

9. Roger P. Peterson and Timothy D. Peterson, *Is Short-Term Mission Really Worth the Time and Money?* (Minneapolis: STEM Ministries, 1991), 28.

10. Stan Guthrie, *Missions in the Third Millennium: 21 Key Trends for the 21st Century* (Maryknoll, N.Y.: Orbis, 2000), 89.

11. David Hayse, interview by Charles Gailey (December 10, 2001).

12. Ken Baker, "Boomers, Busters, and Missions: Things Are Different Now," *Evangelical Missions Quarterly,* vol. 33, no. 1 (January 1997), 70-77.

13. Craig Sheppard, e-mail to Howard Culbertson (September 13, 2006).

14. Reuben Staines, "Church Leaders Condemn 'Religious Killing' of Kim Sun-il," *The Korea Times* (July 15, 2004).

15. John Piper, *Let the Nations Be Glad!* (Grand Rapids: Baker, 1993), 111.

16. Douglas W. Terry, "Short-termers over the Long Run: Assessing Missional Effective-

ness of Non-Career, Mid-term Nazarene Missionaries," unpublished dissertation (Asbury Theological Seminary, 2002), 10.

17. Ibid., 199.

18. Ibid., 201.

19. Margaret Carlson, "All Together Now," *TIME,* vol. 159, no. 6 (February 11, 2002), 33.

Chapter 10

1. Sherwood Eddy, *Pathfinders of the World Missionary Crusade* (New York: Abingdon-Cokesbury, 1945), 131.

2. Elisabeth Elliot, *The Shadow of the Almighty* (New York: Harper and Row, 1958), 15.

3. Jay Gary, "Agenda for Students in the 80s: The Phenomena of Youth Mission Movements in History," *International Journal of Frontier Missions,* vol. 1:1 (January 1, 1984), 25.

4. George Verwer, "If You're Not Called to Stay, Then Go!" cassette tape (Oasis Audio, June 2000).

5. Claudia Stevenson, *World Mission* (October 1991), 18.

6. That phrase "Fear the LORD," which is frequently used in Scripture, does not mean panic or terror but rather an awe that would be expected on the human side of a divine/human covenant relationship.

7. John Seaman, e-mail to Howard Culbertson (July 22, 2006).

8. Charles Hadden Spurgeon, *Lectures to My Students* (Grand Rapids: Zondervan Publishing House, 1954), 26.

9. Roger Winans, *Gospel over the Andes* (Kansas City: Beacon Hill Press, 1955), 17.

10. Quoted in Curtis Hutson, *Punch Lines* (Murfreesboro, Tenn.: Sword of the Lord Publishers, 2000), 154. Variations of this are also credited to G. K. Chesterson, Thomas Carlyle, and Charles Haddon Spurgeon.

11. For a look at the rich and varied ministry of William Carey, see Vishal and Ruth Mangalwadi, "Who (Really) Was William Carey," in *Perspectives on the World Christian Movement,* ed. Winter and Hawthorne, 525-28.

12. Mark Elmore, lecture to cultural anthropology class (Bethany, Okla.: Southern Nazarene University, August 26, 2006).

13. Quoted in James Dobson, *Straight Talk to Men and Their Wives* (Waco, Tex.: Word Publishing Company, 1980), 92.

14. Kimberly Jayne Rushing, term paper (Southern Nazarene University, Spring 2000).

15. Esther Carson Winans, handwritten note on her application for missionary service, circa 1914 (Kansas City: Nazarene Theological Seminary Library collection).

Chapter 11

1. Harold Lindsell, "Fundamentals for a Philosophy of the Christian Mission," *The Theology of the Christian Mission,* ed. Gerald Anderson (New York: McGraw-Hill, 1961), 239.

2. Quoted in *The Fundamentalist,* vol. 20, no. 1 (May/June 2006), 3.

3. Donald A. McGavran, *Understanding Church Growth,* rev. ed. (Grand Rapids: Eerdmans, 1980), 40.

4. Wesley L. Duewel, *Ablaze for God* (Grand Rapids: Zondervan, 1989), 238.

5. Quoted in J. Herschel Caudill, "The Church That Stands," *Vital Christianity,* vol. 99, no. 12 (June 24, 1979), 3.

6. Johnstone and Mandryk, *Operation World,* 460.

7. David Mosher, e-mail to Charles R. Gailey (May 16, 1997).

8. David Mosher, e-mail to Charles R. Gailey (October 8, 1997).

9. Paul Orjala, *Get Ready to Grow* (Kansas City: Beacon Hill Press of Kansas City, 1978), 105.

10. Quoted in Robert E. Webber, *Ancient-Future Evangelism: Making Your Church a Faith-Forming Community* (Grand Rapids: Baker, 2003), 13.

11. Paul G. Hiebert, *Anthropological Insights for Missionaries* (Grand Rapids: Baker Books, 1985), 93-94.

12. Brett Elder, "Dismantling the Ecclesiastical Welfare System," *Occasional Bulletin, Evangelical Missiological Society,* vol. 15, no. 3 (Fall 2003), 2.

13. Fred Barlow, *Profiles in Evangelism* (Murfreesboro, Tenn.: Sword of the Lord Publishers, 1976), 33-34.

14. Philip Schaff, *Medieval Christianity,* vol. 4 of *History of the Christian Church* (Grand Rapids: Eerdmans, 1979), 94.

15. Basil Miller, *Miracle in Cape Verde: The Story of Everette and Garnet Howard* (Kansas City: Beacon Hill Press, 1950), 100.

16. Quoted in Edward R. Dayton and David A. Fraser, *Planning Strategies for World Evangelization* (Grand Rapids: Eerdmans, 1990), 175.

17. Gailyn Van Rheenen, *Missions: Biblical Foundations and Contemporary Strategies* (Grand Rapids: Zondervan, 1996), 141-42.

18. Tim Eby, "Hope," in L. David Duff, *To the Ends of the Earth* (Kansas City: Nazarene Publishing House, 2001), 40-41.

Chapter 12

1. Some of the material in this chapter appeared previously in Charles Gailey, "Switching Channels—Paradigm Shifts in Mission," *Called to Teach,* ed. Gail Sawrie (Kansas City: Nazarene Publishing House, 2002).

2. David Barrett and Todd Johnson, "Annual Statistical Tables," *International Bulletin of Missionary Research,* vol. 29, issue 1 (January 2005), 25.

3. Pat Morley, "24 Leadership Ideas for Your Men's Ministry," *A Look in the Mirror* newsletter, no. 126.

4. Ray Bakke, *Urban Christian* (Downers Grove, Ill.: InterVarsity, 1987), 28.

5. Robert A. Blincoe, U.S. director of Frontiers, e-mail to Howard Culbertson (August 23, 2006).

6. Quoted in Clive Price, "It's God's Hour for Iran," *Charisma* (June 2004), 65.

7. Consultation on Mission Language and Metaphors, unpublished document (School of World Mission, Fuller Theological Seminary, June 1-3, 2000), 1.

8. Phil Parshall, *Muslim Evangelism: Contemporary Approaches to Contextualization* (Waynesboro, Ga.: Gabriel Publishing, 2003), 29-30.

9. H. L. Richard, "Rethinking Forum Convenes in Chicago," *Mission Frontiers* (May-June 2004), 9.

10. Butler, *State of the Church and World Evangelism,* 14.

11. Don Richardson, *Eternity in Their Hearts* (Ventura, Calif.: Regal Books, 1981), 32.

12. John D. Ellenberger, "Is Hell a Proper Motivation for Missions?" *Through No Fault of Their Own: The Fate of Those Who Have Never Heard,* ed. William V. Crockett and James G. Sigountos (Grand Rapids: Baker, 1991), 223.

13. Paul Hiebert, "Flaw of the Excluded Middle," *Missiology* 10:1 (January 1982), 35-47, and later reprinted in his book *Anthropological Reflections on Missiological Issues* (Grand Rapids: Baker, 1994).

14. For an in-depth review of this book, see Charles Gailey, "Review of *Engaging the Enemy: How to Fight and Defeat Territorial Spirits* by C. Peter Wagner," *Missiology,* vol. 22 (April 1994), 250.

Chapter 13

1. Harold Briley, "An Adventurer with a Purpose," *The Times* (London, England) (May 15, 1995).

2. John R. Mott, *The Evangelization of the World in This Generation* (New York: Student Volunteer Movement for Foreign Missions, 1901), 145.

3. Mendell Taylor, *Fifty Years of Nazarene Missions,* vol. 1 (Kansas City: Nazarene Publishing House, 1952), 9.

4. Ralph Winter, quoted in "Reaching New Heights and Hearts," *Mission Frontiers* (March 2001), 34.

5. Kenneth W. Osbeck, *Devotional Warm-Ups for the Church Choir* (Grand Rapids: Kregel Publications, 2001), 46.

6. William Remfry Hunt, *Heathenism Under the Searchlight: The Call of the Far East* (London: Morgan and Scott, 1908), 139.

7. R. A. Torrey, *The Power of Prayer* (Grand Rapids: Zondervan, 1963 reprint [c. 1924 by Fleming H. Revell]), 65.

8. David Penman, quoted in John Piper, *A Godward Life: Savoring the Supremacy of God in All of Life* (Sisters, Oreg.: Multnomah, 1997), 155.

9. Jan A. B. Jongeneel, "The Legacy of Francois Elbertus Daubanton," *International Bulletin of Missionary Research,* vol. 29, issue 2 (April 2005), 95.

10. John R. Mott, *The Pastor and Modern Missions: A Plea for Leadership in World Evangelization* (New York: Student Volunteer Movement for Foreign Missions, 1904), 50, 52-53.

11. Mike Stachura, "Passing the Torch," presidential keynote address, regional conferences, Advancing Churches in Missions Commitment (Fall 1996).

12. Steve Cooley, "The Call of Susan Fitkin," *Herald of Holiness* 74, no. 20 (October 15, 1985), 9.

13. Phyllis Perkins, *Women in Nazarene Missions: Embracing the Legacy* (Kansas City: Nazarene Publishing House, 1994), 77.

14. Quoted in Dave Geisler, "Keith Green Commands a New Generation to Go into Missions," *Mission Frontiers* (August 1999), 43.

Chapter 14

1. Leonard Sweet, *SoulTsunami* (Grand Rapids: Zondervan, 1999), 17.

2. "The Past Imperfect," *TIME* (July 15, 1996), 44. Some dispute whether Thomas Watson actually said this.

3. Gustav Warneck, *Outline of a History of Protestant Missions from the Reformation to the Present Time,* 3rd ed. (New York: Fleming H. Revell, 1904), 54.

4. Quoted in Fleming, *Marks of a World Christian,* 96.

5. Stan Davis and Christopher Meyer, "What Will Replace the Tech Economy?" *TIME* (May 22, 2000), 77.

6. Butler, *State of the Church and World Evangelism,* 18.

7. David Bryant, "Concerts of Prayer," *Mission Frontiers* (March 1983), 8.

8. A. B. Simpson, "Mission Work," *The Word, Work, and World* 9 (special number, 1887), 104.

9. Jerry Gass, online class submission for the "Global Evangelism" course at Nazarene Bible College, Colorado Springs (September 1, 2006).

10. Rick Warren, *The Purpose-Driven Life* (Grand Rapids: Zondervan, 2002), 297, 300, 301, 304.

11. Barrett and Johnson, "Annual Statistical Tables," 29.

12. John A. Siewert and Dotsey Welliver, ed., *Mission Handbook: U.S. and Canadian Ministries Overseas, 2001-2003* (Wheaton, Ill.: EMIS, 2000), 45.

13. Barrett and Johnson, "Annual Statistical Tables," 29.

14. "Christian Persecution," *NCN Weekly Summary* (January 21, 2000), 1.

15. Brent Hulett, e-mail to Charles R. Gailey (January 2000).

16. Terry Read, "Needed: A Theology of Suffering," *Holiness Today* (August 2001), 27.

17. Quoted in Charles R. Gailey, "Persecution Today: A New Holocaust," *Holiness Today,* vol. 4, no. 11 (November 2002), 14.

18. Quoted in James Eckman, *Exploring Church History* (Wheaton, Ill.: Crossway Books, 2002), 19.

19. Russell Shubin, "What Is True Spirituality?" *Mission Frontiers* (March-April, 1999), 16.

20. Ibid.

21. Elisabeth Elliot, personal conversation with Charles Gailey (Alton Bay, N.H., September 1, 2002).

22. Read, "Needed: A Theology of Suffering," 28.

23. This story was originally told in Gailey, "Persecution Today: A New Holocaust," 14.

24. This story was originally published in Gailey, *Mission in the Third Millennium,* 82-84.

25. Quoted from an e-mail sent to Charles Gailey in June 2000.

Appendix

1. Franklin Cook, e-mail to Howard Culbertson (December 11, 2006).

GLOSSARY

4-14 window—period of life from 4 to 14 years of age, a time when many people accept Christ and when many missionaries receive their call

10/40 Window—Luis Bush's designation for that area or window of the globe that lies between 10 degrees and 40 degrees north of the equator and stretches east from North Africa to Asia

Abrahamic covenant—Yahweh's promise to give Abraham a great name, a large family, and land with the understanding that he would pass on divine blessings to all peoples

acculturation—process by which an adult learns a new culture

action-to-information ratio—amount of information it takes to move people to action

Alopen—a missionary, likely of Nestorian tradition, who took the gospel to China in 635

animism—belief that daily life is an interaction with supernatural spirits that can be manipulated

apostle—from a Greek word that means "one sent forth"; its meaning thus parallels that of *missionary*, which comes from a Latin word meaning "sent one"

appropriate technology—technology particularly suited to the culture and environment where it is used

Augustine—a Benedictine commissioned in 596 by Gregory the Great as leader of a missionary group being sent to England

bicultural person—someone who has learned two cultures well enough to be seen as an insider in either one

bonding—forming of close relationships between expatriate missionaries and their adopted cultures

Carey, William—bivocational English Baptist pastor who became a pioneer missionary to India in 1792 and is now known as the father of the modern missionary movement

catalyst—in Christian mission, an outsider such as a missionary who initiates and facilitates but does not become a permanent part of the situation

church planting—establishment of new Christian congregations as an integral part of an outreach strategy

closure—finishing the Great Commission task of making disciples in every people group

colporteur—person using the itinerant selling of Bibles and religious books as an evangelistic strategy

contextualization—clothing the essentials of the gospel, including the church, in the forms of a culture so that insiders do not see the gospel or the church as foreign imports

creative access areas—places in the world that are politically resistant or even closed to traditional Christian missionary activity and where Christians seek to minister in creative ways such as teaching English, doing medical work, getting a job, or setting up a business

cultural adjustment—four- to five-stage emotional roller-coaster process of acculturation that includes gloomy and depressing times as well as exhilarating ones

cultural anthropology—study of humanity, especially as it relates to cultures

cultural evolution—a now outdated theory that the cultural universals of all societies are moving from simple to complex and from primitive to more civilized

cultural relativity—the attempt to understand societies and people groups on their own terms and with their own value systems

cultural universals—categories of things like communication, law, economics, and religious systems that occur in every culture

culture—complex, integrated coping mechanism consisting of learned concepts and behavior, underlying perspectives (worldview), resulting products, customs and rituals, and material artifacts

culture-bound—in linguistics, those words used in a language that are very difficult to express in another language because they refer to something present only in one particular culture

culture shock—part of the cultural adjustment process in which feelings of disorientation and frustration are experienced as people try to assimilate unfamiliar things of a new culture

dependency—lack of independence or self-sufficiency; in Christian mission it usually refers to financial dependency

Diaspora—the dispersion or scattering of a people group outside of their native area

dynamic equivalence—thought-for-thought translation style first articulated by Eugene Nida that attempts to evoke the same response in readers that was experienced by the original readers

ecclesiology—beliefs about the nature, function, and purpose of church, a doctrine that missiologist John Howard Yoder said is inextricably linked to missiology

enculturation—process in which children learn the culture of the society in which they are raised; sociologists give the name socialization to this process

ethnocentrism—judging things in other cultures by the values and motivations of one's own

excluded middle—as it relates to Christian mission, the idea that all that exists is God and the created world; there are no other significant supernatural realities

exegeting the culture—the process of analyzing and interpreting the attitudes, customs, and ideas of a particular area, including the various social, religious, economic, and other cues and clues by which those within a society make sense of their own activities

expatriate (often shortened to **expat**)–someone who is in a country other than that of his or her upbringing

faith missions–individuals or organizations who have no parent body helping to mobilize financial support; the largest Protestant missionary sending organizations are now faith missions; "praying in support" is often the phrase used to talk about how finances are sought after

fieldwork—living among a people for the purpose of learning their culture

form—object, sound, or action to which people have attached special meaning

fourth self—Paul Hiebert's call for self-theologizing to be added to the three-selfs of Venn and Anderson

frontier missions—missionary efforts in unreached or underevangelized areas

function—significance or meaning placed upon an object, sound, or action by a particular culture

functional substitute—alternative form that provides the basically same function for a culture as the original

futurology—forecasting the future based on current trends

gateway cities—100 cities that missiologists consider key doorways through which the gospel may flow to unreached cultural groups

general call—the call to the Church as a whole to get the gospel to every person; by implication, then, every Christian is to be a witness for God

globalization—the unprecedented 20th- and 21st-century integration of economic, cultural, political, and social systems across political boundaries and geographic distances

glocalization—a word combining globalization and localization to describe the emergence of local adaptations within the larger processes of globalization

gôyim—Hebrew word used about 500 times in the Old Testament that means "nations" or "peoples"

Great Commission—Jesus' words in Matthew 28:19-20 in which He sends His followers to all nations; words that are sometimes called the marching orders of the Church

Haystack Prayer Meeting—an 1806 prayer meeting for world evangelism by Williams College students who had sought shelter from rain in the lee of a haystack

heart language—a person's first language; also called native language or mother tongue

holistic—the perspective that sees the emotional, spiritual, social, and mental well-being of people as one unified package

homogenous unit principle—Donald McGavran's enunciation of the idea that people like to become Christian without feeling they have to cross social, class, economic, or cultural barriers

identification—assuming the characteristics of others in order to create a bond; one of the characteristics of mission that grounds it in the divine Trinity

incarnational—living out the life of Christ and the ideals of His kingdom before unbelievers

inclusivism—view that while Christ alone saves, a person could conceivably be led to respond to God's grace through natural revelation or even visions and dreams

indigenization—transforming something to fit a local culture so that it has a feel of belonging to that environment; a concept similar to though not identical to contextualization

indigenous church—a church that looks and feels like it belongs in a given cultural context rather than being a foreign import

informant—in linguistics, a native speaker of a language who helps someone trying to learn it; in anthropology, an insider of a culture who helps an outsider understand it

International Day of Prayer for the Persecuted Church—day of prayer in mid-November observed on behalf of those churches in areas where there is governmentally sanctioned persecution

inverted homesickness—term used by Samuel Zwemer to describe the feelings missionaries have when upon returning to their own homeland they have an intense longing to go back to their place of missionary service

***JESUS* film**—Campus Crusade for Christ's film on the life of Christ that is used as an evangelistic tool; the most-watched full-length film in history

Judson, Adoniram—missionary to Burma in early 1800s; one of the pioneers of the modern missionary movement in the United States

labels—when referring to people, the prejudicial use of geographic or biological references

language—structured system of arbitrary symbols, usually vocal, by means of which people interact and cooperate

Lausanne Covenant—a comprehensive manifesto promoting worldwide Christian evangelism that was written and adopted by 2,300 evangelicals at the 1974 International Congress on World Evangelization in Lausanne, Switzerland

Law of Apostasy—Islamic law based on the *Hadith,* which allows the killing of any Muslim who converts to Christianity

linguist—specialist in languages

Macedonian call—a call for Paul, already a missionary, to begin evangelizing in Europe

magical approach—effort to manipulate the supernatural in order to secure one's own desires or will

majority world—non-western or non Euro-American nations comprising approximately two-thirds of the world's land area, and in which reside approximately two-thirds of the world's population

mass evangelism—communication of the gospel to large numbers of people at the same time

mentor—one who provides guidance and recommendations to someone regarding his or her behavior and courses of action

Mills, Samuel—leader in 19th-century mission in the United States who was instrumental in founding the Board of Commissioners for Foreign Missions in 1810

mimicry—in language learning, trying to copy a speaker after closely observing the movements of that person's teeth, lips, tongue, and tone

Missio Dei—Latin phrase meaning the "mission of God"

missiologist—scholar whose teaching and writing shapes the study and doing of mission

missiology—literally "the study of mission"; a discipline that integrates theology, history, and the social sciences as they relate to global mission

mission—the attempt to fulfill God's call to make disciples of all people

mission fatigue syndrome—when mission vision and passion dims or fails to be embraced by individuals, continued exposure to mission stories and motivational attempts may produce only bored yawns

Missional Effectiveness Index—evaluative tool developed by Douglas Terry to gauge mission volunteers' efficaciousness

missionary—a person who, in response to God's call and gifting, is sent across cultural barriers to proclaim the gospel and be a catalytic leader in the development and multiplication of indigenous churches

missionary call—deep, underlying conviction that God is directing a person into missionary service; may take many different forms and may be ascertained either gradually or suddenly

missionary orders—Roman Catholic groups such as the Benedictines, Franciscans, Dominicans, Carmelites, and Jesuits who carried on that church's global outreach

mission-minded pastor—a pastor who understands the biblically centered character of mission and who acts accordingly

modality—an inclusive community such as the Church that may have within it smaller, task-oriented groups called "sodalities"

Moffat, Robert—missionary to Africa sent out by the London Missionary Society in 1816 and whose ministry inspired David Livingstone to become a missionary

monotheism—belief that there is only one God

Moravians—Germanic group of Pietists who became a strong force for revival and mission in the 18th century

Morrison, Robert—first Protestant missionary to reach China (1807)

Muhammad—man born in Mecca in 570 whom Muslims consider to be God's final and most important prophet

multiplication mentality—philosophy of mission that expects rapid growth from the replication of disciples, small groups, leaders, and congregations

mutuality—a reciprocal relationship of interdependence and sharing that benefits the whole (as in the global church)

new paradigms—fresh thought patterns or models of explaining and reflecting

nominalism—in Christian missions, the understanding that many people identified as adherents of various religions are not fervent believers of those religions

nonverbal communication—gestures, silence, spacing, and other behaviors that can be powerful communication means

non-Western—the majority world outside of the Euro-American or Western cultures

panta ta ethnē—Greek phrase in the Great Commission that means "all nations" or "all peoples"

parachurch organizations—autonomous ministry groups that work collaboratively outside of and across denominational lines in mission, social welfare, and evangelism

paradigm shifts—changes or alterations in patterns or frameworks of perceiving, reflecting, and acting

partnership—cooperative relationship of shared responsibility

paternalism—acting on behalf of other people without their permission, often creating dependency

Patrick of Ireland—an ex-slave whose 28 years of missionary ministry in Ireland in the fifth century resulted in the planting of 700 churches

Paul of Tarsus—one of the first missionaries commissioned in the Book of Acts who helped the gospel spread beyond the Judaic culture

Pax Romana (or Roman Peace)—a 150-year peaceful period during the height of the Roman Empire that saw the creation of roads and social and political structures that inadvertently aided the spread of Christianity

people blindness—malady afflicting churches and leaders that makes particular people groups within their ministry area seem invisible

persecuted church—churches in areas where there is systematic governmental persecution or persecution of a minority by a majority group

personal evangelism—one-on-one attempts to invite individuals into a relationship with the Lord Jesus Christ

philosophy of mission—system of principles shaping how global mission is done

Pietists—spiritual movement originating with Philip Spener (1635-1705) that stressed the cultivation of devotion to God and whose intense spirituality gave birth to global mission endeavors

pneumatology—in Christian theology, the doctrine of the person and work of the Holy Spirit

postmodernity—the aspects of culture, contemporary art, economics, and social conditions resulting from globalization, consumerism, fragmentation of authority, and the commoditization of knowledge of late 20th and early 21st centuries

power encounter—phrase coined by Alan Tippet to describe God's activity in direct opposition to evil spiritual powers

prevenient grace—John Wesley's term for God's grace that precedes or goes before and prepares

Qur'an (Koran)—sacred text of Islam, which consists of documents supposedly received through divine revelation over a period of about 20 years by Muhammad

racism—the linking of physical characteristics and culture, often resulting in erroneous views of another group of persons

receptivity—gauge of openness to the gospel on the part of an individual or a culture

reciprocity—exchanges between people who see themselves as equals

redemptive analogies—Don Richardson's term for elements within a culture that anticipate the gospel

regular missions—mission efforts in areas that are defined as reached

religious approach—an attitude of submission to and worship of the supernatural as contrasted with the magical approach, which attempts to manipulate supernatural forces

reverse culture shock—feeling of disorientation and frustration experienced by missionaries returning to their home culture; some prefer to say reentry shock

reverse mission—those who have gone somewhere to minister find themselves being equally ministered to

short-term mission—cross-cultural mission experiences that last from a few days up to about two years; some use the label "midterm mission" to describe those experiences that last from three months to two years or more

Sinai covenant—covenant in Exodus 19 in which God calls His people to be a holy nation and a kingdom of priests

sodality—a voluntary, task-oriented association that has been established for a specific purpose (such as in doing cross-cultural missionary outreach)

soteriological—referring to the doctrine of salvation

strategy—overall plan or method as to how one goes about reaching a goal

strategic partnerships—those liaisons, especially between denominations and parachurch organizations, that are significant in accomplishing world evangelization

Student Volunteer Movement—organization that caused a groundswell of missionary enthusiasm among young people in the late 19th and early 20th centuries and resulted in 20,000 Westerners becoming expatriate missionaries

syncretism—fusing of elements of two differing religious systems to create a hybrid belief system

Taylor, J. Hudson—missionary to China whose founding of the China Inland Mission in 1865 focused Protestant missionary attention on unreached inland areas

tentmakers/tentmaking—those who take a secular job in another culture with the intention of being involved in making disciples and planting churches in that culture

Theological Education by Extension—way of providing leadership training in which the school goes to the student

three-self formula—self-government, self-support, and self-propagation, proposed by Henry Venn and Rufus Anderson in the 1850s and used with great success by John Nevius in Korea

trade language—a language, usually a pidgin but which can be a major language spoken elsewhere, such as Hindi or English, that is used for communication between speakers of different native languages

truth encounter—way of delivering gospel content that primarily depends on an apologetics mode of persuasion

unreached people groups—any group that does not have a church within it capable of effectively evangelizing that group

urbanization—the process of rural populations moving to cities

volunteerism—working for others without expecting pay or other tangible gain

von Zinzendorf, Nicholas—German count who sheltered Moravian refugees in the 18th century and was instrumental in their becoming a missionary movement

Wesley, John—missionary to Georgia; founder of Methodism along with his brother Charles

Western (or West)—Euro-America (Canada and Europe) plus Australia and New Zealand

world Christian—a disciple for whom God's global cause has become an integrating, overriding priority

BIBLIOGRAPHY

Allen, Roland. *Missionary Methods: St. Paul's or Ours?* reprint ed. Grand Rapids: Eerdmans, 1962 [originally published 1912].

Bakke, Ray. *Urban Christian.* Downers Grove, Ill.: InterVarsity, 1987.

Borthwick, Paul. *How to Be a World-Class Christian: You Can Be a Part of God's Global Action,* reprint ed. Waynesboro, Ga.: Send the Light, 2004 [originally published 1991].

———. *Youth and Missions.* Waynesboro, Ga.: Gabriel, 1998.

Bosch, David. *Transforming Mission: Paradigm Shifts in Theology of Mission.* Maryknoll, N.Y.: Orbis Books, 1991.

Butler, Phill. *The Power of Partnership.* Seattle: InterDev, 1998.

———. *The State of the Church and World Evangelism at the End of the '90s.* Seattle: InterDev, 1999.

Chandler, Paul-Gordon. *God's Global Mosaic: What We Can Learn from Christians Around the World.* Downers Grove, Ill.: 2000.

Costas, Orlando. *The Church and Its Mission: A Shattering Critique from the Third World.* Wheaton, Ill.: Tyndale House Publishing, 1977.

Crockett, William V., and James G. Sigountos. *Through No Fault of Their Own: The Fate of Those Who Have Never Heard.* Grand Rapids: Baker, 1991.

Dayton, Edward R., and David A. Fraser. *Planning Strategies for World Evangelization.* Grand Rapids: Eerdmans, 1990.

Dean, Judith M., Julie Schaffner, and Stephen L. S. Smith, ed. *Attacking Poverty in the Developing World: Christian Practitioners and Academics in Collaboration.* Monrovia, Calif.: World Vision, 2005.

Elmer, Duane. *Cross-Cultural Conflict: Building Relationships for Effective Ministry.* Downers Grove, Ill.: 1993.

———. *Cross-Cultural Connections: Stepping Out and Fitting in Around the World.* Downers Grove, Ill.: InterVarsity Press, 2002.

———. *Cross-Cultural Servanthood: Serving the World in Christlike Humility.* Downers Grove, Ill.: InterVarsity Press, 2006.

Escobar, Samuel E. *The New Global Mission: The Gospel from Everywhere to Everyone.* Downers Grove, Ill.: InterVarsity Press, 2003.

Fleming, Dean. *Contextualization in the New Testament: Patterns for Theology and Mission.* Downers Grove, Ill.: InterVarsity Press, 2005.

Glasser, Arthur F., and Donald A. McGavran. *Contemporary Theologies of Mission.* Grand Rapids: Baker, 1983.

Hahn, Ferdinand. *Mission in the New Testament.* London: SCM Press, 1965.

Hampton, Vinita, and Carol Plueddemann. *World Shapers.* Wheaton, Ill.: Harold Shaw Publishers, 1991.

Hastings, Adrian. *A World History of Christianity.* Grand Rapids: Eerdmans, 1999.

Hesselgrave, David J. *Communicating Christ Cross-Culturally: An Introduction to Missionary Communication.* Grand Rapids: Zondervan, 1978.

———. *Paradigms in Conflict: 10 Key Questions in Christian Missions Today.* Grand Rapids: Kregel Publications, 2005.

———. *Today's Choices for Tomorrow's Mission: An Evangelical Perspective on Trends and Issues in Missions.* Grand Rapids: Academie Books, 1988.

Hesselgrave, David J., and Edward Rommen. *Contextualization: Meanings, Methods, and Models.* Grand Rapids: Baker, 1989.

Hiebert, Paul G. *Anthropological Insights for Missionaries.* Grand Rapids: Baker, 1985.

———. *Anthropological Reflections on Missiological Issues.* Grand Rapids: Baker, 1994.

———. *Cultural Anthropology.* Grand Rapids: Baker, 1983.

Hiebert, Paul G., and Eloise Hiebert Meneses. *Incarnational Ministry: Planting Churches in Band, Tribal, Peasant, and Urban Societies.* Grand Rapids: Baker Academic, 1996.

Hunsberger, George R., and Craig Van Gelder. *The Church Between Gospel and Culture.* Grand Rapids: Eerdmans, 1996.

Hunter, George G., III. *The Celtic Way of Evangelism.* Nashville: Abingdon Press, 2000.

———. *To Spread the Power.* Nashville: Abingdon Press, 1987.

Hutchison, William. *Errand to the World: American Protestant Thought and Foreign Missions.* Chicago: University of Chicago, 1987.

Jenkins, Philip. *The Next Christendom: The Coming of Global Christianity.* New York: Oxford University, 2002.

Johnstone, Patrick. *The Church Is Bigger than You Think.* Pasadena, Calif.: William Carey Library, 1998.

Johnstone, Patrick, and Jason Mandryk. *Operation World.* Pasadena, Calif.: William Carey Library, 2001.

Kaiser, Walter C., Jr. *Mission in the Old Testament: Israel as a Light to the Nations.* Grand Rapids: Baker, 2000.

Köstenberger, Andreas J., and Peter T. O'Brien. *Salvation to the Ends of the Earth: A Biblical Theology of Mission.* New Studies in Biblical Theology. Downers Grove, Ill.: InterVarsity Press, 2001.

Kraft, Charles. *Anthropology for Christian Witness.* Maryknoll, N.Y.: Orbis, 1996.

Kraft, Charles, and Marguerite G. Kraft. *Christianity in Culture: A Study in Dynamic Biblical Theologizing in Cross-cultural Perspective,* 25th anniversary ed. Maryknoll, N.Y.: Orbis, 2005.

LaGrand, James. *The Earliest Christian Mission to "All Nations" in the Light of Matthew's Gospel.* Grand Rapids: William B. Eerdmans Publishing Company, 1995.

Latourette, Kenneth Scott. *A History of Christianity,* rev. ed. Peabody, Mass.: Prince Press, 1997.

Lingenfelter, Sherwood. *Agents of Transformation: A Guide for Effective Cross-Cultural Ministry.* Grand Rapids: Baker, 1996.

———. *Transforming Culture.* Grand Rapids: Baker, 1998.

Lingenfelter, Sherwood, and Marvin Mayers. *Ministering Cross-Culturally: An Incarnational Model for Personal Relationships,* 2nd ed. Grand Rapids: Baker, 2003.

McKaughan, Paul, Dellanna O'Brien, and William O'Brien. *Choosing a Future for U.S. Missions.* Monrovia, Calif.: MARC, 1998.

Miley, George. *Loving the Church, Blessing the Nations.* Waynesboro, Ga.: Authentic Publishing, 2003.

Moreau, Scott, et al., eds. *Evangelical Dictionary of World Missions.* Grand Rapids: Baker, 2000.

Moreau, Scott, Gary Corwin, and Gary McGee. *Introducing World Missions: A Biblical, Historical, and Practical Survey.* Grand Rapids: Baker Academic, 2004.

Neill, Stephen. *A History of Christian Missions,* 2nd ed. New York: Penguin Books, 1986.

Netland, Harold. *Encountering Religious Pluralism: The Challenge to Christian Faith and Mission.* Downers Grove, Ill.: InterVarsity Press, 2001.

Newbigin, Lesslie. *The Open Secret: An Introduction to the Theology of Mission.* Grand Rapids: Eerdmans, 1995.

Nida, Eugene. *Customs and Cultures: Anthropology for Christian Missions,* reprint ed. Pasadena, Calif.: William Carey Library, 1982 [originally published 1954].

Noll, Mark A. *Turning Points: Decisive Moments in the History of Christianity.* Grand Rapids: Baker, 2000.

Orjala, Paul R. *God's Mission Is My Mission.* Kansas City: Nazarene Publishing House, 1985.

Palen, John. *The Urban World.* New York: McGraw Hill, 1997.

Parker, Fred J. *Mission to the World.* Kansas City: Nazarene Publishing House, 1985.

Parshall, Phil. *Muslim Evangelism: Contemporary Approaches to Contextualization.* Waynesboro, Ga.: Gabriel/Authentic Media, 2003.

Parsons, Martin. *Unveiling God: Contextualizing Christology for Islamic Culture.* Pasadena, Calif.: William Carey Library, 2005.

Penny, Russell L., ed. *Overcoming the World Missions Crisis: Thinking Strategically to Reach the World.* Grand Rapids: Kregel Publications, 2001.

Peterson, Roger, Gordon Aeschilman, and R. Wayne Sneed. *Maximum Impact Short-Term Mission: The God-Commanded, Repetitive Deployment of Swift, Temporary, Non-Professional Missionaries.* Minneapolis: STEM Press, 2003.

Piper, John. *Let the Nations Be Glad!* 2nd ed. Grand Rapids: Baker, 2003.

Plueddemann, Jim, and Carol Plueddemann. *Witness to All the World: God's Heart for the Nations.* Wheaton, Ill.: Harold Shaw, 1996.

Pocock, Michael, Gailyn Van Rheenen, and Douglas McConnell. *The Changing Face of World Missions: Engaging Contemporary Issues and Trends.* Grand Rapids: Baker Academic, 2005.

Reapsome, Jim, and John Hirst. *Innovation in Mission: Insights into Practical Innovations Creating Kingdom Impact.* Waynesboro, Ga.: Authentic, 2007.

Saint, Steve. *The Great Omission.* Seattle: YWAM Publishing, 2001.

Sanders, John. *No Other Name: An Investigation into the Destiny of the Unevangelized.* Grand Rapids: Eerdmans, 1992.

Shenk, Wilbert R. *Henry Venn: Missionary Statesman.* Maryknoll, N.Y.: Orbis Books, 1983.

Siewert, John A., and Dotsey Welliver, eds. *Mission Handbook: U.S. and Canadian Ministries Overseas, 2004-2006,* 19th ed. Wheaton, Ill.: EMIS, 2004.

Sjogren, Bob. *Unveiled at Last.* Seattle: YWAM Publishing, 1992.

Sjogren, Bob, and Bill and Amy Stearns. *Run with the Vision.* Minneapolis: Bethany House, 1995.

Spencer, Aida Besancon, and William David Spencer. *The Global God: Multicultural Evangelical Views of God.* Grand Rapids: Baker Books, 1998.

Stearns, Bill and Amy. *2020 Vision: Amazing Stories of What God Is Doing Around the World.* Minneapolis: Bethany House, 2005.

Stott, John, and Robert T. Coote, eds. *Gospel and Culture.* Pasadena, Calif.: William Carey Library, 1979.

Sweet, Leonard. *SoulTsunami.* Grand Rapids: Zondervan, 1999.

Tallman, Ray. *Introduction to World Mission.* Dubuque, Iowa: Kendall/Hunt, 1989.

Telford, Tom, Lois Shaw, and Leith Anderson. *Today's All-Star Missions Churches: Strategies to Help Your Church Get into the Game.* Grand Rapids: Baker, 2001.

Thomas, Norman E. *Classic Texts in Mission and World Christianity.* American Society of Missiology Series, no. 20. Maryknoll, N.Y.: Orbis Books, 1995.

Tippet, Alan. *Introduction to Missiology.* Pasadena, Calif.: William Carey Press, 1987.

Tucker, Ruth. *From Jerusalem to Irian Jaya: A Biographical History of Christian Missions.* Grand Rapids: Zondervan, 1983.

———. *Guardians of the Great Commission.* Grand Rapids: Academie, 1988.

Van Engen, Charles. *God's Missionary People.* Grand Rapids: Baker, 1991.

________. *Mission on the Way.* Grand Rapids: Baker, 1996.

Van Rheenen, Gailyn. *Missions: Biblical Foundations and Contemporary Strategies.* Grand Rapids: Zondervan, 1996.

Walston, Vaughn, and Robert Stevens, eds. *African-American Experience in World Mission: A Call Beyond Community.* Pasadena, Calif.: William Carey Library, 2002.

Winter, Ralph D., and Steven C. Hawthorne, eds. *Perspectives on the World Christian Movement,* 3rd ed. Pasadena, Calif.: William Carey Library, 1999.

Woodberry, John Dudley. *Reaching the Resistant: Barriers and Bridges for Mission.* Pasadena, Calif.: William Carey Library, 1998.

Zumwalt, John Willis. *Passion for the Heart of God.* Choctaw, Okla.: HGM Publishing, 2000.

INDEX

E

F

G

H